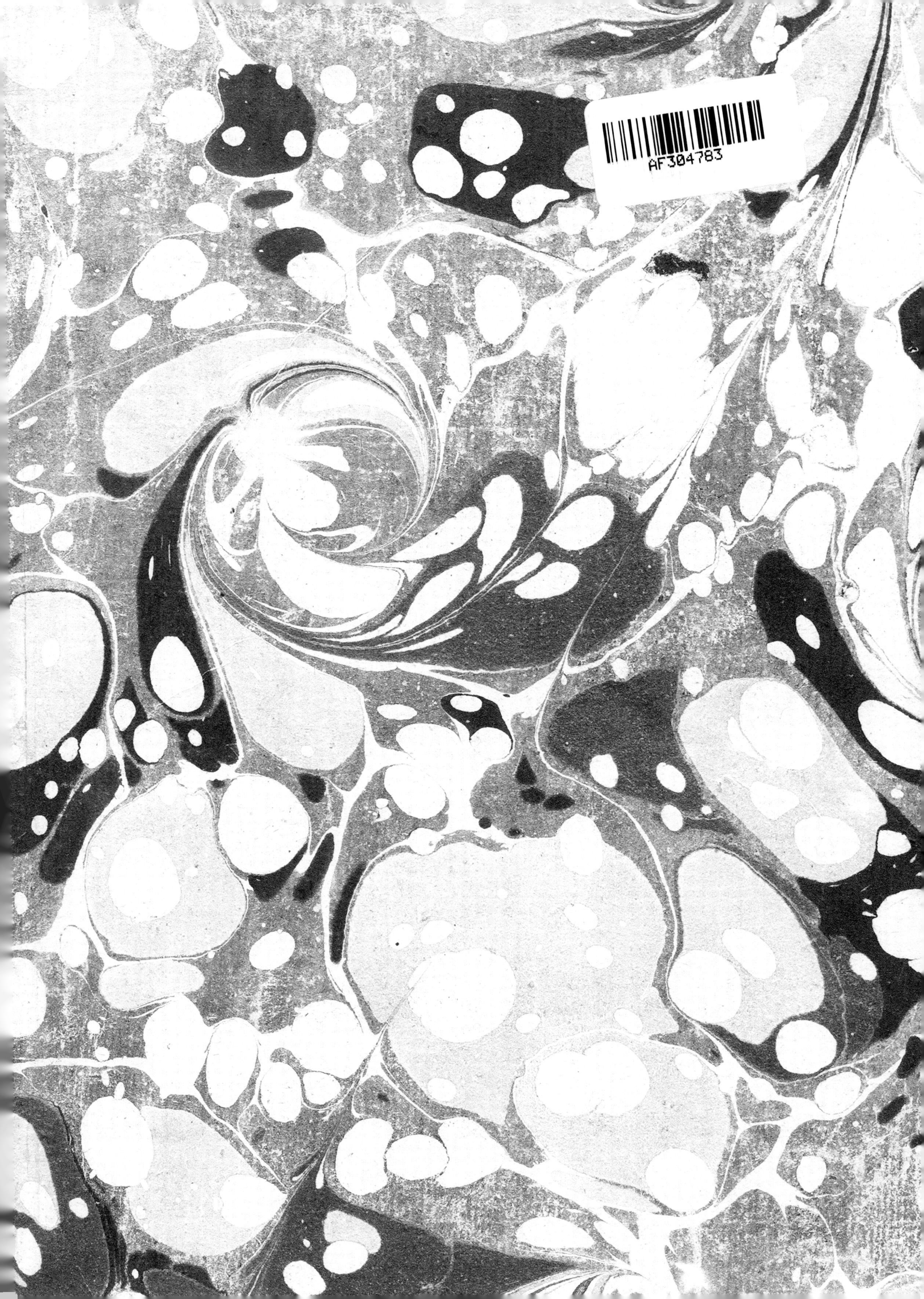

AF304783

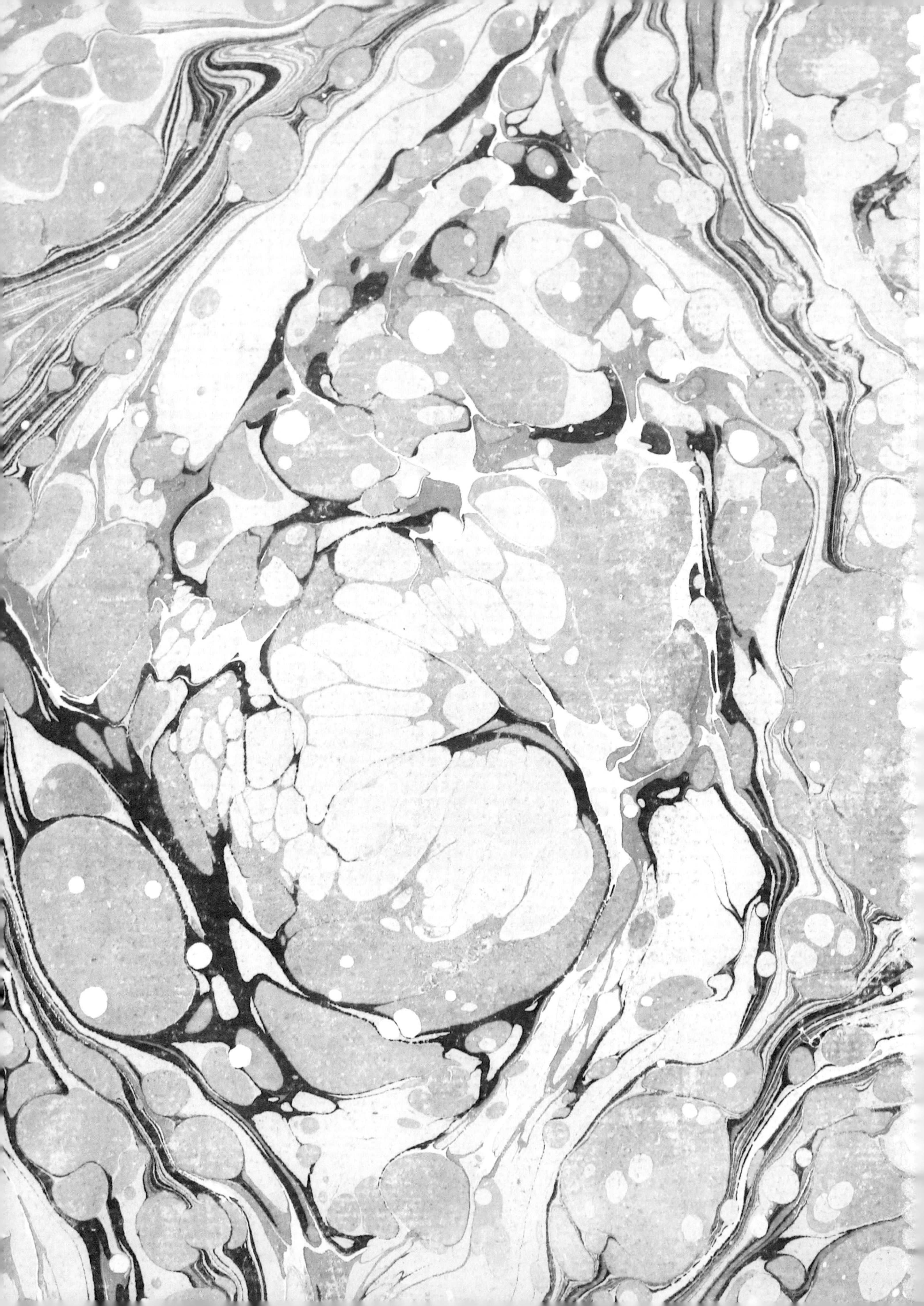

JOCHEN PLOGSTIES

KÜSSE AM NACHMITTAG
KISSES IN THE AFTERNOON

HIRMER

JOCHEN PLOGSTIES

KÜSSE AM

NACHMITTAG

KISSES IN

THE AFTERNOON

LXXIV FARBTAFELN

Inhaltsverzeichnis / Table of contents

When I saw Jochen Plogsties's paintings for the first time four years ago, I was immediately convinced that they suggested a possibility of figurative painting, which in its conception and execution represents a potential further development of established practices.

Being a master-class student of Neo Rauch is not always a blessing, for it can be difficult to avoid the pitfall of exhibiting possible similarities. One way round this is to radically renounce the model. Instead of recounted stories, as ambiguous as they might be, instead of new protagonists and stagings, which ultimately will always have to bear comparison with the master, Plogsties decided on tackling canonical visual models. He has drawn inspiration from exhibition catalogues of Old Masters such as Rembrandt, Cranach or Vermeer, and later from Picasso. More recently, he has turned to magazine covers and album sleeves. His investigation of these images focuses on their composition, colour and style of painting—as well as the question of possible variances. What changes when the original size of the paintings is radically reduced or enlarged? What happens when one takes up the chosen visual model literally—together with the captions and white margins of the catalogue page? Finally, how does the impression change when the originally fine painting on panel is transposed to rough burlap? Plogsties is not concerned, however, with duplication, such as that of "Appropriation Art"; he needs the model as his inspiration, just like the landscape painter needs nature.

Each painting is created in a three-way dialogue between model, eye and hand. Only during the process of painting does the artist understand which decisions his predecessors took while constructing their pictures. One often hears artists say that a picture speaks to them once the answers have been found. Plogsties paints some motifs repeatedly, according to other models with another colour temperature, another page layout; he varies the painting's dimensions. Although he adopts the same motif, a completely new picture emerges. The right of all painted pictures to uniqueness.

It is a pleasure for us to offer Jochen Plogsties a first prominent presentation in Germany with this exhibition at the kestnergesellschaft. Many paintings will be displayed for the very first time. I would like to thank him for the many talks we have had in his Leipzig studio and, of course, for his graphic editions, which he has made exclusively available to the members of the kestner-gesellschaft.

Arne Linde, from the Leipzig gallery that represents him, deserves my special gratitude for her exemplary and unstinting support for the exhibition and for liaising with the lenders, whom I likewise wish to thank for their trust. I'd like to extend my sincere gartitude to Steffen Hildebrand and Dr. Dr. Thomas Rusche for their unwavering commitment to the exhibition.

The Leipziger Volkszeitung played an essential part in the discovery of the artist. In 2011 the newspaper awarded him its Art Prize, which Neo Rauch had won a few years before. I would like to thank the newspaper for its commitment, especially to this exhibition.

My heartfelt thanks also go to the Kulturstiftung des Freistaates Sachsen and the Förderkreis der kestnergesellschaft for their continuing and generous support.

And last but not least, I wish to thank Lotte Dinse, who, in close cooperation with the artist, has compellingly curated the exhibition and conceived the idea for the catalogue. Her essay for the catalogue demonstrates a fine sensitivity for painting and scholarly competence with regard to visual strategies, making Jochen Plogsties' work accessible to us.

Veit Görner

Ich war sofort überzeugt — nachdem ich Jochen Plogsties Bilder erstmals vor vier Jahren sah —, dass sich hier eine Möglichkeit figurativer Malerei andeutet, die in ihrer Konzeption und Ausführung ein Erweiterungspotenzial tradierter Praktiken darstellt.

Meisterschüler von Neo Rauch zu sein ist nicht immer nur ein Segen, denn die Fallgrube möglicher Ähnlichkeiten kann verdammt groß sein. Ein Ausweg ist die radikale Abkehr vom Vorbild. Statt erzählter Geschichten — so uneindeutig sie auch immer sein mögen —, statt neuer Protagonisten und Kulissen, die letztlich doch immer wieder dem Vergleich mit dem Meister standhalten müssen, entschied sich Plogsties für die Auseinandersetzung mit kanonisierten Bildvorlagen. Er lässt sich von Ausstellungskatalogen europäischer Altmeister wie Rembrandt, Cranach oder Vermeer inspirieren, später auch von Picasso. Zuletzt kamen Titelseiten von Illustrierten und Plattencover dazu. Seine Untersuchung gilt der Komposition, der Farbigkeit und Malweise dieser Bilder und der Frage nach möglichen Varianzen. Was ändert sich, wenn man die Originalgröße der Bilder radikal verkleinert oder vergrößert? Wenn man die auserwählte Bildvorlage wortwörtlich übernimmt — mit Bildunterschriften und weißen Rändern der Katalogseite? Und schließlich, wie verändert sich die Anmutung, wenn ursprüngliche Feinmalerei auf Holz mit groben Pinseln auf rauen Rupfen übertragen wird? Plogsties geht es aber nicht um identische Reduplikationen, wie etwa bei der „Appropriation Art" — er braucht die Vorlage als Inspiration wie der Landschaftsmaler die Natur.

Das Bild entsteht im Dialog zwischen Vorlage, Auge und Hand. Erst im Malprozess versteht der Maler, welche Entscheidungen sein Vorläufer getroffen hat, um ein Bild zu bauen. Wenn die Antworten gefunden worden sind, hört man von Künstlern oft, dass das Bild zu ihnen spricht. Manche Motive malt Plogsties mehrfach, nach anderen Vorlagen mit anderer Farbtemperatur, anderem Seitenlayout; er variiert die Bildgrößen. Obwohl das gleiche Motiv, entsteht so ein vollkommen neues Bild. Das Recht aller gemalten Bilder auf Einzigartigkeit.

Es ist uns ein großes Vergnügen, Jochen Plogsties mit dieser Ausstellung in der kestnergesellschaft einen ersten prominenten Auftritt in Deutschland ermöglichen zu können. Viele Bilder sind überhaupt erstmals zu sehen. Ich danke ihm sehr für die vielen Gespräche in seinem Leipziger Atelier und natürlich auch für seine Editionen, die er exklusiv den Mitgliedern der kestnergesellschaft zur Verfügung gestellt hat.

Arne Linde, seiner Galeristin in Leipzig, gilt mein besonderer Dank für die perfekte und großzügige Unterstützung der Ausstellung und den Kontakt zu den Leihgebern, denen ich ebenfalls herzlich für ihr Vertrauen danken möchte. Zudem gilt mein aufrichtiger Dank Steffen Hildebrand und Dr. Dr. Thomas Rusche, die die Ausstellung mit großem Engagement unterstützt haben.

Einen wesentlichen Anteil an der Entdeckung des Künstlers hat die Leipziger Volkszeitung. Sie verlieh ihm 2011 ihren Kunstpreis, der Jahre zuvor auch schon Neo Rauch zuteilwurde. Für ihr Engagement, insbesondere für die aktuelle Ausstellung, möchte ich mich ausdrücklich bedanken.

Für weitere und großzügige Förderung danke ich ganz herzlich der Kulturstiftung des Freistaates Sachsen und dem Förderkreis der kestnergesellschaft.

Last but not least danke ich Lotte Dinse, die in enger Zusammenarbeit mit dem Künstler Ausstellung und Katalog überwältigend kuratiert und szenografiert hat. Ihr Katalogessay zeugt von hoher Sensibilität gegenüber Malerei sowie wissenschaftlicher Kompetenz in bildnerischen Strategien und macht uns das Werk von Jochen Plogsties sehr zugänglich.

The conscious decision to work with the pre-existing visual motifs of others instead of inventing new subjects of his own represents, in a programmatic manner, a fundamental transformation in Jochen Plogsties's artistic practice. What at first appears to be conceptual calculation is in fact an unpretentious and—in light of the mass of existing and reproducible images—even logical attitude: taking what is already there, what can be appropriated and found in the form of printed materials, everyday objects or on the Internet. Plogsties is interested in a broad spectrum of visual motifs from the past and the present, which he grants equal importance and integrates into his artistic production. His point of departure are the reproductions of well-known artworks by old and new masters, as well as the secular images and photographs that surround him in his own lifeworld. Whereas in the past four years Plogsties selected motifs above all from portrait painting from the Renaissance—and later from early Modernism—in more recent works he has also turned to record covers, animal pictures from the Internet and photographs by famous contemporary artists such as Cindy Sherman. In his work Jochen Plogsties engages with a central phenomenon of art history, as old as art itself: the copying and reproducing of specific models in art.[1] There is hardly an issue in Western art and cultural history which has been as extensively and controversially debated by artists, theoreticians and critics as the visual categories of original and copy, as well as the related question of the value placed on originality and individuality. Depending on the respective social, cultural and economic context of each epoch, the copy has fulfilled different functions associated with the changing value that has been placed on the original and the copy.[2] Jochen Plogsties reflects on and explores the varying uses of, motives for and contexts of copying in art, not only by means of the artistic form of the copy itself, but also by the selection of specific visual models. Yet limiting the examination of his works solely to the aspect of copying is inadequate. Plogsties repeatedly takes up certain pictures derived from reproduced models and lays them bare by means of various strategies. We see, therefore, a certain motif, and we see a copy; between them a difference arises, and thus

---

[1]

Ariane Mensger, »Déjà-vu. Von Kopien und anderen Originalen«, in: *Déjà-vu? Die Kunst der Wiederholung von Dürer bis Youtube*, Staatliche Kunsthalle Karlsruhe/Staatliche Hochschule für Gestaltung Karlsruhe, Karlsruhe 2012, p. 30.

[2]

While in Antiquity and the Middle Ages the copying of models or of already-existing artworks was generally accepted, serving as a widespread method of preserving tradition and quality, in the Renaissance artistic invention was regarded as the pinnacle of artistic production. This helped to establish the ideal of the original and its associated qualitative attributes of individuality, creativity and personality. During this period the practice of copying not only became a fixed part of the training received at art academies, but the growing art market brought the painted copy to the fore as a medium used to reproduce prized originals. Up to the 19th century there existed many painting workshops in which copies of famous masters, such as Cranach or Brueghel, were turned out. This increased the geographical area in which an artist was known. This form of reproduction can be regarded at the same time as a precursor of the distribution of technically reproduced artworks in the 20th century—with the objective of making an artwork available to everyone at an affordable price. By the invention of the colour lithograph at the very latest the artistic copy had lost its significance. At the end of the 19th century, moreover, the value placed on the practice of copying changed. The Impressionists rejected academic art education, which had included copying on its syllabus, and distanced themselves from the mimetic function of painting, in favour of more individualised forms of representation. This development was pioneering for the radical paradigm shift that was Modernism. The avant-garde's belief in progress forbade any type of imitation of past styles or of resorting to art-historical predecessors. Art was to refer only to itself and not subordinate itself to any model. At one stroke copying was out. See Romana Rebbelmund, *Appropriation Art, die Kopie als Kunstform im 20. Jahrhundert*, Frankfurt am Main 1999, p. 56ff.

Lotte Dinse

Die bewusste Entscheidung, mit bereits vorhandenen, fremden Bildmotiven zu arbeiten, statt neue, eigene Sujets zu erfinden, stellt in programmatischer Hinsicht einen elementaren Wandel in Jochen Plogsties künstlerischer Praxis dar. Was zunächst an konzeptuelles Kalkül denken lässt, ist in Wirklichkeit eine unprätentiöse und – in Anbetracht der massenhaft existierenden und reproduzierten Bilder – sogar naheliegende Haltung: das zu nehmen, was bereits da ist, was in Form von Druckerzeugnissen, Alltagsobjekten oder im Internet abrufbar und anzueignen ist. Plogsties interessiert sich für ein breites Spektrum vergangener und gegenwärtiger Bildmotive, die er gleichwertig behandelt und in seine künstlerische Produktion integriert. Ausgangspunkt seiner Arbeiten sind Reproduktionen bekannter Kunstwerke Alter und Neuer Meister sowie profane Bilder und Fotografien, die ihn in seiner eigenen Lebenswelt umgeben. Während Plogsties die Auswahl seiner Motive in den vergangenen vier Jahren vor allem auf Porträtmalerei der Renaissance – später auch der Klassischen Moderne – fokussierte, bezieht er in seinen neueren Arbeiten auch Plattencover, Tierabbildungen aus dem Internet sowie Fotografien von bekannten KünstlernInnen wie Cindy Sherman ein. Mit seinen Arbeiten thematisiert Jochen Plogsties ein zentrales Phänomen der Kunstgeschichte, das so alt ist wie die Kunst selbst: das Kopieren und Reproduzieren besonderer Vorbilder in der Kunst.[1] Kaum ein Thema ist in der abendländischen Kunst- und Kulturgeschichte von Künstlern, Theoretikern und Kritikern so umfassend und kontrovers diskutiert worden wie die beiden Bildkategorien Original und Kopie und die damit verbundene Frage nach dem Stellenwert von Originalität und Individualität. Abhängig vom jeweiligen gesellschaftlichen, kulturellen und wirtschaftlichen Kontext einer jeden Epoche erfüllte die Kopie in der Kunst unterschiedliche Funktionen, die mit differierenden Wertschätzungen von Original und Kopie einhergingen.[2] Nicht nur mittels der künstlerischen Form der Kopie selbst, sondern auch anhand der spezifischen Auswahl von Bildvorlagen reflektiert und untersucht Jochen Plogsties die verschiedenen Funktionen, Motive und Kontexte

[1] Ariane Mensger, »Déjà-vu. Von Kopien und anderen Originalen«, in: *Déjà-vu? Die Kunst der Wiederholung von Dürer bis Youtube*, Staatliche Kunsthalle Karlsruhe/Staatliche Hochschule für Gestaltung Karlsruhe, Karlsruhe 2012, S. 30.

[2] Während in der Antike und im Mittelalter das Kopieren von Vorbildern bzw. bereits vorhandener Kunstwerke allgemein anerkannt und als gängige Praxis vor allem der Wahrung von Tradition und Qualität diente, galt in der Renaissance die künstlerische Erfindung als Maxime künstlerischen Schaffens. Damit etablierten sich erstmals die Idee des Originals und die daran geknüpften

something new. Jochen Plogsties's paintings offer a number of readings, enabling the observer to approach what is seen from a multiplicity of perspectives: What do the selected motifs tell us and why did the artist choose these in particular? What do the historical visual models tell us about contemporary conditions of the production, reception and distribution of artworks? In which formal-aesthetic and narrative context are the individual subjects related to one another? What is the difference between looking at the copy of a popular visual motif, firmly anchored in the collective memory, and of an anonymous photograph? How are Plogsties's works related to the Western myth of original uniqueness? And to what extent does his approach differ from his historical predecessors who employed copying as an art form?

The appropriation of images from others as a genuine form of artistic expression was established in the 1960s by the latest with the works, among other artists, of Elaine Sturtevant, known for her almost exact copies of works by Jasper Johns, Claes Oldenburg, Andy Warhol and many other artists of her generation. An essential difference between Sturtevant's works and those that approximately 20 years later were to be summed up as "Appropriation Art",[3] lies in the fact that she made her copies from originals, while Mike Bidlo and Sherrie Levine, for example, worked with reproductions. Appropriation Art is positioned within the context of the Postmodern discourse on issues of authorship, originality and authenticity in a media-dominated society[4] and has often been interpreted as a provocative, subversive renunciation of the apodictic claim to originality and autonomy of Modernism. Sherrie Levine, for instance, photographed reproductions of well-known photographs from books. That her photographs were appropriations of already-existing artworks was reflected in such titles as *After Walker Evans* or *After Alexander Rodchenko*. Jochen Plogsties goes one step further. The titles of his works consist of a number that suggests a date or a series and the (fragmentary) title of the copied work. In this manner he refers to the existing artwork. The number that precedes the title, however, indicates that his copy is a work of genuine artistic production. Plogsties emphasises in the title his proximity to and, at the same time, his independence from the visual model, which itself is depicted in his pictures in an exaggerated form. Instead of following the strict concept, like Levine, of making the appropriated pictures in the same size as the reproductions, Plogsties prefers, not only with regard to the painting's format, to take a freer, more radical approach. While the reproduction itself, as regards image detail and colour, distorts the original, Plogsties adds further changes to his reproductions. Although he makes an almost exact copy of the composition of the picture that is his model, the style of painting, the choice of colours and materials, of size and degree of completion, are all subject to decisions made consciously or unconsciously.

This approach is especially noticeable in 24_14 (**Souvenir du Maroc**) from 2014. The idea behind the picture that served as the model here is—if one is not familiar with the original—hardly recognisable. It seems as though Plogsties stopped the process of appropriation at a moment when the chosen motif had not yet been transferred to the canvas. The blue copying grid stands out prominently; various colours applied with broad strokes are visible within the individual fields on the canvas. Everything is ready for transferring the motif from the model to the canvas, yet the artist declares the painting in this early state as finished. The example demonstrates that here a subjectively marked process of appropriation, adaption and abstraction is taking place, sometimes subtly, sometimes inscribed noticeably in his pictures.

3
Christoph Zuschlag observes that the definition of »Appropriation Art« is problematic. In this text I use the term to refer to the conceptual art movement arising at the end of the 1970s in New York. See Christoph Zuschlag, »Die Kopie ist das Original«, in: *Déjà-vu? Die Kunst der Wiederholung von Dürer bis YouTube*, Staatliche Kunsthalle Karlsruhe/ Staatliche Hochschule für Gestaltung Karlsruhe, Karlsruhe 2012, pp. 126–135.

4
Ibid.

des Kopierens in der Kunst. Die Betrachtung seiner Arbeiten lediglich auf den Aspekt des Kopierens zu reduzieren, greift meines Erachtens jedoch zu kurz. Plogsties wiederholt bestimmte Bilder nach reproduzierten Vorlagen und legt dies anhand unterschiedlicher Strategien offen. Wir sehen also ein bestimmtes Motiv und wir sehen eine Kopie, und dazwischen tritt eine Differenz und somit etwas Neues zutage. Jochen Plogsties Bilder offerieren somit unterschiedliche Lesarten, die dem Betrachter eine multiperspektivische Annäherung an das zu Sehende ermöglichen: Was erzählen die ausgewählten Motive und wieso wählt der Künstler gerade diese aus? Was erzählen die historischen Bildvorlagen über gegenwärtige Bedingungen der Produktion, Rezeption und Distribution von Kunstwerken? In welchem formal-ästhetischen und narrativen Kontext stehen die einzelnen Sujets zueinander? Welchen Unterschied macht es, die Kopie eines im kollektiven Gedächtnis verankerten, populären Bildmotivs oder die einer anonymen Fotografie zu betrachten? Wie verhalten sich Plogsties Arbeiten zum abendländischen Mythos originärer Einmaligkeit? Und inwiefern unterscheidet sich sein Ansatz von dem historischer Vorgänger, die das Kopieren als Kunstform praktizierten?

Die Aneignung fremder Bilder als genuine künstlerische Ausdrucksform etablierte sich frühestens in den 1960er-Jahren, unter anderem mit Elaine Sturtevant, die durch ihre nahezu exakten Kopien von Werken Jasper Johns, von Claes Oldenburg, Andy Warhol und vielen anderen Künstlern ihrer Generation bekannt geworden ist. Ein zentraler Unterschied zwischen Sturtevants Arbeiten und den künstlerischen Äußerungen, die etwa zwanzig Jahre später unter dem Label »Appropriation Art«[3] gefasst wurden, besteht darin, dass sie ihre Kopien nach Originalen anfertigte, während beispielsweise Mike Bidlo und Sherrie Levine mit Reproduktionen arbeiteten. Appropriation Art steht im Kontext des postmodernen Diskurses um Fragen nach Autorschaft, Originalität und Authentizität in der mediengeprägten Gesellschaft[4] und wurde oft als provokativ-subversive Absage an den apodiktischen Anspruch auf Originalität und Autonomie der Moderne interpretiert. Sherrie Levine fotografierte beispielsweise Reproduktionen bekannter Fotografien aus Büchern ab. Dass es sich bei ihren Fotografien um Aneignungen bereits vorhandener Kunstwerke handelt, belegte sie mit Werktiteln wie *After Walker Evans* oder *After Alexander Rodchenko*.

Jochen Plogsties geht noch einen Schritt weiter. Seine Werktitel setzen sich aus einer Nummer, die an eine Datierung oder Seriennummer denken lässt, und dem (fragmentarischen) Titel des kopierten Werkes zusammen. Damit offenbart auch er die Referenz auf ein bestehendes Kunstwerk. Die Nummer, die er im Titel voranstellt, verweist jedoch darauf, dass es sich bei seiner Kopie um ein Werk genuiner Kunstproduktion handelt. Plogsties unterstreicht bereits im Werktitel seine Nähe und gleichzeitige Autonomie gegenüber der Bildvorlage, die in den Bildern selbst in zugespitzter Form dargestellt wird. Statt wie Levine dem strengen Konzept zu folgen, die angeeigneten Bilder stets in der Größe anzufertigen, die auch der Größe der Reproduktion entspricht, pflegt Plogsties nicht nur in Bezug auf die Bildformate einen freieren, radikaleren Umgang. Während die Reproduktion hinsichtlich Bildausschnitt und Farbigkeit bereits eine Verfremdung des Originals darstellt, fügt Plogsties seinen Nachschöpfungen weitere Veränderungen hinzu. Zwar kopiert er die einem Bild zugrundeliegende Komposition nahezu exakt, doch Malstil, Farb- und Materialwahl, Bildgröße und Grad der Vollendung unterliegen Entscheidungen, die er bewusst oder auch unbewusst trifft.

Qualitätsmerkmale wie Individualität, Kreativität und Persönlichkeit. Zu dieser Zeit entwickelte sich die Praxis des Kopierens nicht nur zum festen Bestandteil der Ausbildung an den Akademien, sondern mit dem wachsenden Kunstmarkt trat die gemalte Kopie vor allem als Medium der Vervielfältigung begehrter Originale erstmals in den Vordergrund. Bis ins 19. Jahrhundert gab es zahlreiche Malereiwerkstätten, in denen Kopien bekannter Meister wie Cranach oder Brueghel angefertigt wurden. Dadurch erweiterte sich der räumliche Radius, in dem ein Künstler bekannt war. Diese Form der Reproduktion lässt sich zugleich als frühes Pendant zur Distribution technisch reproduzierter Kunstwerke im 20. Jahrhundert verstehen – mit dem Ziel, ein Kunstwerk preisgünstig für jedermann verfügbar zu machen. Spätestens mit der Erfindung der Farblithografie verlor die künstlerische Kopie jedoch an Bedeutung. Im ausgehenden 19. Jahrhundert änderte sich zudem die Wertschätzung gegenüber der Praxis des Kopierens. Die Impressionisten lehnten sich gegen die akademische Ausbildung auf, zu der ja bis dahin das Kopieren gehörte, und lösten sich von der Abbildfunktion der Malerei zugunsten individualistischer Darstellungsweisen. Diese Entwicklung war Wegbereiter für den radikalen Paradigmenwechsel der Moderne. Das Fortschrittsdenken der Avantgarden verbot jegliche Form der Nachahmung vergangener Stile oder den Rückgriff auf kunstgeschichtlich Vorhandenes. Die Kunst sollte sich allein auf sich selbst beziehen und sich keinem Vorbild unterordnen. Kopieren in der Kunst war mit einem Schlag out. Vgl. Romana Rebbelmund, *Appropriation Art. die Kopie als Kunstform im 20. Jahrhundert*, Frankfurt am Main 1999, S. 56ff.

3
Christoph Zuschlag konstatiert, dass die Definition dessen, was als »Appropriation Art« bezeichnet werden kann, sehr schwierig ist. Ich beziehe mich in diesem Text auf die Ende der 1970er-Jahre in New York entstandene konzeptuelle Kunstrichtung. Vgl. Christoph Zuschlag, »Die Kopie ist das Original«, in: *Déjà-vu? Die Kunst der Wiederholung von Dürer bis Youtube*, Staatliche Kunsthalle Karlsruhe/Staatliche Hochschule für Gestaltung Karlsruhe, Karlsruhe 2012, S. 126–135.

4
Ebd.

The mimetic imitation of the reproduction is not a priority for Plogsties, rather, the utilisation of his particular painterly possibilities, limits and decisions in the process of copying. He is concerned with tracing the specific qualities and characteristics of the original, which as a consequence of the photographic reproduction have faded into the background. Jochen Plogsties thus approaches the painterly parameters of a certain model by scrutinising one or several reproductions step-by-step and experiencing it or them through another medium. While the conceptual approach, the questioning of the conditions under which a work of art is produced and received in the age of mechanical and digital reproduction, is indicative of Appropriation Art, for Plogsties the intensive engagement with the medium of the respective visual model—which in most cases is painting—is at the fore. He examines the relationships between the painterly and the technical reproduction of a painting. What is conveyed by the mechanical scan process is translated back into painting. In this process Plogsties reconstructs the historical steps that a painter—in some cases—went through many years before him and that the reproduction ignores or has replicated only relatively precisely.

At the same time he explores his visual models with regard to their flexibility and malleability. How much unused visual potential lies in a model? How can specific parameters be varied in a motif that remains identical, so that the original message of the picture is deflected, causing it to take another direction? Instead of "copying as art form", an essential aspect of this approach is free translation, the repetition of an existing work in the present under changed circumstances. By means of various painterly strategies Plogsties lends the motifs a perplexing character. Certain subjects are immediately recognisable, yet at the same time the specific painterly moment that was so characteristic of the respective epoch or artist is missing. Instead, Plogsties is much more concerned with depicting the repeated motifs via his own means. A constant feature of many of his pictures is the rough canvas that shimmers through the depiction. This effect is especially prevalent in paintings such as 2_13 (**Portrait of Maria de' Medici**), 9_13 (**Arab, Saddling his Horse**), 10_13 (**Mona Lisa**) or 5_14 (**Mary and Child**). Instead of fine brushstrokes that allow a precise working out of details, Plogsties's coarse and flat manner of painting often blurs the contours. He thus imparts a deliberately unfinished and imperfect quality to his pictures.

Plogsties's painting 7_12 (**Portrait of a Man in a Red Turban**) is based on a reproduction of the *Portrait of a Man in a Red Turban* (1433) by Jan van Eyck. This panel depicts the painter in three-quarter view and is considered the first autonomous self-portrait in the Early Modern Period.[5] Van Eyck painted himself when he was at the pinnacle of his artistic career. He had just successfully completed the Ghent Altarpiece, which brought him material wealth, and he married in the same year the self-portrait was completed. In a certain sense he represents the prototype of the successful man, as is also reflected in the execution of the painting. The man's face appears as though it were illuminated, clearly highlighted against the black background. The man's features express brilliance, dignity and self-confidence. Plogsties painted this motif twice in 2012, in two different formats. Both versions represent a radical deviation from the original—not only with regard to the painting's large size in his 255 x 180 cm version. Here, in contrast to the original, the entire figure of the man fades into the background. This is not only because the composition is slightly modified and the head with the large chaperon is therefore smaller, thus occupying less pictorial space. The effect arises primarily because the man's face is painted over with red and black, so that it is hardly distinguishable from his clothes and the background. Because of the face's colour, applied in rough brushstrokes that

5
Andreas Beyer, *Das Porträt in der Malerei*, Munich 2002, p. 43.

Besonders deutlich ist dieser Ansatz in 24_14 (**Souvenir du Maroc**) von 2014 sichtbar. Die Idee des Bildes, das hier als Vorlage diente, ist – kennt man das Original nicht – kaum zu erkennen. Es scheint, als hätte Plogsties den Prozess der Aneignung in einem Moment beendet, bei dem das ausgewählte Motiv noch gar nicht auf die Leinwand gebracht war. Das blaue Übertragungsraster sticht besonders hervor, verschiedene mit groben Strichen aufgetragene Farben sind innerhalb der einzelnen Felder auf der Leinwand organisiert. Alles ist vorbereitet, um das Motiv von der Vorlage auf die Leinwand zu übertragen, doch der Künstler erklärt das Bild bereits in diesem Stadium als beendet. Das Beispiel zeigt, dass hier ein subjektiv geprägter Prozess von Aneignung, Adaption und Abstraktion stattfindet, der sich seinen Bildern mal subtil, mal offenkundig einschreibt.

Bei Plogsties steht nicht die mimetische Nachahmung der Reproduktion im Vordergrund, sondern das Ausloten eigener malerischer Möglichkeiten, Grenzen und Entscheidungen im Vorgang des Kopierens. Es geht es um das Aufspüren spezifischer Qualitäten und Merkmale des Originals, die infolge der fotografischen Reproduktion in den Hintergrund treten. Dabei nähert sich Jochen Plogsties den malerischen Parametern einer bestimmten Vorlage, indem er eine oder mehrere Reproduktionen Schritt für Schritt abtastet und somit durch ein anderes Medium hindurch erfährt. Während für die Appropriation Art der konzeptuelle Ansatz, die medialen Rahmenbedingungen der Produktion und Rezeption des Kunstwerks im Zeitalter seiner technischen und digitalen Reproduzierbarkeit zu hinterfragen, konstitutiv ist, steht bei Plogsties die intensive Auseinandersetzung mit der medialen – und zwar zumeist malerischen – Konstitution seiner jeweiligen Bildvorlage im Vordergrund. Er untersucht dabei die Beziehung zwischen der malerischen und der technischen Reproduktion einer Malerei. Das, was der mechanische Scanprozess liefert, übersetzt er zurück in Malerei. Innerhalb dieses Prozesses rekonstruiert Plogsties die historischen Schritte, die ein Maler – in einigen Fällen – viele Jahre vor ihm unternommen hat und die bei der Reproduktion ignoriert oder nur annähernd genau wiedergegeben wurden.

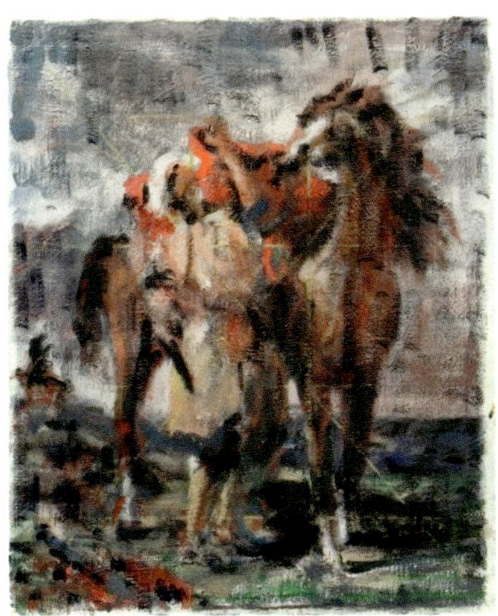

9_13

Zugleich lotet er seine Bildvorlagen in Bezug auf deren Flexibilität und Dehnbarkeit aus. Wie viel ungenutztes bildnerisches Potenzial steckt in einer Vorlage? Wie können spezifische Parameter bei gleichbleibendem Motiv so variiert werden, dass die ursprünglich intendierte Bildaussage in eine andere Richtung gelenkt wird? Zentral für diesen Ansatz ist weniger die »Kopie als Kunstform« als der Aspekt der freien Übersetzung, der Wieder-Holung eines bestehenden Werkes in die Gegenwart unter veränderten Bedingungen. Mittels unterschiedlicher malerischer Strategien verleiht Plogsties den Motiven dabei einen irritierenden Charakter. Bestimmte Sujets erkennt man zwar auf Anhieb wieder, zugleich fehlt aber das spezifisch malerische Moment, das für die jeweilige Epoche oder die individuelle Handschrift eines bestimmten Künstlers so prägend war. Vielmehr geht es Plogsties darum, die wiederholten Motive mit seinen eigenen Mitteln darzustellen. Ein zentrales Merkmal ist, dass in vielen seiner Bilder die raue Leinwand durchschimmert. Dieser Effekt ist in Bildern wie 2_13 (**Portrait of Maria de Medici**), 9_13 (**Araber, sein Pferd sattelnd**), 10_13 (**Mona Lisa**) oder 5_14 (**Maria mit dem Kinde**) besonders stark ausgeprägt. Statt feiner Pinselstriche,

resemble wounds, the portrayed man does not radiate grandeur, vitality or pride; instead Plogsties turns the figure into its opposite, creating the image of a shrunken, wounded, withdrawn, almost sinister man. Whether through such interventions he intends to narrate the precarious situation of contemporary artists—beyond all the pomp and glamour—or whether his depiction simply makes visible the layers of paint of the production process, remains unclear. For the observer it is not immediately evident whether such variants arise from the given conditions of the reproduced model, from a conscious reinterpretation or destructive gesture of the artist, or whether they are the traces of multiple attempts at appropriation. Whatever the case may be, the example demonstrates that the repetition of a certain motif always stimulates reflection on the meaning of the depiction and on the manner of its painterly appropriation.[6]

Plogsties not only repeats certain visual subjects, but also shows how the originals are reproduced. He thus paints, for example, the white or coloured margins of a book's page or of a postcard. In addition, in many of his paintings the grid structure is visible, revealing the technical procedure employed by the artist. With the grids he not only indicates that his paintings are copies of copies, but also brings himself into the picture and suggests his own "presence". Such signs can be understood as "visible markings of the producer".[7] Isabelle Graw, who regards the medium of painting as a form of the production of signs characterised by "indexicality", applies this term—originally coined by Charles S. Peirce and used to refer to photography—to painting, observing that painting "lives from the suggestion that the absent artistic subject appears in it".[8] Referring to the painting technique employed by Gerhard Richter to make blurred copies of photographs, Graw writes that "the photographic quality thus helps these pictures to make a reference to life, which is then ultimately reshaped by the painter's signature. One gets both from Richter—the trace of the reality of life and the suggestion of the painter's presence."[9]

In relation to Plogsties's work, it could be correspondingly said that one gets both from him, too—the reference to the original artwork and the suggestion of his own presence. The visual discourse does not take place—as in the case of Appropriation Art—primarily on a meta-level, but rather is a basic component of the artistic process itself, since painting—in contrast to photography—cannot produce an exact copy of a reproduction. Instead, Plogsties is much more interested in the variance that arises in the process of repetition. He is concerned with a purposeful, subjective comprehension of the conditions that underlie the painted—in contrast to a mechanical—copy. An independent artistic accomplishment takes place in this process of comprehension, which is based on a complex relationship of proximity-distance to the copied model. The more exact Plogsties follows the model, the more his individuality—and thus his distance to the original—comes to the fore.

By working with reproductions instead of with the originals, he also draws attention to questions regarding the conditions of the production and the reception of the work of art in the digital age. With his works he patently demonstrates a type of art reception that seems to have become a natural mode of our time: artworks are primarily experienced via publications, magazines or on the Internet, instead of face-to-face in the context of a museum. In addition, Plogsties works with numerous popular works of art history such as the *Mona Lisa*, *The Birth of Venus* or *The Girl with the Pearl Earring*, which populate our daily life as innumerable reproductions in the form of postcards, posters and everyday ob-

---

6
Plogsties proceeded in a similar manner with another model by Jan van Eyck. He copied *Portrait of a Man with a Blue Chaperon* twice, with one version in a much larger format. This larger picture, 1_12 (**Man with a Blue Chaperon**) from 2012, evidences clear traces of several painterly "attempts" at the figure's face and hands. It appears as though Plogsties's painting makes the different facets of one and the same person visible or shows them under changed conditions. In contrast to the figure in its smaller version from 2011, the man appears older, worried and ill.

7
Isabelle Graw / Peter Geimer, *Über Malerei: Eine Diskussion*, Berlin 2012, p. 40.

8
Ibid., p. 29.

9
Ibid., p. 44.

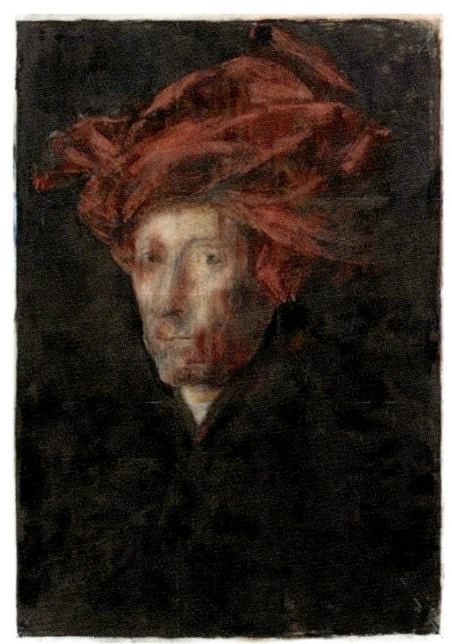

7_12

die eine präzise Ausarbeitung von Details erlauben, verschwinden bei Plogsties Konturen oft durch seine grobe und flächige Malweise. Dadurch schreibt er seinen Bildern das gewollt Unfertige und Unperfekte ein.

Plogsties Bild 7_12 (**Bildnis eines Mannes mit rotem Turban**) beruht auf einer Reproduktion des Gemäldes *Bildnis eines Mannes mit rotem Turban* (1433) von Jan van Eyck. Das Bild zeigt den Maler in Dreiviertelansicht und gilt als erstes autonomes Selbstbildnis der Neuzeit.[5] Van Eyck malte sich selbst, als er sich auf dem Höhepunkt seiner künstlerischen Laufbahn befand. Gerade hatte er erfolgreich den Genter Altar vollendet, was ihm zu materiellem Wohlstand verhalf, und im Entstehungsjahr des Selbstporträts heiratete er. In gewisser Weise stellt er somit den Prototypen eines erfolgreichen Mannes dar, was sich auch in der Ausführung des Gemäldes widerspiegelt. Das Gesicht des Mannes wirkt wie angestrahlt und hebt sich dadurch vor dem sonst schwarzen Hintergrund deutlich ab. Die Gesichtszüge drücken Glanz, Würde und Selbstbewusstsein aus. Plogsties hat das Motiv im Jahr 2012 gleich zweimal in unterschiedlichen Formaten gemalt. Beide Versionen stellen eine radikale Abweichung vom Original dar – wobei sich diese in dem 255 × 180 cm großen Bild nicht nur auf die Bildgröße bezieht. Im Gegensatz zum Original tritt die gesamte Figur des Mannes optisch in den Hintergrund. Das liegt nicht nur daran, dass der Bildausschnitt leicht verändert ist und der Kopf mit dem üppigen Chaperon etwas kleiner ausfällt und somit weniger Bildraum beansprucht. Die Wirkung kommt vor allem dadurch zustande, dass sich das Gesicht des Mannes kaum von Kleidung und Hintergrund abhebt, da es rötlich-schwarz übermalt ist. Durch die Gesichtsfarbe, die aufgrund des groben Pinselstrichs an Blessuren denken lässt, strahlt der Porträtierte weder Erhabenheit noch Vitalität oder Stolz aus, sondern Plogsties verkehrt die Figur ins Gegenteil, indem er das Bild eines eingefallenen, versehrten, zurückgezogenen, beinahe unheimlich wirkenden Mannes entwirft. Ob er mittels solcher Interventionen die prekäre Situation eines zeitgenössischen Künstlers – jenseits von Glanz und Glamour – erzählt oder ob seine Darstellungsweise lediglich die im Produktionsprozess entstandenen Malschichten sichtbar macht, bleibt allerdings unklar. Für den Betrachter ist nicht auf Anhieb nachvollziehbar, ob solche Varianzen den gegebenen Bedingungen der reproduzierten Vorlage, einer bewussten Umdeutung oder destruktiven Geste des Künstlers entspringen oder ob sie Spuren multipler Aneignungsversuche sind. Das Beispiel zeigt jedoch, dass die Wiederholung eines bestimmten Motivs stets eine Reflexion auslöst, die sich auf die Bedeutung des Dargestellten und auf die Form der malerischen Aneignung selbst beziehen lässt.[6]

Plogsties wiederholt aber nicht nur bestimmte Bildsujets, sondern zeigt auch, wie die Originale abgebildet sind. So malt er beispielsweise auch die weißen oder farbigen Flächen einer Buchseite oder Postkarte mit. Außerdem lässt sich auf zahlreichen seiner Bilder eine Rasterstruktur erkennen, die über die technische Vorgehensweise des Künstlers Aufschluss gibt. Damit verweist er nicht nur darauf, dass es sich bei seinen Bildern um Kopien von Kopien handelt, sondern bringt damit sich selbst ins Spiel und suggeriert seine eigene »Anwesenheit«. Solche Setzungen lassen

5
Andreas Beyer, *Das Porträt in der Malerei*, München 2002, S. 43.

6
Ähnlich verfährt Plogsties auch bei einer weiteren Bildvorlage von Jan van Eyck. *Bildnis eines Mannes mit blauem Chaperon* hat er ebenfalls zweimal kopiert, wobei er eine Version wieder in deutlich größerem Format fertigte. Auf dem größeren Bild 1_12 (**Mann mit blauem Chaperon**) von 2012 sind im Gesicht und an den Händen der Figur deutliche Spuren mehrerer malerischer »Anläufe« zu sehen. Es ist, als mache Plogsties Bild verschiedene Facetten ein und derselben Person sichtbar oder als zeige er sie unter veränderten Bedingungen. Im Gegensatz zu der Figur in seiner kleineren Version von 2011 wirkt der Mann hier kränklich, gealtert, betrübt.

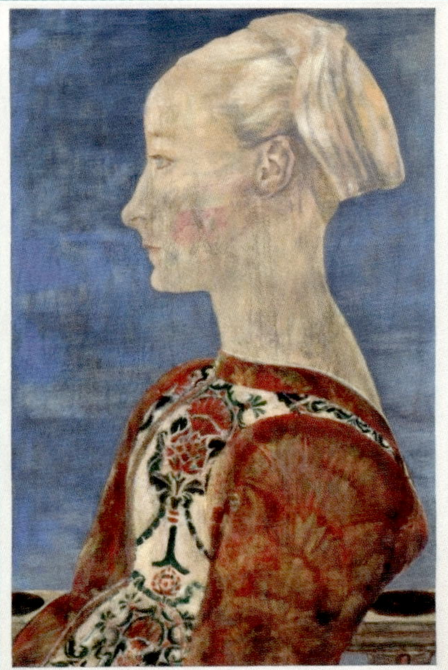

28_14

jects such as cups, bookmarks, pillowcases, T-shirts, etc. The issues of the commercialisation and trivialisation of artworks linked to their mass reproduction have been dealt with in a provocative and critical manner by Marcel Duchamp, Andy Warhol as well as other artists who have worked with quotes and copies. Yet, this discussion is not crucial for approaching Jochen Plogsties's work. The type of repetition that Plogsties practises does not principally reflect a subversive, critical attitude towards the contemporary conditions of the production, reception and distribution of artworks, but rather a profound curiosity for specific visual motifs and compositions, which appear particularly prominent, attractive, difficult or perplexing to the artist in connection with their reproduction. Elevating the reproduction to a model should be understood here not as the rejection of the original, but rather as an artistic experiment and at the same time a technical challenge. Which painterly parameters of a large painting can be found in the format of a small postcard? How does a motif change when the new version is radically different in size from the original? Often, Plogsties does not work with a single model, but compares different reproductions when working on a certain motif. Why are the slightest variations in colours of different reproductions of the same motif more or less difficult to reproduce? In order to answer such questions, several attempts are necessary. The process of precisely seeing, painting and the ensuing positioning—of how close he comes to the model—can take weeks or months.

A considerable deviation from the size of the model is evidenced in Plogsties's 28_14 (**Portrait of a Young Lady in Profile**). Antonio del Pollaiuolo created the original painting in 1465 with the dimensions of 52.5×36.5 cm; Plogsties enlarged it to 270×190 cm. Female profile portraits were a favourite subject of Florentine paintings in the 15th century. Pollaiuolo's painting differs from similar portraits in that he concentrates not just on the woman's face, but also on her corporeality. He achieves this by turning the body slightly to the left and by stressing the haptic materiality of the dress.[10] The face, in contrast, appears stony, almost marble-like. It is not a depiction of the sitter but of established ideals of beauty. In his version, Plogsties does not repeat those details that constituted the innovative moment or unique characteristic of the painting in its day. The patterns on the dress in his picture seem blurred. Just like in his 7_12 (**Portrait of a Man in a Red Turban**), the face does not appear regular and is less doll-like compared to the original; instead, underlying layers of paint shimmer through and rough brushstrokes are plainly visible. By means of such inaccuracies Plogsties makes clear that an original portrait is also a reproduction. In portraying a sitter, a painter makes unconscious decisions based on the social and cultural conventions of the age as well as his or her own perception. A painted portrait is per se a variant of the model. For Jochen Plogsties this effect is amplified when he paints persons whose perception has already been filtered through the eyes of another artist. He investigates how such infinitely continuable processes of repetition transform the appearance and charisma of a person and how one's own memories of a specific person—perhaps from one's own environment—can be inscribed in this process.

10
See note 5, p. 65.

sich als »sichtbare Markierungen des Produzenten« verstehen.[7] Isabelle Graw, die das Medium Malerei als eine Form der Zeichenproduktion begreift, welche sich durch Indexikalität auszeichnet, überträgt den von Charles S. Peirce geprägten und ursprünglich auf die Fotografie bezogenen Begriff der Indexikalität auf die Malerei und konstatiert, dass diese »von der Suggestion lebe, dass das abwesende Künstlersubjekt in ihr aufscheint«.[8] In Bezug auf die malerische Technik, mit der Gerhard Richter Fotografien unscharf abmalte, schreibt Graw: »Somit verhilft das Fotografische diesen Bildern zu einem Lebensbezug, der von der Signatur des Malers am Ende doch überformt wird. Man bekommt bei Richter beides — den Verweis auf Lebenswirklichkeit *und* die Suggestion der Anwesenheit des Malers.«[9]

Bezogen auf Plogsties Arbeiten könnte man entsprechend sagen, dass man bei ihm ebenfalls beides bekommt — den Verweis auf das Originalkunstwerk *und* die Suggestion seiner eigenen Anwesenheit. Der bildnerische Diskurs findet hier nicht vorrangig — wie das bei der Appropriation Art der Fall war — auf einer Metaebene statt, sondern ist elementarer Bestandteil des künstlerischen Produktionsprozesses selbst, da die Malerei im Gegensatz zur Fotografie keine exakte Abbildung einer Reproduktion leisten kann. Vielmehr interessiert sich Plogsties für die Varianz, die im Prozess der Wiederholung entsteht. Es geht um ein dezidiertes, subjektives Nachvollziehen der Bedingungen, die der malerischen Kopie im Gegensatz zu einer mechanischen zugrunde liegen. Innerhalb dieses Nachvollzugs findet eine autonome künstlerische Leistung statt, die auf einem komplexen Nähe-Distanz-Verhältnis zur kopierten Vorlage beruht. Je exakter Plogsties sich an die Vorlage hält, desto deutlicher tritt seine Individualität in den Vordergrund und somit wiederum eine Distanz zum Original.

Indem Plogsties mit reproduzierten Vorlagen arbeitet anstelle von Originalen, lenkt er den Blick auch auf die Frage nach den Bedingungen der Produktion und Rezeption von Kunstwerken im digitalen Zeitalter. Mit seinen Arbeiten demonstriert er geradezu eine Form der Kunstrezeption, die ein selbstverständlicher Modus unserer Zeit zu sein scheint: Kunstwerke werden vorrangig über Publikationen, Zeitschriften oder im Internet betrachtet statt face to face im musealen Kontext. Zudem arbeitet Plogsties mit zahlreichen populären Werken der Kunstgeschichte wie beispielsweise *Mona Lisa, Die Geburt der Venus* oder *Das Mädchen mit dem Perlenohrring*, die aufgrund zahlloser Reproduktionen in Form von Postkarten, Postern, Alltagsgegenständen wie Tassen, Lesezeichen, Kissenbezügen, T-Shirts usw. in unserem Alltag kursieren. Die mit der massenhaften Reproduktion einhergehenden Aspekte der Kommerzialisierung und Trivialisierung von Kunstwerken sind von Marcel Duchamp, Andy Warhol und anderen Künstlern, die sich mit Zitaten und Kopien beschäftigt haben, auf provokative und kritische Weise thematisiert worden. Meines Erachtens ist diese Diskussion aber nicht ausschlaggebend für eine Annäherung an Jochen Plogsties Werk. Die Form der Wiederholung, die Plogsties praktiziert, spiegelt nämlich nicht in erster Linie eine subversive, kritische Haltung gegenüber zeitgenössischen Rahmenbedingungen der Produktion, Rezeption und Distribution von Kunstwerken wider, sondern eine unbefangene Neugier gegenüber spezifischen Bildmotiven- und -kompositionen, die dem Künstler im Kontext ihrer Reproduktion besonders auffällig, attraktiv, schwierig oder irritierend erscheinen. Die Reproduktion zur Vorlage zu erheben ist hier weniger als Absage an das Original zu verstehen, sondern als künstlerisches Experiment und technische Herausforderung zugleich. Welche malerischen Parameter eines ur-

7 Isabelle Graw und Peter Geimer, *Über Malerei. Eine Diskussion*, Berlin 2012, S. 40.

8 Ebd., S. 29.

9 Ebd., S. 44.

Aside from the specifically painterly issues explored by Plogsties, the question of the selection of visual motifs provides an indication of what motivation actually drives his practice of repetition. In particular popular, familiar works have not only already been repeatedly quoted by other artists, but these images circulate in the form of innumerable reproductions in our lifeworlds today and are the subject of films and books. Countless legends and myths entwine around these works; they seem to have possessed a secret ever since their creation that neither artists nor theoreticians have been able to uncover. What hides behind a painting such as the *Mona Lisa*, which has driven scholars until the present day to conduct extensive research on the real person behind the portrait?[11] On account of their enormous popularity and the questions that the above-mentioned paintings have raised until today, it is difficult to look at them without their "mythical baggage".[12] Plogsties dares to undertake this in order to comprehend the mystery and singularity of these paintings. This process recalls what Walter Benjamin described in his text *Einbahnstraße* (1928): "The power of a country road is different when one is walking along it from when one is flying over it by airplane. In the same way, the power of a text is different when it is read from when it is copied out. […] Only the copied text thus commands the soul of him who is occupied with it, whereas the mere reader never discovers the new aspects of his inner self that are opened by the text."[13] The thought expressed here, "that only whoever copies a text can truly understand its transformative power",[14] can undoubtedly be transposed to the copying of a painting.

Plogsties paints his pictures after reproductions, but he paints them with knowledge of the originals—only he does not (usually) look at them during the painting process. He does not deny that by means of his work process he learns much—about his own habits and peculiarities when painting, but also about compositions that other painters before him conceived. Is Plogsties completely untouched by the modem dogma of originality that appropriation artists before him attempted to subvert and ultimately only served? In the epoch of avant-gardes, practices of copying, quoting and repetition were deemed a betrayal of the autonomy of art.[15] With its rigorous rejection of any form of mimesis, indebted to its age's general idea of progress, Modernism idealised the qualities of originality and individuality to such an extent that art acquired a well-nigh religious status.[16] The artist, only by creating what was new, thus became a creator. Not until the middle of the 20th century was the Modernist paradigm radically questioned and contested, by means of various strategies, by different art movements such as minimal art, concept art, pop art and appropriation art. According to them different techniques of copying, reproducing and quoting became conceptually significant, but were to be understood in most cases as "acts of resistance".[17]

Wolfgang Ullrich observes in a younger generation of artists such as Silke Wagner, Klaus Mosettig, Tatjana Doll or Claudia Angelmaier, all of whom work with reproduction and repetition, that, unlike their predecessors, they are not intent on provocation and denial, but rather a serious engagement with the models: "They create repetitions not to make things easy for themselves, instead they are much more concerned with comprehending the work step for step, analytically, and in a controlled manner. Just like someone who slowly spells out a complicated word, in order to absorb it and to make it completely present, artists today carry out efforts to help models take form once more as consciously as possible."[18] Linked to this is a completely transformed conception of art, which Gerhard Richter had questioned in his complex of works *Forty-eight Portraits*, a series of portraits painted after encyclopaedia illustrations. Markus Lüpertz likewise frustrates the expectation that

11
»The most recent efforts to positively establish the identity once and for all prompted a search for the tomb of Lisa del Giocondo, to use her skull in an attempt to reconstruct her face. Since 2011 archaeologists have looked for her final resting place in the monastery of Sant Orsola in Florence.« Julia Bock, *Die stille Macht vertrauter Motive: Bewusste und unbewusste Adaption, Zitation und Wahrnehmung von Kunst in der Populärkultur und ihr möglicher Nutzen für die Museumspädagogik*, Göttingen 2013, p. 121.

12
Ibid.

13
See note 3, p. 126; quote taken from Walter Benjamin, *One-Way Street and Other Writings*, translated by Edmund Jephcott, London 1979, p. 50.

14
Ibid.

15
Wolfgang Ullrich, »Wiederholung als Ritual«, in *Déjà-vu? Die Kunst der Wiederholung von Dürer bis YouTube*, Staatliche Kunsthalle Karlsruhe/Staatliche Hochschule für Gestaltung Karlsruhe, Karlsruhe 2012, p. 139.

16
Ibid., p. 140.

17
Ibid., p. 141.

18
Ibid., p. 144.

sprünglich großformatigen Gemäldes lassen sich im Format einer Postkarte noch nachvollziehen? Und wie verändert sich ein Motiv, wenn die eigene Version radikal von der Größe des Originals abweicht? Oft arbeitet Plogsties nicht mit nur einer einzigen Vorlage, sondern vergleicht mehrere Reproduktionen, wenn er an einem bestimmten Motiv arbeitet. Warum lassen sich leichteste Variationen der Farben in verschiedenen Reproduktionen desselben Motivs leichter oder schwieriger wiedergeben? Um diesen Nachvollzug zu leisten, braucht es oft mehrere Anläufe. Der Prozess des genauen Sehens, Malens und der anschließenden Standortbestimmung – wie nah er der Vorlage gekommen ist – dauert wochen- und monatelang.

Eine starke Abweichung zur Originalgröße nimmt Plogsties beispielsweise auch mit 28_14 (**Bildnis einer jungen Frau im Profil**) vor. Antonio del Pollaiuolo fertigte das Motiv 1465 im Format 52,5 × 36,5 cm, Plogsties vergrößert es auf 270 × 190 cm. Weibliche Profilbilder waren im 15. Jahrhundert populäre Bildsujets. Das Gemälde von Pollaiuolo gilt als Darstellung, die von anderen Bildern seiner Zeit dadurch abweicht, dass er sich nicht nur auf das Gesicht der Frau konzentrierte, sondern auch deren Körperlichkeit thematisierte. Dies erreichte er durch den leicht nach links gewendeten Körper und die haptisch wirkende Stofflichkeit der Kleidung.[10] Das Gesicht dagegen wirkt steinern, marmorn. Das Antlitz orientierte sich weniger am eigentlichen Vorbild, sondern entspricht dem tradierten Schönheitsideal. In seiner Wiederholung gibt Plogsties genau jene Details nicht wieder, die damals das innovative Moment oder Alleinstellungsmerkmal des Gemäldes darstellten. In seinem Bild wirken die Muster auf dem Kleid verschwommen. Wie bei 7_12 (**Bildnis eines Mannes mit rotem Turban**) wirkt das Gesicht nicht ebenmäßig und im Gegensatz zum Original weniger puppenhaft, sondern es lassen sich durchscheinende untere Malschichten und grobe Pinselstriche erkennen. Mittels solcher Ungenauigkeiten macht Plogsties deutlich, dass auch ein originales Porträt bereits eine Reproduktion darstellt. Indem ein Maler sein Modell porträtiert, trifft er unwillkürlich Entscheidungen, die den gesellschaftlichen und kulturellen Konventionen seiner Zeit sowie seiner ureigenen, persönlichen Wahrnehmung geschuldet sind. Ein gemaltes Porträt stellt also per se eine Abweichung vom Vorbild dar. Für Jochen Plogsties multipliziert sich dieser Effekt, indem er Personen abmalt, deren Wahrnehmung bereits durch die Augen eines anderen Künstlers gefiltert ist. Er untersucht, wie sich durch solche unendlich fortsetzbaren Wiederholungsprozesse das Aussehen und die Ausstrahlung einer Person verändern und wie sich diesem Prozess eigene Erinnerungen an eine bestimmte Person – möglicherweise auch aus seinem privaten Umfeld – einschreiben lassen.

Neben solchen spezifisch malerischen Fragestellungen, die Plogsties untersucht, gibt auch die Frage nach der Auswahl seiner Bildmotive Aufschluss darüber, aus welcher Motivation heraus die Praxis der Wiederholung hier eigentlich stattfindet. Gerade die populären, vertrauten Werke sind nicht nur bereits von anderen Künstlern immer wieder zitiert worden, diese Bilder zirkulieren in Form unzähliger Reproduktionen in unserer heutigen Lebenswelt und sind Gegenstand von Kinofilmen und Büchern. Es ranken sich unzählige Legenden und Mythen um die Werke, sie scheinen ein Geheimnis zu enthalten, das seit ihrer Entstehung auch von Künstlern und Theoretikern nicht gelüftet werden konnte. Was steckt hinter einem Gemälde wie *Mona Lisa*, das Wissenschaftler bis heute dazu veranlasst, aufwändige Recherchen zu der echten Person, die sich hinter dem Porträt verbirgt, zu betreiben?[11] Aufgrund ihrer enormen Popularität und der Fragen, die die oben genannten

10
Wie Anm. 5, S. 65.

11
»Die jüngsten Bestrebungen, die Identität ein für alle Mal zu klären, gingen dahin, das Grab von Lisa del Gicondo zu finden, um anhand ihres Schädels eine Gesichtsrekonstruktion zu versuchen. Seit 2011 suchten Archäologen nach ihrer letzten Ruhestätte im Kloster Sant Orsola in Florenz«; Julia Bock, *Die stille Macht vertrauter Motive. Bewusste und unbewusste Adaption, Zitation und Wahrnehmung von Kunst in der Populärkultur und ihr möglicher Nutzen für die Museumspädagogik*, Göttingen 2013, S. 121.

the artist has merely to produce what is new and never-before-seen, stating that "painting consists of the further development of what has come before and the avant-garde today is found in tradition and its continuation".[19] The artist today is not necessarily a creative originator, rather he or she creates out of the wide-ranging content of pre-existing artworks, in order to subject them to a revision with the aid of "interpretive and renewing practices".[20]

This applies to Jochen Plogsties, too. His exploration and reconstruction of already-existing images is a form of visualisation, closely linked to the process of memory. In his novel *Repetition*, Peter Handke writes: "And remembering did not mean the past returned, rather the past indicated its place by returning. When I remembered, I felt: that was how the experience was, exactly like that! And thus this first became conscious, nameable, voiced and definite for me; and that is why remembering is for me not an arbitrary act of thinking back, but rather a being-at-work, and the work of remembering assigns to what has been experienced its place, whose life-preserving consequence is the story, which can always move into an open telling, into larger life, into invention."[21] Memory as visualization and repetition of something that already took place, that already exists, constitutes the poetics underlying Jochen Plogsties's works.

19
Cordula Meier, *Kunst und Gedächtnis: Zugänge zur aktuellen Kunstrezeption im Licht digitaler Speicher*, Munich 2002, p. 42.

20
See note 15, p. 144.

21
Peter Handke, *Die Wiederholung*, Frankfurt am Main 1992, p. 110.

Appropriation of one's own

Bilder bis heute aufwerfen, ist es vermutlich sehr schwierig, sie ohne ihren »mythischen Ballast«[12] zu betrachten. Plogsties wagt dieses Unterfangen, um die Rätselhaftigkeit und Besonderheit dieser Bilder nachzuvollziehen. Dieser Vorgang erinnert an das, was Walter Benjamin in seiner 1928 erschienenen Schrift *Einbahnstraße* beschreibt: »Die Kraft der Landstraße ist eine andere, ob einer sie geht oder im Aeroplan darüber hinfliegt. So ist auch die Kraft des Textes eine andere, ob einer ihn liest oder abschreibt. [...] So kommandiert allein der abgeschriebene Text die Seele dessen, der mit ihm beschäftigt ist, während der bloße Leser die neuen Ansichten seines Innern nie kennen lernt ...«[13] Der hier ausgedrückte Gedanke, »dass nur wer einen Text abschreibt, wirklich seine verändernde Kraft versteht«,[14] lässt sich zweifellos auch auf das Abmalen eines Bildes beziehen.

Plogsties malt seine Bilder zwar nach Reproduktionen, aber er malt sie im Wissen um die Originale — bloß schaut er sie während des Malprozesses (meist) nicht an. Auch leugnet er nicht, dass er durch seine Arbeitsweise viel lernt – über seine eigenen Angewohnheiten und Eigenheiten beim Malen, aber vor allem auch über Kompositionen, die andere Maler vor ihm erfanden. Ist Plogsties vom modernen Originalitätsdogma, das schon die Appropriation Artists zu unterwandern versuchten und letztlich doch bedienten, völlig unberührt? Im Zeitalter der Avantgarden galten Praktiken des Kopierens, Zitierens und Wiederholens als Verrat an der Autonomie der Kunst.[15] Die Moderne mit ihrer – dem allgemeinen Fortschrittsdenken jener Zeit verpflichteten – rigorosen Ablehnung jeder Form der Mimesis verklärte den Stellenwert von Originalität und Individualität derart, dass die Kunst einen religiösen Status erlangte.[16] Der Künstler, indem er ausschließlich Neues kreierte, agierte somit als Schöpfer. Erst Mitte des 20. Jahrhunderts wurde das moderne Paradigma vonseiten unterschiedlicher Richtungen wie Minimal Art, Concept Art, Popart und Appropriation Art radikal in Frage gestellt und mittels unterschiedlicher Strategien angefochten. Bereits hier kamen verschiedene Techniken wie Kopieren, Reproduzieren und Zitieren konzeptuell zum Tragen, sind jedoch vielfach als »Akte des Widerstands«[17] zu verstehen.

Wolfgang Ullrich attestiert einer jüngeren Generation von Künstlern wie Silke Wagner, Klaus Mosettig, Tatjana Doll oder Claudia Angelmaier, die sich mit Reproduktionen und Wiederholungen auseinandersetzen, dass sie es nicht mehr auf Provokation und Verweigerung anlegen, sondern dass ihre Arbeiten eine ernsthafte Auseinandersetzung mit den Vorbildern darstellen: »Wiederholt wird also nicht, um es sich leicht zu machen, vielmehr geht es darum, das Werk Schritt für Schritt analytisch und kontrolliert nachzuvollziehen. So wie jemand ein kompliziertes Wort langsam nachbuchstabiert, um es aufzunehmen und ganz zu vergegenwärtigen, üben sich Künstler heute darin, Vorbildern möglichst bewusst erneut zur Gestalt zu verhelfen.«[18] Damit verbunden ist ein vollkommen verändertes künstlerisches Selbstverständnis, das Gerhard Richter bereits 1972 mit seinem Werkkomplex *Achtundvierzig Porträts*, einer Serie von Porträts, die er nach Lexikonabbildungen malte, hinterfragte. Auch Markus Lüpertz stellt sich gegen die Erwartung, dass vom Künstler lediglich Neues und noch nicht Gesehenes produziert werde, und konstatiert, »dass die Malerei in der Weiterentwicklung von Überliefertem bestehe und Avantgarde heute in der Tradition und deren Fortsetzung stecke«.[19] Der Künstler ist heute nicht mehr zwangsläufig ein kreativer Schöpfer, sondern er schöpft aus den mannigfaltigen Beständen schon existierender Kunstwerke, um diese mithilfe »interpretierender und erneuernder Praktiken«[20] einer Revision zu unterziehen.

12 Ebd.

13 Wie Anm. 3, S. 126.

14 Ebd.

15 Wolfgang Ullrich, »Wiederholung als Ritual«, in: *Déjà-vu? Die Kunst der Wiederholung von Dürer bis Youtube*, Staatliche Kunsthalle Karlsruhe/Staatliche Hochschule für Gestaltung Karlsruhe, Karlsruhe 2012, S. 139.

16 Ebd., S. 140.

17 Ebd., S. 141.

18 Ebd., S. 144.

19 Cordula Meier, *Kunst und Gedächtnis. Zugänge zur aktuellen Kunstrezeption im Licht digitaler Speicher*, München 2002, S. 42.

20 Wie Anm. 15, S. 144.

Dies trifft auch auf Jochen Plogsties zu. Sein Ausloten und Nachvollziehen bereits vorhandener Bilder ist eine Form der Vergegenwärtigung, die eng verwandt ist mit dem Prozess des Erinnerns. In dem Roman *Die Wiederholung* von Peter Handke heißt es: »Und Erinnerung hieß nicht: Was gewesen war, kehrte wieder; sondern: Was gewesen war, zeigte, indem es wiederkehrte, seinen Platz. Wenn ich mich erinnerte, erfuhr ich: So war das Erlebnis, genau so!, und damit wurde mir dieses erst bewusst, benennbar, stimmhaft und spruchreif, und deshalb ist mir die Erinnerung kein beliebiges Zurückdenken, sondern ein Am-Werk-Sein, und das Werk der Erinnerung schreibt dem Erlebten seinen Platz zu und der ist am Leben haltende Folge, der Erzählung, die immer wieder übergehen kann ins offene Erzählen, ins größere Leben, in die Erfindung.«[21] Das Erinnern als Vergegenwärtigung und Wiederholung von etwas, das bereits stattgefunden hat, das bereits existiert, ist die Poetik, die Jochen Plogsties Werken zugrunde liegt.

[21] Peter Handke, *Die Wiederholung*, Frankfurt am Main 1992, S. 110.

Andreas Reckwitz

Künstler-Kreateure

[…] Im Kunstfeld versammeln sich seit dem letzten Drittel des 18. Jahrhunderts disparate Elemente, die sich als »künstlerisch« verstehen. Die Kunst erlangt als ein soziales Feld dadurch ihre Identität, dass es ihr gelingt, genuin ästhetisch orientierte Praktiken auszubilden, die sich andere, bisher historisch mit ihnen kombinierte Handlungs- und Denkweisen, so das Religiöse, das sozial Gesellige (etwa der höfischen Gesellschaft), teilweise auch das Moralische, auf Distanz halten. Das Kunstfeld schließt unterschiedliche Künste ein, die jedoch nach der einflussreichen Definition von Batteux nun alle einheitlich als »Kunst« klassifiziert werden,[1] und es entwickelt sich in den verschiedenen europäischen Gesellschaften nicht völlig synchron. Es umfasst Artefakte, vor allem die Kunstwerke, singuläre und abgrenzbare Objekte wie Gemälde, Skulpturen, Musikstücke und literarische Texte, aber auch Gebäude, die der Ausstellung und Aufführung dieser Objekte dienen (Museen, Theater, Konzerthäuser etc.). Es schließt die Praktiken der Herstellung der Kunstwerke, ihrer Verbreitung – über den Kunst- und Literaturmarkt – und Ausstellung sowie ihrer Verarbeitung durch den Rezipienten ein. Es umfasst die Sozialisation des Künstlers und des Rezipienten. Es schließt die Vergemeinschaftung von Künstlern in entsprechenden Milieus und Stadtvierteln ebenso ein wie das gesellschaftliche Wissen bezüglich des Ästhetischen, das in der Philosophie, der Kulturkritik und der Literatur kursiert.

Dieses heterogene Feld erlangt seine Form zunächst insbesondere durch eine Umstrukturierung der künstlerischen Herstellungspraxis und ihres Trägers, des Künstlers.[2] Es positioniert das Künstlersubjekt als Produzenten *neuartiger* ästhetischer Objekte, die jeweils mit den sozialen Erwartungen des ästhetisch Üblichen brechen. Diese kulturelle Entwicklung setzt den Diskurs der Genie-

[1] Vgl. Charles Batteux, *Les beaux arts réduits à un même principe*, Paris 1773.

[2] Zum Künstler insgesamt vgl. nur Jörg Völlnagel und Moritz Wullen (Hrsg.), *Unsterblich! Der Kult des Künstlers*, München 2008; Martin Hellmold u. a. (Hrsg.), *Was ist ein Künstler? Das Subjekt der modernen Kunst*, München 2003.

ästhetik voraus, der sich Mitte des 18. Jahrhunderts in Deutschland, England und Frankreich etabliert. Die Genieästhetik modelliert den Künstler als »schöpferischen« Hervorbringer von Werken, die gegen die bestehenden Regeln verstoßen, die überraschen und in diesem Sinne neuartig sind,[3] und gewinnt ihre Identität aus der Abgrenzung gegenüber der humanistischen und klassizistischen Nachahmungsästhetik. Eine semantische Vorbereitung findet sich im ausgehenden 17. Jahrhundert im Rahmen der »Querelle des Anciens et des Modernes«, in der die Funktion der Kunst als antiklassizistische, am Neuen orientierte Aktivität vorformuliert wird. Während die Nachahmungsästhetik die Aufgabe des Künstlers in der Anwendung und perfektionierten Umsetzung der Regeln idealer Kunst, damit in der virtuosen Reproduktion des Alten und Universalen festmachte, erfindet die neue Ästhetik den Künstler als Antikopisten, als Schöpfer origineller Werke, die sich nicht mehr aus allgemeingültigen Regeln ableiten lassen.[4] Damit wird auch eine eindeutige Differenz zwischen Kunst und Kunsthandwerk möglich und nötig.[5]

Im Zentrum der Genieästhetik steht ein subjektivistisches Zuschreibungsschema der Produktion des Neuen: Sie rechnet das jeweilige Kunstwerk einem individuellen, nicht austauschbaren »Schöpfer« zu, dessen Psyche mit außeralltäglichen Eigenschaften ausgestattet scheint. »Genie« ist eine Umschreibung dieser Qualitäten. Wenn Alexander Gerard 1774 in seinem *Essay on Genius* definiert, »das Genie umfasst im Kern die Fähigkeit zur Erfindung (inventio), welche es einem Menschen ermöglicht, in der Wissenschaft neue Entdeckungen zu machen oder originelle Kunstwerke zu produzieren«,[6] dann wird deutlich, dass es sich um ein Dispositionskonzept handelt. Es bezeichnet ein Vermögen zur *inventio* im Gegensatz zur *imitatio* des Regelkanons. Grundlegend ist hier die angenommene Parallele zwischen der Nichtregelhaftigkeit des Werkes und der des Autors, die beide mit dem Begriff der »Originalität« versehen werden. Wenn das Kunstwerk sich durch Originalität auszeichnen will, dann muss auch der Künstler als Schöpfer ein »Original« sein, und beide scheinen durch eine Beziehung des Ausdrucks (Expression) miteinander verbunden: Die Einzigartigkeit des Künstlers drückt sich in der des Werkes aus. In der Antike wurde diese Genialität mit dem angeborenen Ingenium begründet, in der Frühen Neuzeit mit der Inspiration, wobei beides religiös konnotiert ist. Das moderne Verständnis des Genies ist weitgehend säkularisiert, auch wenn metaphorische Bezüge zum Göttlichen die Faszination für die Außeralltäglichkeit des Künstlers fördern.[7]

Im Rahmen der Kartografie der sich ökonomisierenden, verrechtlichenden und politisierenden Gesellschaft der Moderne besetzt das Künstlersubjekt soziologisch damit zunächst einen besonderen Ort: Es ist ein *Exklusivtypus* und damit eine merkwürdige Doppelfigur. Der Künstler ist einerseits ein sozial identifizierbarer Typus, der spezialisierte Leistungen erbringt, die Produktion von Kunstwerken. Aber er ist zugleich eine sozial exklusive Figur, denn nicht jeder kann Künstler sein oder werden. Das Künstlertum soll vielmehr »außeralltägliche« Eigenschaften erfordern, die sich gegen eine soziale Inklusion sperren und die im Rahmen der Geniekultur als *genius* und *ingenium* umschrieben werden. Wenn soziale Inklusion meint, dass potenziell jede Person an einem sozialen Zusammenhang partizipieren darf, sofern sie entsprechende Voraussetzungen erwirbt, und im Prinzip auch jeder diese erwerben kann, dann bedeutet Exklusivität, dass eine solche universalisierte Teilhabe grundsätzlich nicht möglich ist.[8] Genau dies trifft auf den Künstler zu, und zwar in einem besonderen Sinne. Der Künstler entspricht nämlich weder der alten Exklusivklasse noch der neuen Leistungsinklusion: Weder beruht seine Exklusivität wie beim Adel des Ancien Régime auf seiner Herkunft noch stehen seine Leistung und sein Status potenziell jedem offen, wie dies offiziell für

3

Vgl. auch Nathalie Heinich, *La gloire de Van Gogh. Essai d'anthropologie de l'admiration*, Paris 1991.

4

Vgl. Jochen Schmidt, *Die Geschichte des Genie-Gedankens in der deutschen Literatur, Philosophie und Politik 1750–1945*, Bd. 1, Darmstadt 1985; Edgar Zilsel, *Die Entstehung des Geniebegriffs. Ein Beitrag zur Ideengeschichte der Antike und des Frühkapitalismus* [1926], Hildesheim/New York 1972; Hans Brög, *Zum Geniebegriff. Quellen, Marginalien, Probleme*, Ratingen 1973.

5

In mancher Hinsicht kann die Genieästhetik auf Elemente des Individualismus in der Renaissancekunst zurückgreifen. Dieser ideenhistorische Bezug ist ein klassischer Topos; vgl. nur Alessandro Conti, *Der Weg des Künstlers*, Berlin 1998.

6

Alexander Gerard, *An Essay on Genius*, London 1774, S. 8 (Übersetzung A. R.).

7

Shaftesbury nennt den Dichter »einen zweiten Schöpfer (maker), geradezu einen Prometheus«; vgl. Anthony Shaftesbury, Soliloquy, or, Advice to an Author [1710], in: ders., *Characteristics of Men, Manners, Opinions, and Times*, Bd. 1, London 1900, S. 103–234, hier S. 136.

8

Zum Konzept der Inklusion vgl. Rudolf Stichweh, Inklusion in Funktionssystemen der modernen Gesellschaft, in: Renate Mayntz u. a. (Hrsg.), *Differenzierung und Verselbständigung*, Frankfurt am Main/New York 1988, S. 45–116.

moderne Berufe gilt.[9] Der Künstler ist wie sein Werk stattdessen Gegenstand einer kulturellen Auratisierung: Er erscheint als Individuum, das zu einer außeralltäglichen Perzept- und Affektproduktion fähig ist und sich darin einer graduellen Leistungsbewertung entzieht. Das Künstlersubjekt kann offenbar nur dadurch als jene Instanz etabliert werden, die das ästhetisch Neue hervorbringt, dass diese sogleich genialistisch eingeschränkt wird. Der Künstler ist zwar spezialisiert, so wie andere Professionen, aber im Unterschied zu diesen ist mit seiner Tätigkeit der Anspruch und die Erwartung eines entdifferenzierten und entrationalisierten Bezugs zu einer natürlichen, psychischen und sozialen Totalität verknüpft.[10]

Das moderne Kunstfeld setzt voraus, dass die Fähigkeit des Künstlers zum Neuen mit »Einbildungskraft« (Imagination) als ästhetischer Kompetenz verknüpft ist; das Subjektivierungsprogramm des Künstlers als Originalgenie ist eng mit der Aufwertung dieser Imagination verbunden.[11] Während die Imagination von der Antike bis zur Renaissance als eine primitive und riskante Fähigkeit der Sinne erschien, die entweder als im schlichtesten Sinne registrierend oder aber irrational phantasierend verstanden wurde, dreht das Feld der modernen Kunst diese Wertigkeit um. Nun erscheint die Imagination in ihrer Fähigkeit, durch sinnliche Sensibilität und Kombinationsvermögen das Überraschende hervorzubringen, als Voraussetzung des Originalgenies. Denis Diderot charakterisiert in der *Encyclopédie* den Künstler entsprechend über »geistige Weite, Imaginationskraft und seelische Regsamkeit«. Er sei ein Mensch, »dessen Seele die größte Weite hat, also von allen Dingen Empfindungen erfährt, Anteil an allem nimmt«.[12] Es ist dann konsequent, dass im Rahmen der Genieästhetik die künstlerische Tätigkeit der Tendenz nach entmaterialisiert wird. Die nun strikte Trennung zwischen *ars liberales* und *ars mechanicae*, die Positionierung der Kunst im Singular als Gesamtheit der seit der Antike bekannten einzelnen Künste gegen das bloße pragmatische Handwerk setzt voraus, dass nicht die Bearbeitung des Materials das charakteristische Kennzeichen dieser Tätigkeit ist, sondern die geistige, sinnlich-affektive Gestaltung der Gegenstände. Die künstlerische Praxis erweist sich dann mit Schelling als die »Tätigkeit einer Idee«.

Das, was der Künstler-Kreateur im Rahmen des modernen Kunstfeldes verfertigt, ist somit das individuelle Werk als ein Quasi-Objekt, ein kulturell-materielles Doppel.[13] Es setzt sich aus bestimmten Materialien zusammen, die vom Produzenten arrangiert und vom Rezipienten sinnlich wahrgenommen werden, und diesen werden zugleich kulturelle Bedeutungen zugeschrieben; sie haben eine »Form« und einen »geistigen Gehalt«. Die Werke der Kunst sind dabei so heterogen wie die bürgerlich legitimen Künste selbst: Plastiken und Gemälde, poetische Texte und Prosatexte, in Notenschrift fixierbare und aufgeführte Musikstücke und textuell niedergelegte und ebenso aufgeführte Dramen.[14] Als Kunstwerk im modernen Sinne – ein Konzept, wie es erstmals systematisch in Karl Philipp Moritz' »schönem Kunstwerk« entwickelt wird – teilen diese disparaten Objekte mehrere Eigenschaften.[15] Sie sollen »rein ästhetische« Objekte für zwei Sorten von Subjekten, die Künstler und die Rezipienten, sein. Zugleich soll dem Kunstwerk eine Eigendynamik und Binnenkomplexität zukommen; das Werk erscheint als eine »lebendige, hochorganisierte Natur«.[16] Obwohl dem Kunstwerk im Kontext des bürgerlichen Kunstfeldes zunächst größtenteils innere Einheit und immanente Geschlossenheit zugeschrieben werden, soll es so von vornherein das ästhetisch Neue und Originelle verkörpern, und zwar in zweifacher Hinsicht: Als »historisches Individuum« stellt es sich gegen jeden konventionellen Regelkanon. Zugleich ermöglicht es aus sich selbst heraus immer wieder neue, ihm gemäße Aneignungsweisen.

9

Zu dieser klassischen soziologischen Unterscheidung von ascribed- und achieved-Merkmalen vgl. Parsons, *The Social System*, S. 180ff. Mit den Kunstakademien gibt es seit 1800 trotzdem eine Institution, welche die Lehrbarkeit der Kunst suggeriert und die der Genieästhetik und Kunstreligion entgegensteht.

10

Diese Totalität kann als »Natur«, als »Geschichte«, später auch als »Existenz« begriffen werden, Hölderlin bezeichnet sie als »All-Einheit des Lebens«. Vgl. hierzu Jochen Schmidt, *Die Geschichte des Genie-Gedankens*, S. 404ff.

11

Vgl. Jochen Schulte-Sasse, »Einbildungskraft/Imagination«, in: Karlheinz Barck u. a. (Hrsg.), *Ästhetische Grundbegriffe*, Bd. 2, Stuttgart/Weimar 2001, S. 88–120; James Engell, *The Creative Imagination*, Cambridge 1981.

12

Denis Diderot, »Enzyklopädie oder ein durchdachtes Wörterbuch über die Wissenschaften, die Künste und die Handwerke [1751]«, in: ders., *Philosophische Schriften*, Bd. 1, Berlin 1984, S. 235.

13

Vgl. zum Quasi-Objekt Bruno Latour, *Wir sind nie modern gewesen. Versuch einer symmetrischen Anthropologie* [1991], Berlin 1995, S. 120–132, 175–184.

14

Zur Differenz zwischen den verschiedenen Künsten vgl. systematisch Ursula Brandstätter, *Grundfragen der Ästhetik. Bild, Musik, Sprache, Körper*, Köln/Weimar u. a. 2008, S. 119ff.

15

Karl Philipp Moritz, »Über den Begriff des in sich selbst Vollendeten [1785]«, in: ders. und Horst Günther (Hrsg.), *Werke*, Bd. 2., Frankfurt am Main 1981, S. 543–548. Vgl. zum Begriff des Kunstwerks insgesamt Wolfgang Thierse, »Das Ganze aber ist das, was Anfang, Mitte und Ende hat«, in: *Weimarer Beiträge 36* (1990), S. 240–264.

16

Johann Wolfgang von Goethe, »Über Laokoon [1796], in: ders., *Werke*. Hamburger Ausgabe, Bd. 12, München 1998, S. 56.

Appropriationsverfahren: das relativ Neue

In der postmodernen Kunst bildet sich seit den 1960er-Jahren eine Reihe von Praktiken, die den Anspruch der Originalität und radikalen Neuartigkeit von Kunstwerken problematisieren und neujustieren. Die Kritik am Originalgenie sowie an der Unterscheidung zwischen Original und Kopie ist hier verbreitet, und Rosalind Krauss hat sie als eine Kritik am Mythos des »großen Bruchs« auf den Begriff gebracht.[17] Diese Dekonstruktion des Originalitätsanspruchs sollte man jedoch nicht dahingehend missverstehen, dass in der postmodernen Kunst das künstlerisch Neue aufgegeben würde. Es wird vielmehr relativer und subtiler markiert – und damit potenziert.

Exemplarisch für diese alternativen Produktionsverfahren jenseits des »Originals« sind die Pop Art und Andy Warhols Siebdruckverfahren, die serielle Reproduktion industrieller Formen in der *Minimal Art*, die wir bereits gesehen hatten, schließlich die *Postproduction* und *Appropriation Art*, die auf bestehende kulturelle Objekte, zum Beispiel massenmedial verbreitete Fotografien, zurückgreift.[18] Im Grunde kann man in allen diesen Fällen von Appropriationsverfahren sprechen, denn das Grundmodell der Produktion ist immer das gleiche: Es geht nicht darum, der existierenden Objektwelt ein *ex nihilo* geschaffenes Artefakt *hinzuzufügen*, sondern vielmehr auf die existierende Objekte- und Bedeutungswelt zu antworten, indem man sich vorhandener Dinge *bedient*. Der Künstler wird dann zum »Plagiator« (Sherrie Levine), und die Alltagskultur wird ihm zur »immensen Enzyklopädie, die ihm als Quelle dient«.[19] Dieses Sichbedienen bedeutet jedoch immer eine Resignifizierung: Die Alltagswelt ist der Anfangs-, nicht der Endpunkt des künstlerischen Prozesses. Das Neue ergibt sich nicht in einem genieästhetischen Originalitätsanspruch, sondern nistet sich in die Wiederholung des Gegebenen und Vergangenen ein.

Drei Varianten von Appropriationsverfahren lassen sich voneinander unterscheiden, und überall ergeben sich Modelle dessen, was das *relativ* Neue in der Kunst (und darüber hinaus) bedeuten kann. In einer ersten Version greift man auf bereits vorhandene Dinge zurück. Dies gilt etwa für Duchamps Readymades, später für die Environments von Alan Kaprow mit ihren *junk*-Objekten. Das Neue besteht hier in der Selektion der Gegenstände, ihrer kommentierten oder unkommentierten Rekontextualisierung. Die zweite Variante ist die serielle Produktion identischer Formen. Hier werden Objekte sehr wohl hergestellt, aber sie sind Ergebnis eines industriellen Verfahrens und/ oder es handelt sich um Standardobjekte, die nicht vom Künstler erfunden wurden; zudem werden sie in Serie fabriziert, ähnlich einem Konsumobjekt. Dies gilt für die *Multiples* der *Minimal Art*: Hier ist das Neue im neuartigen räumlichen Arrangement der vertrauten Objekte und in der Atmosphärenkreation zu sehen, die sich aus ihm ergibt.

Eine dritte Variante bildet die Reproduktion medialer Formate, etwa von Fotografien. Warhols klassischer Siebdruck, in dem Porträts prominenter Personen verarbeitet werden, gehört ebenso in diese Gruppe wie Sherry Levines, Cindy Shermans und Elaine Sturtevants Reproduktionen und ihr »Nachstellen« von bekannten Fotografien. Die Reproduktion erweist sich dabei als rekontextualisierende Zitation, deren Unterschied zum Original dadurch allerdings umso auffälliger wird. In dieser Gruppe sind die medialen Originale selbst bereits technische Reproduktionen, sie sind gewissermaßen »Kopien ohne Original« (Derrida). Warhol bedient sich dabei vertrauter Verfahren aus seiner Arbeit als Werbegrafiker und erzielt durch die üppige Farbgebung der Siebdruck-Reproduktionen Verfremdungseffekte.[20] Ein anderes Verfahren wählt Elaine Sturtevants *Postproduction Art*: Wenn sie beispielsweise in der Fotografie *La rivoluzione siamo noi* in die Rolle von Beuys aus

17
Vgl. Rosalinde E. Krauss, *Die Originalität der Avantgarde und andere Mythen der Moderne*, Dresden/Amsterdam 2000, S. 197–219.

18
Vgl. dazu allgemein Romana Rebbelmund, *Appropriation Art*, Frankfurt am Main u. a. 1999; Stefan Römer, *Künstlerische Strategien des Fake*, Köln 2001; Nicolas Bourriaud, *Postproduction*, New York 2002.

19
Sherrie Levine, »Statement«, in: *Mannerism. A Theory of Culture*, Ausst.-Kat. Vancouver Art Gallery, 27. 3.–25. 4. 1982, Vancouver 1982, S. 48.

20
Vgl. Klaus Honnef, *Andy Warhol. 1928–1987*, Köln 2006.

dessen bekanntem, gleichnamigem Porträtfoto von 1972 schlüpft,[21] sie die gleiche Kleidung trägt wie dieser und den energischen Schritt auf den Betrachter zu imitiert, dann entblößt sie in der Subtilität der Differenz des Bildes zum Original letzteres bis zur Kenntlichkeit. Das Neue des *Post-production*-Kunstwerks besteht dann in einer Neuinterpretation des »Originals«, das sich selbst als ein kulturelles Stereotyp erweist. […]

Auszug aus: Die Erfindung der Kreativität. Zum Prozeß gesellschaftlicher Ästhetisierung.
© Suhrkamp Verlag Berlin 2012. S. 60–65, 110–112.
Die englische Übersetzung erscheint 2015 bei Polity Press, Cambridge /
The English edition will be published in 2015 by Polity Press, Cambridge

21 Es handelt sich um einen Offsetdruck auf braunem Tonpapier in 60 Exemplaren, der 1988 entstanden ist.

2014

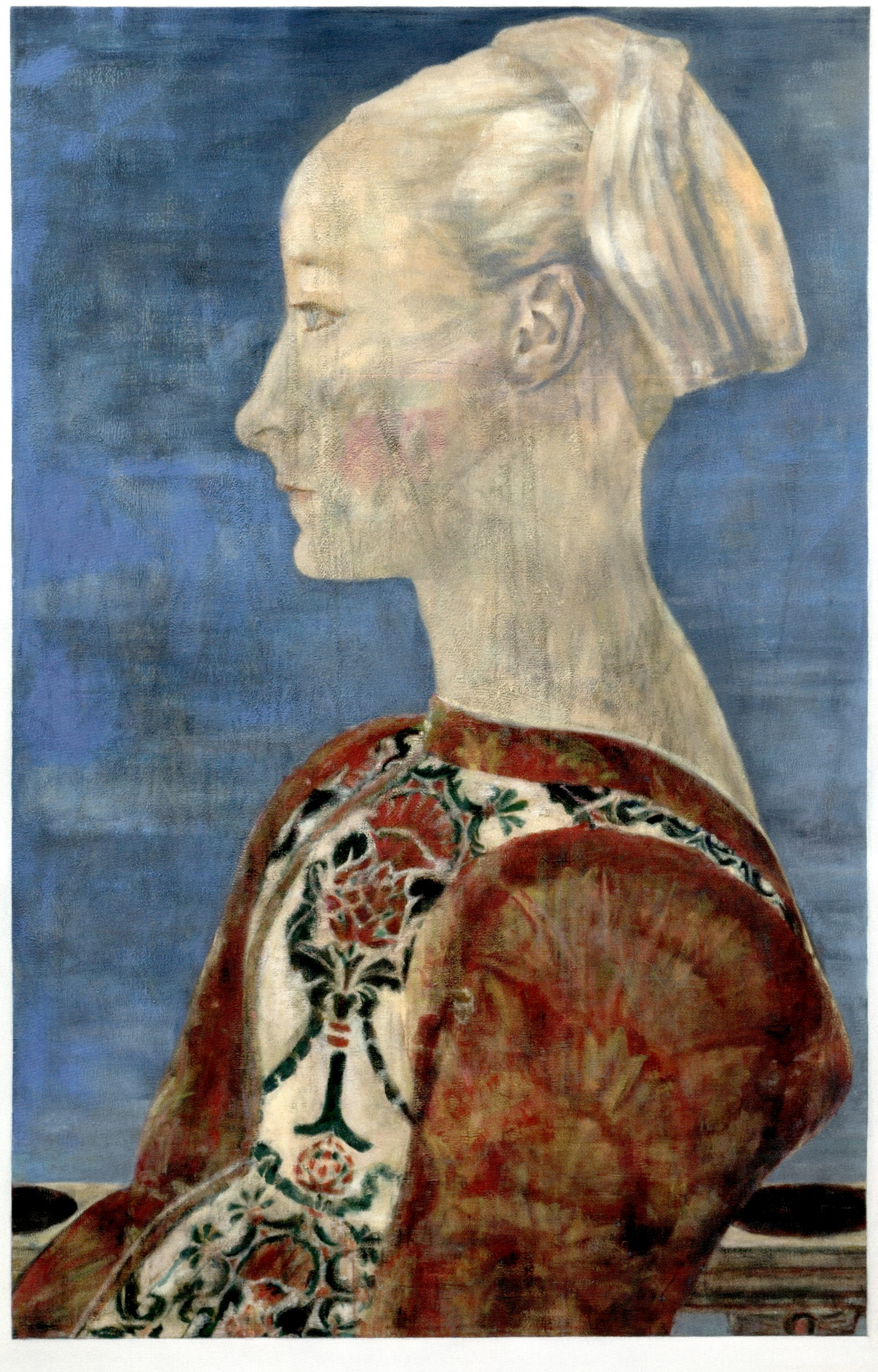

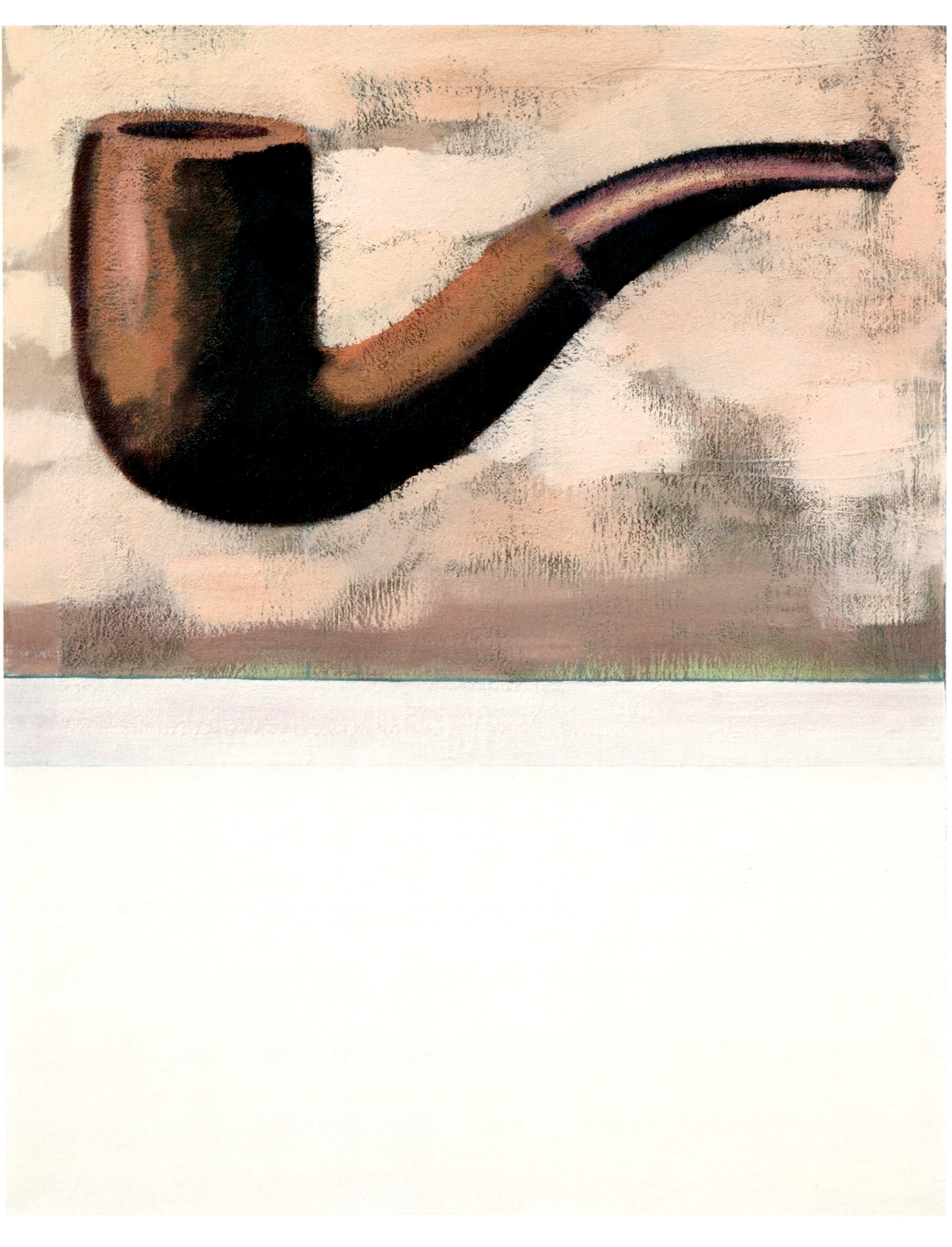

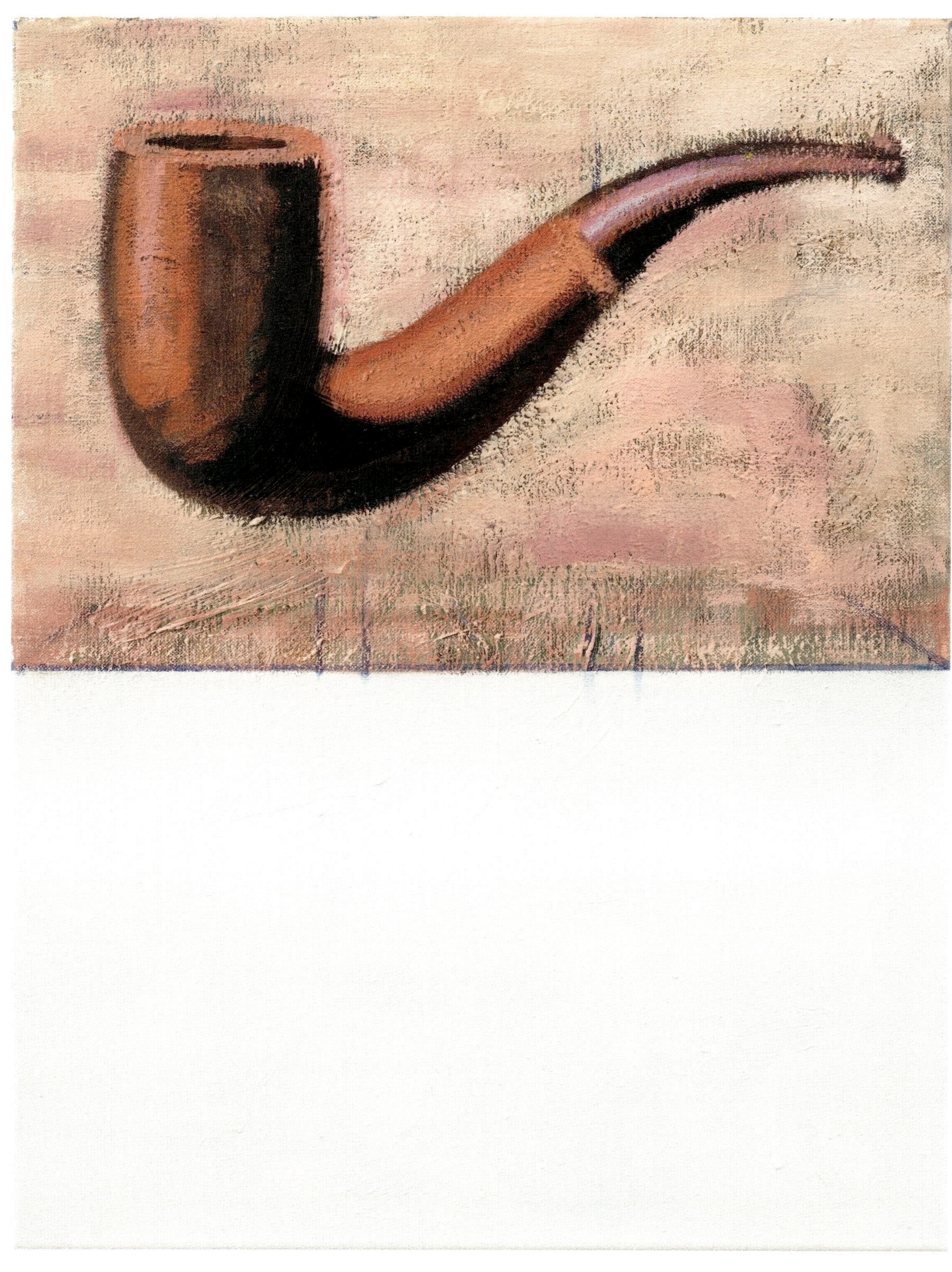

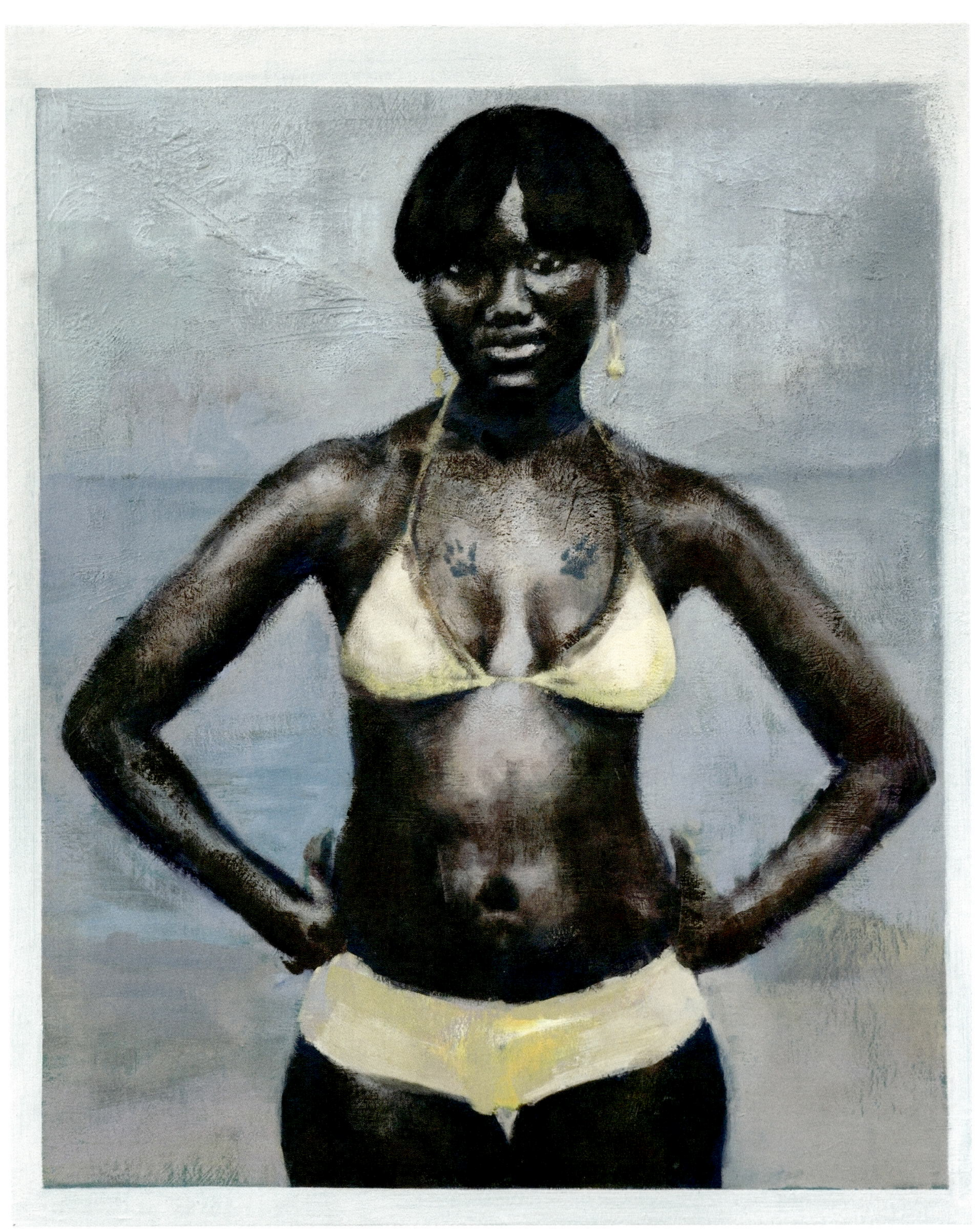

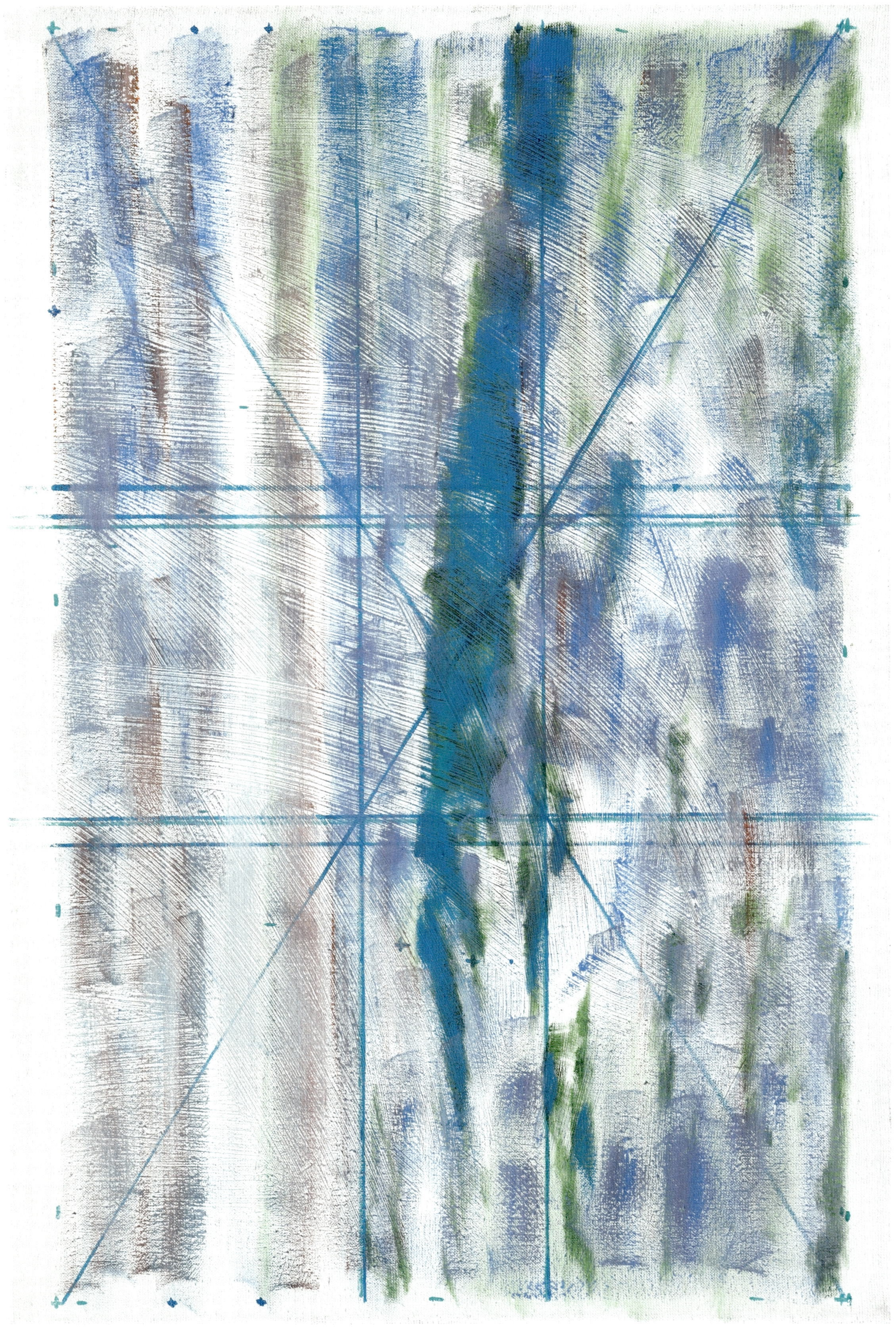

24_14

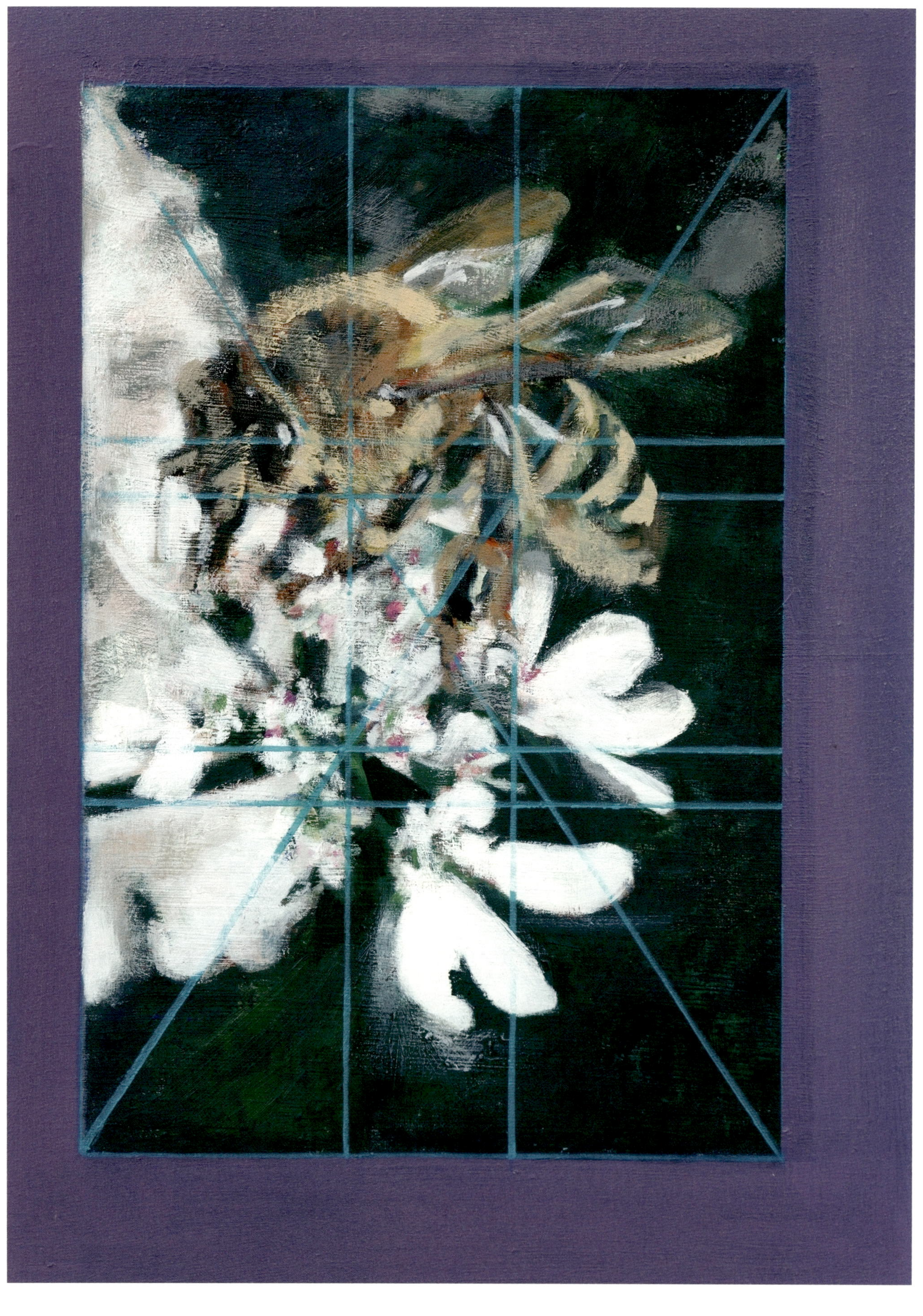

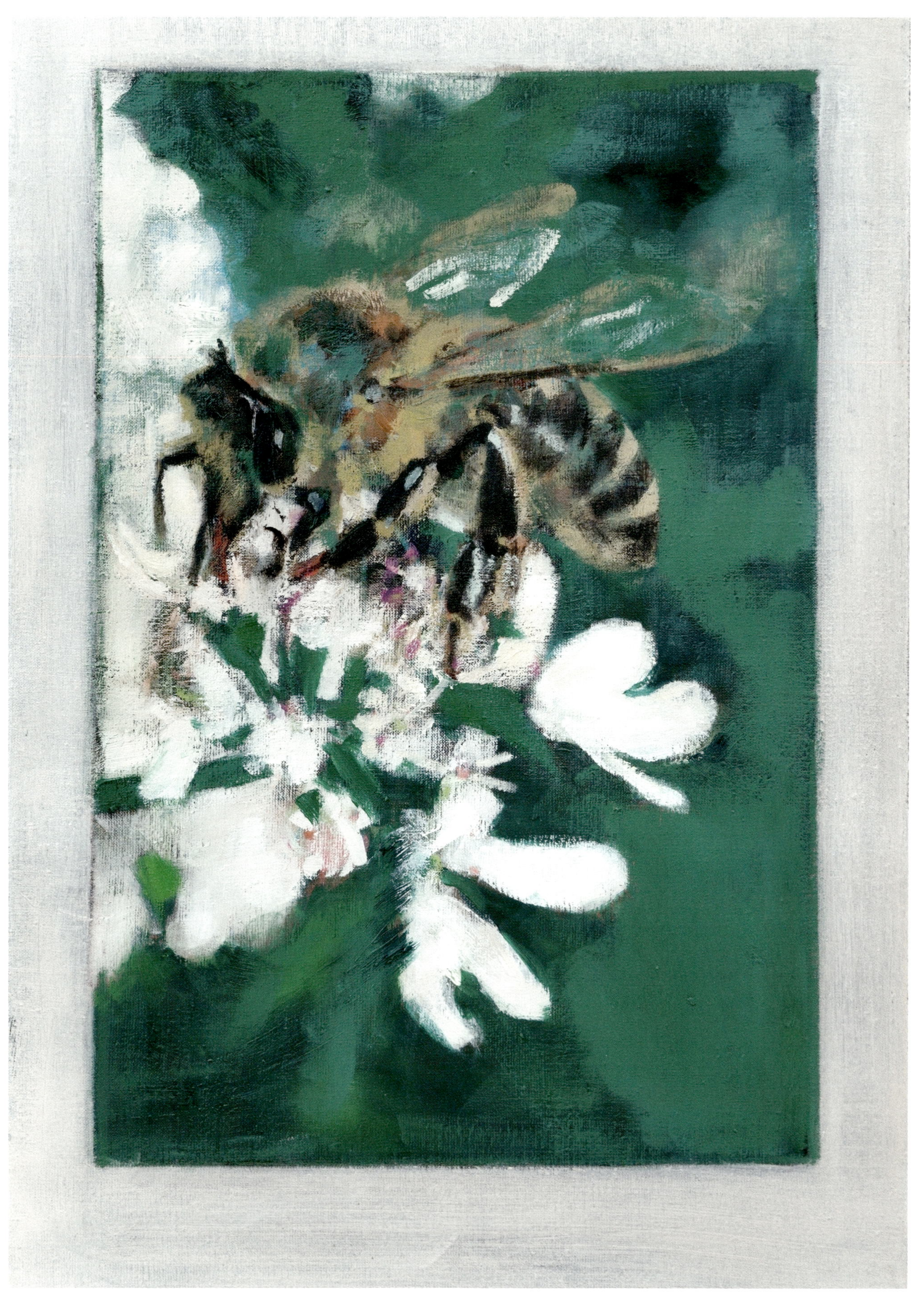

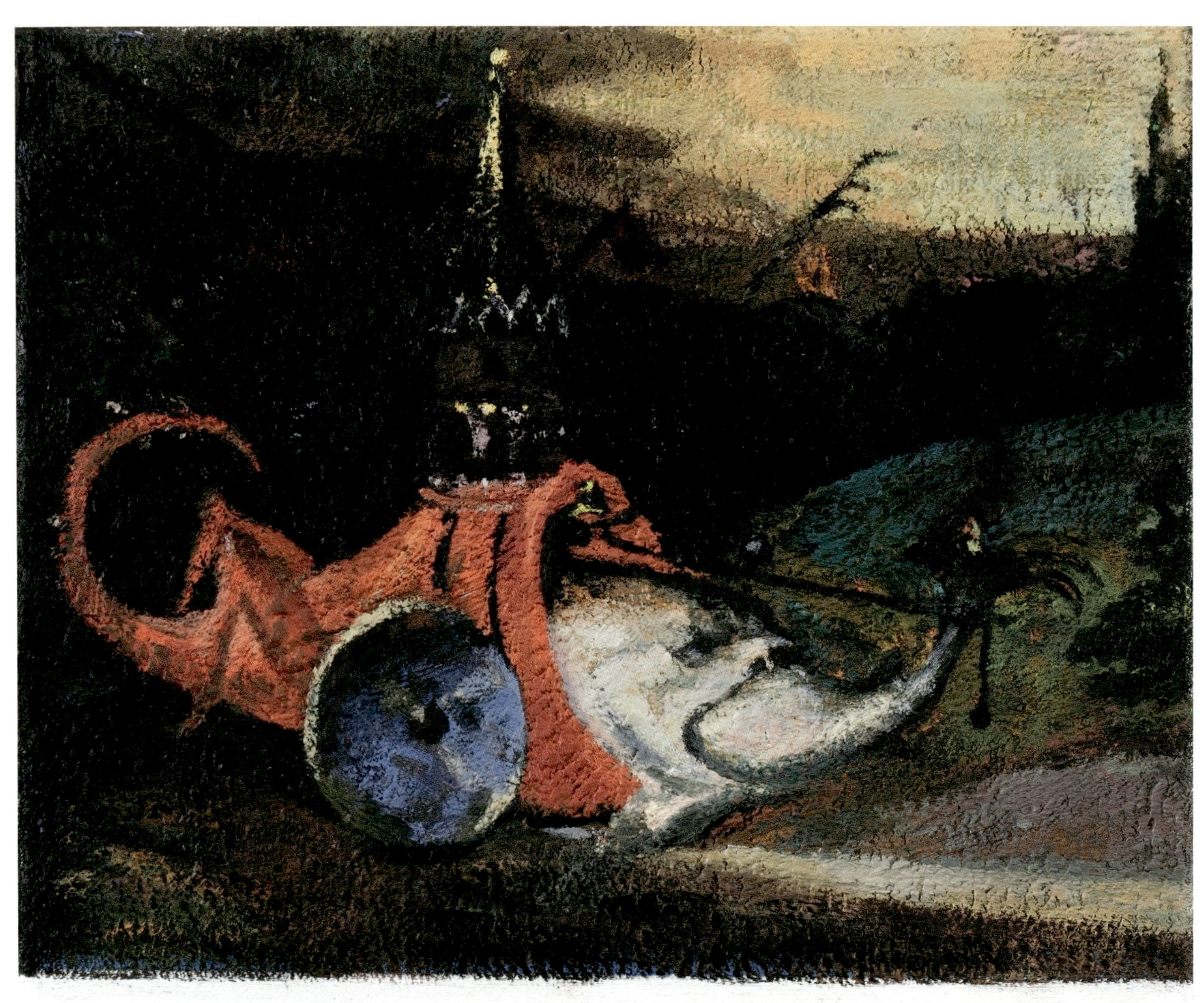

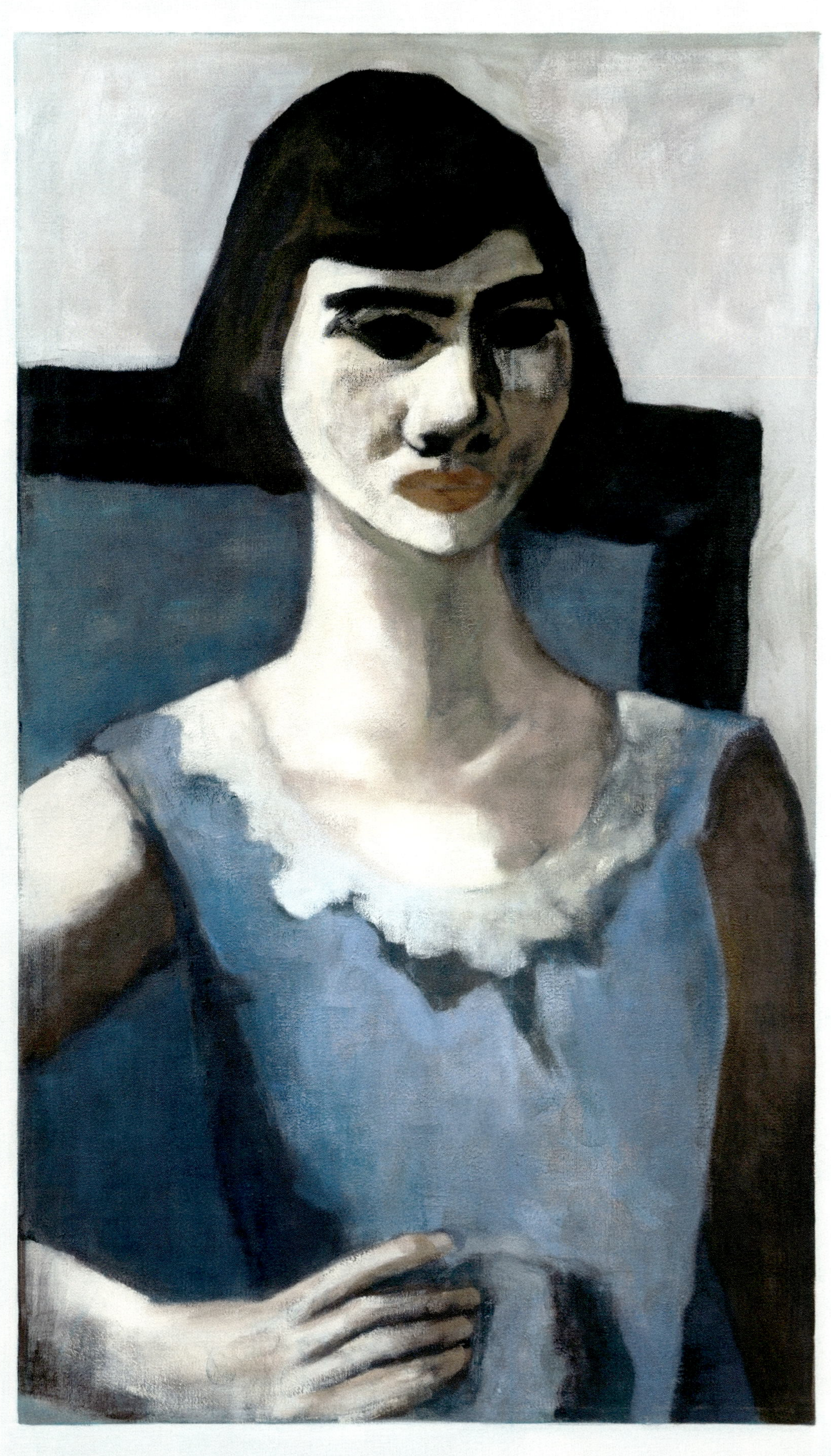

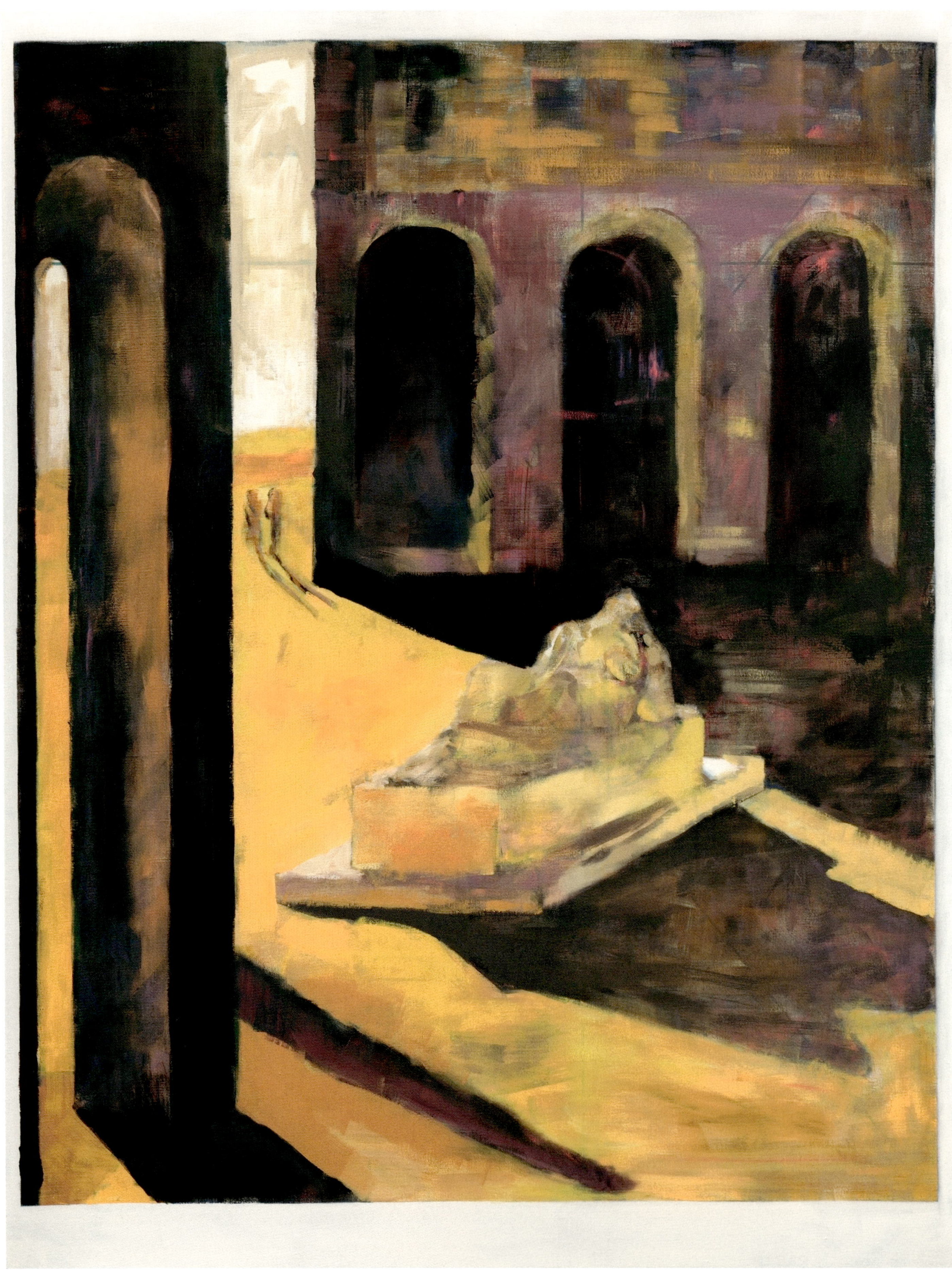

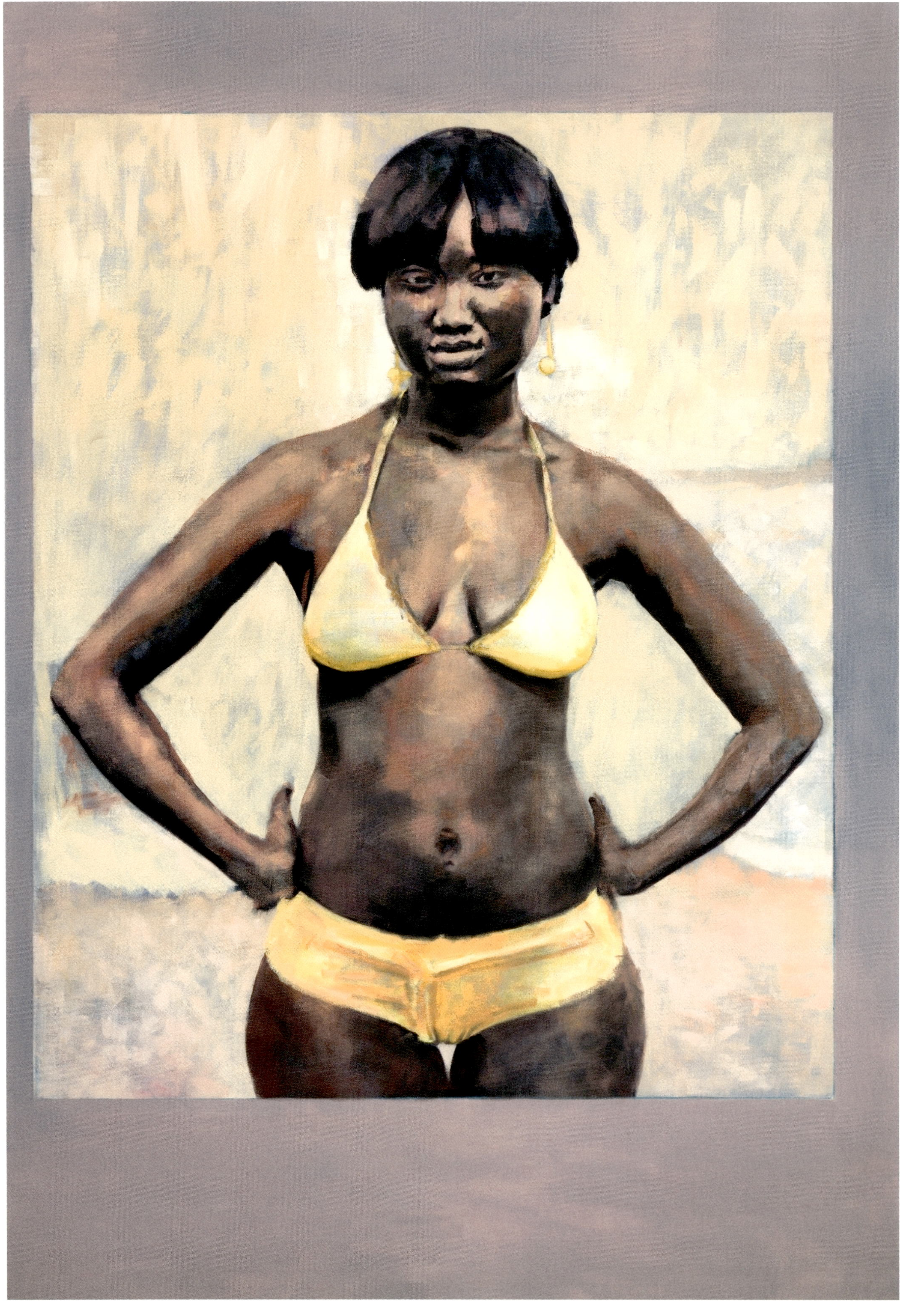

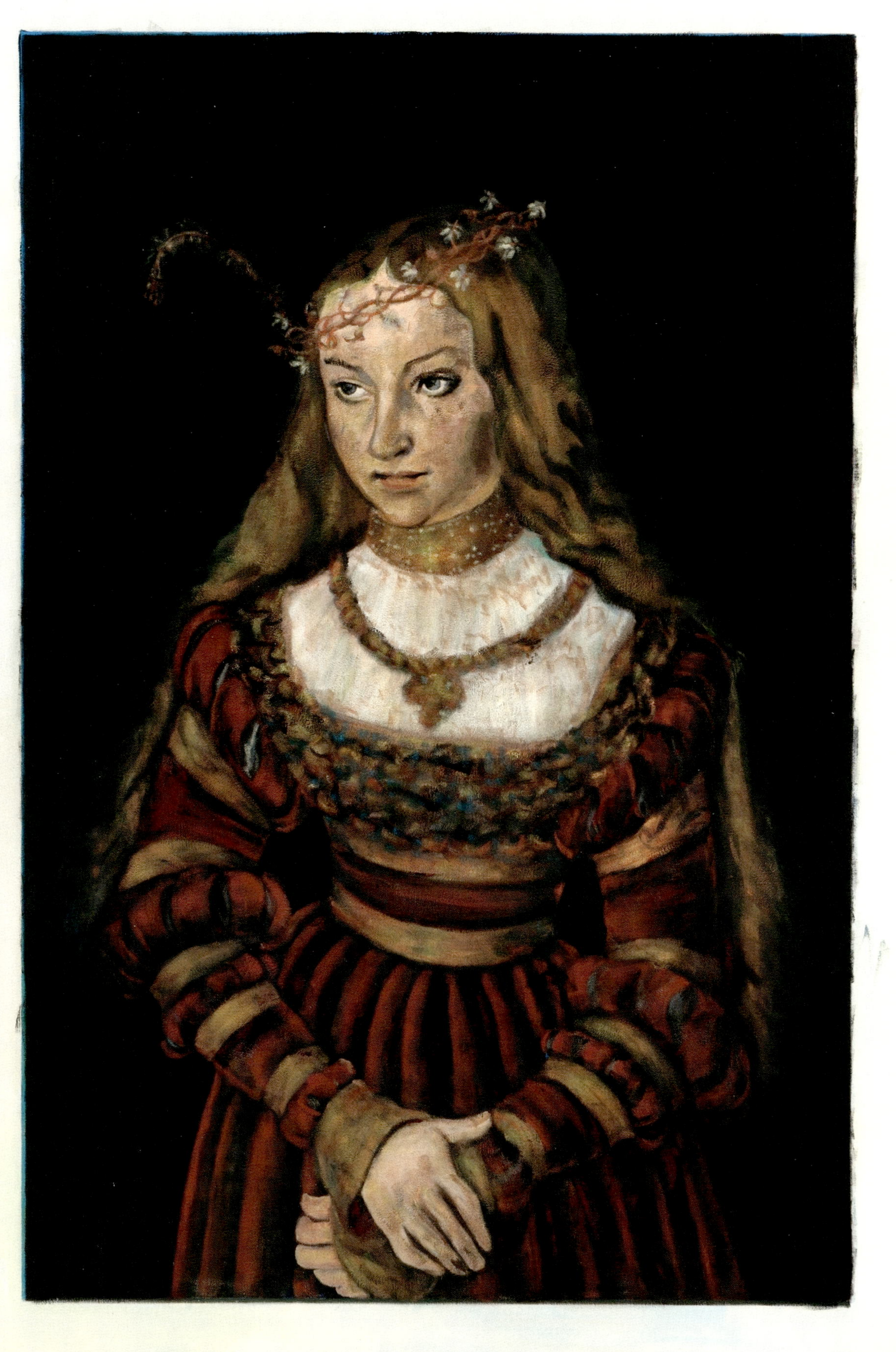

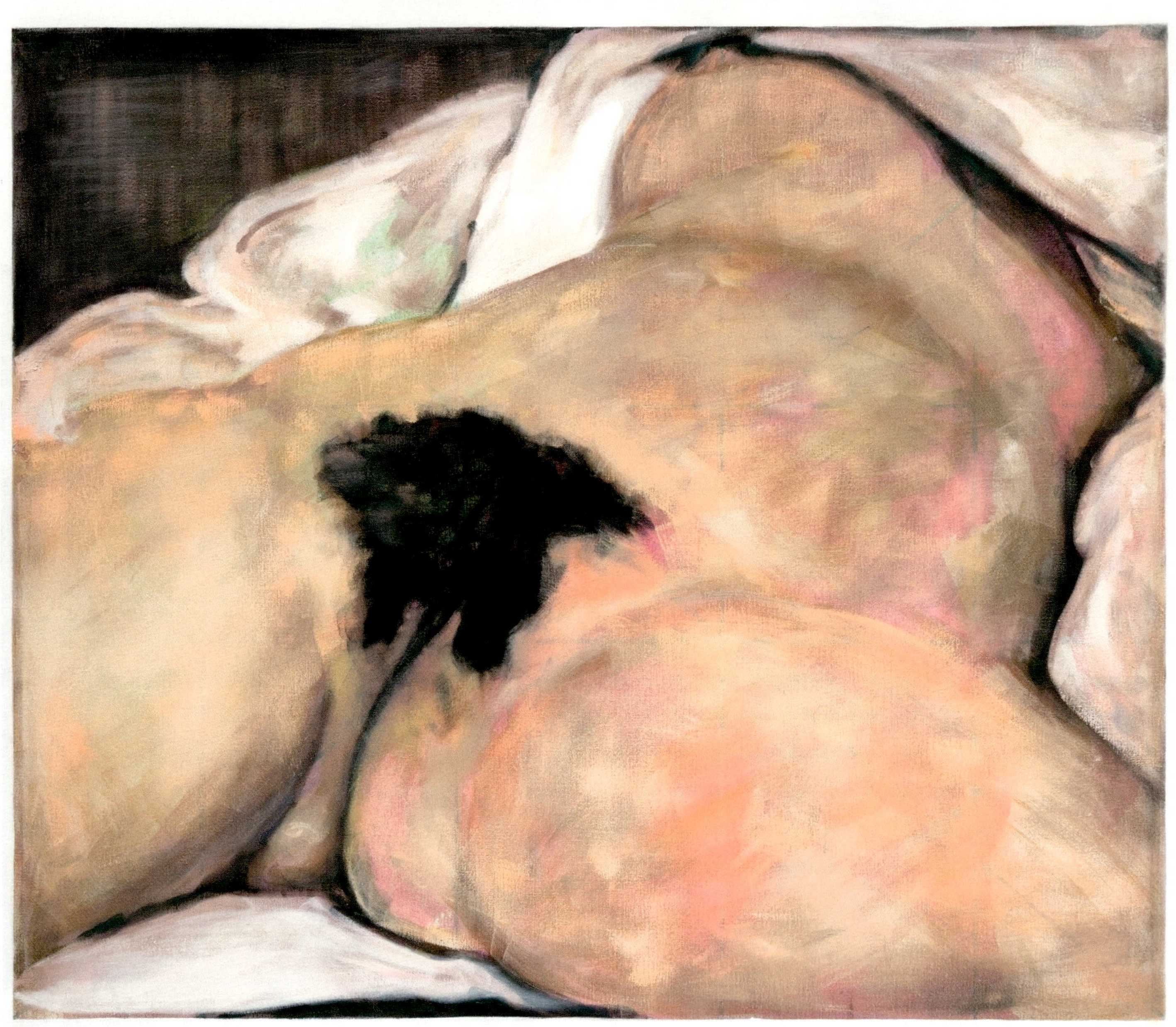

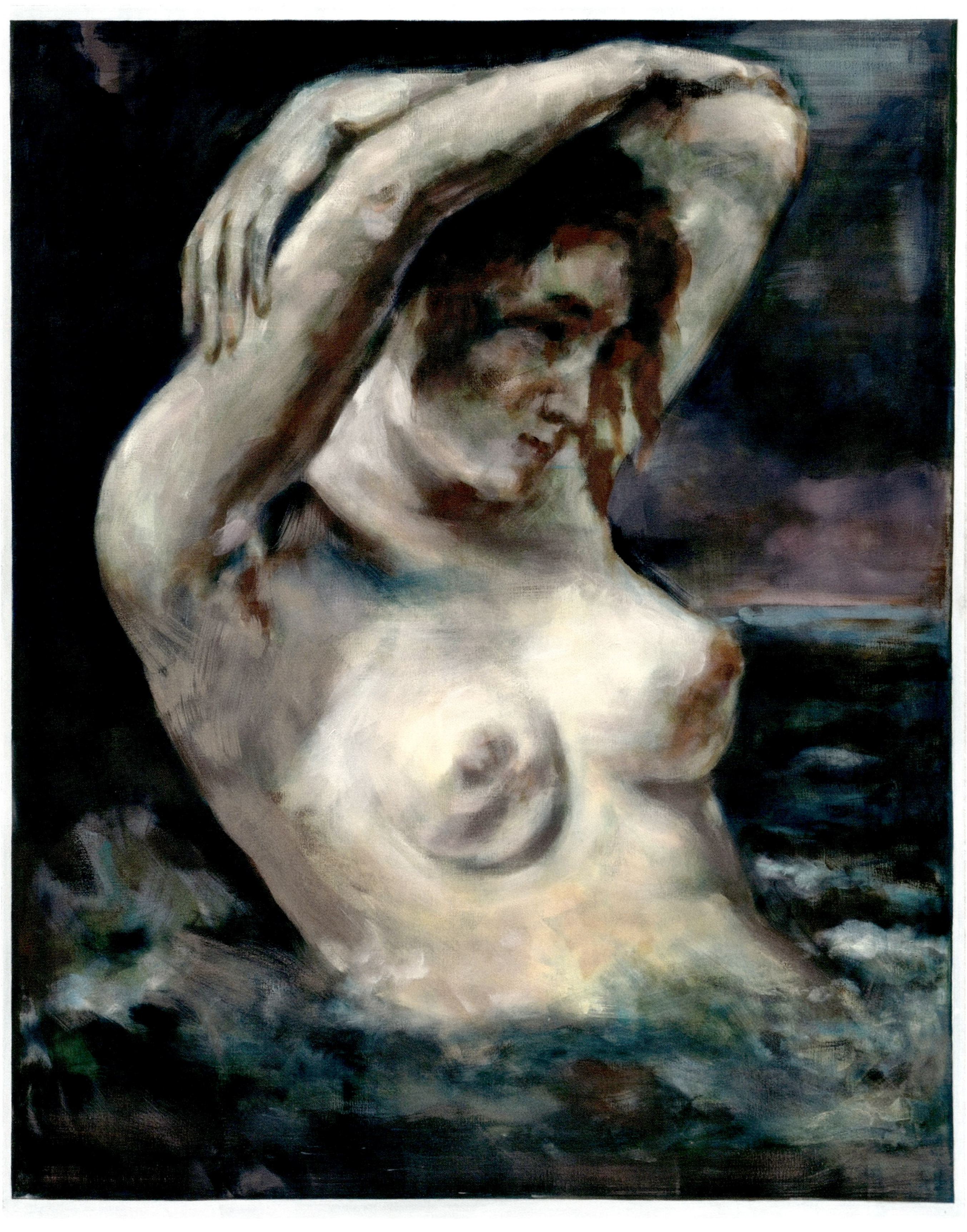

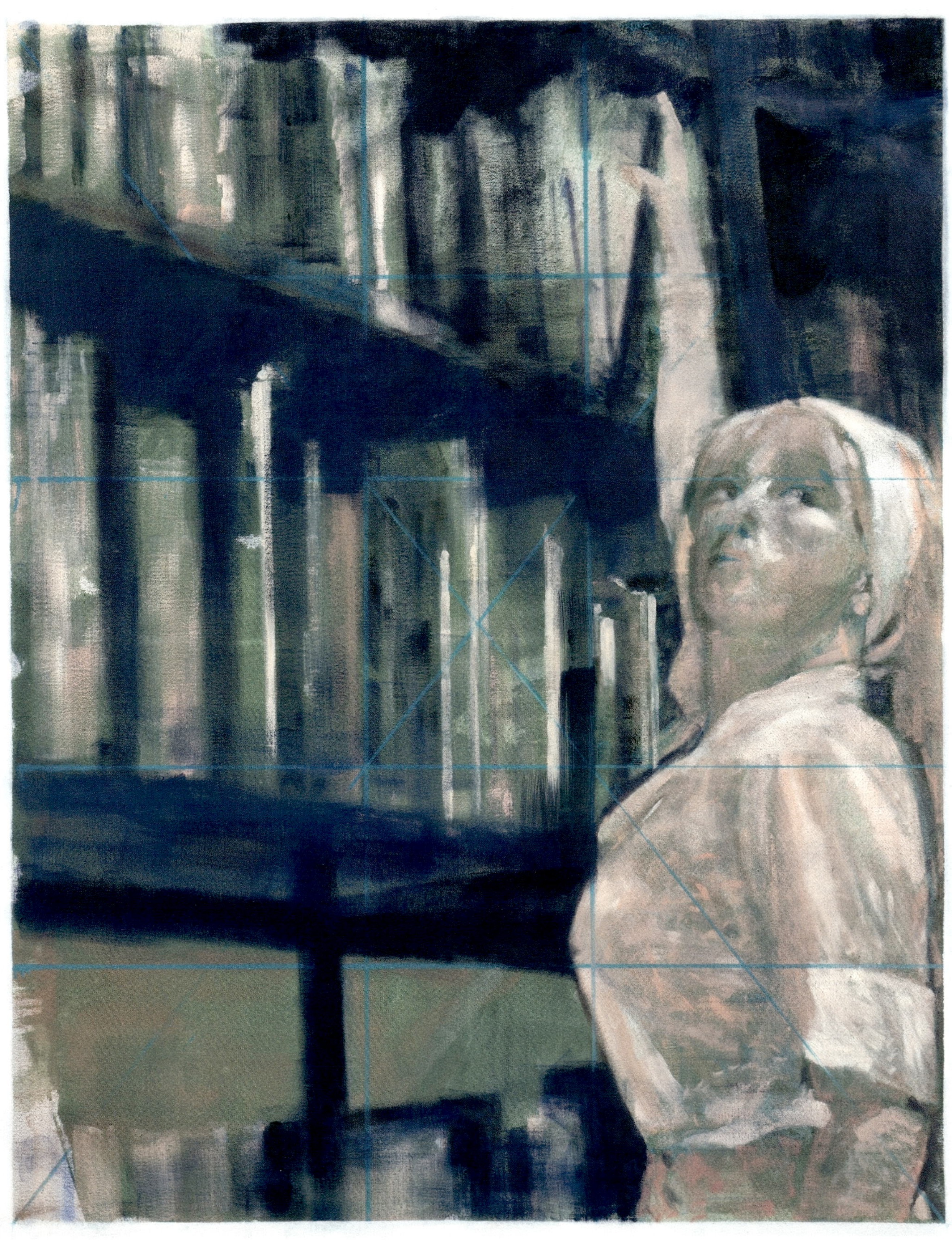

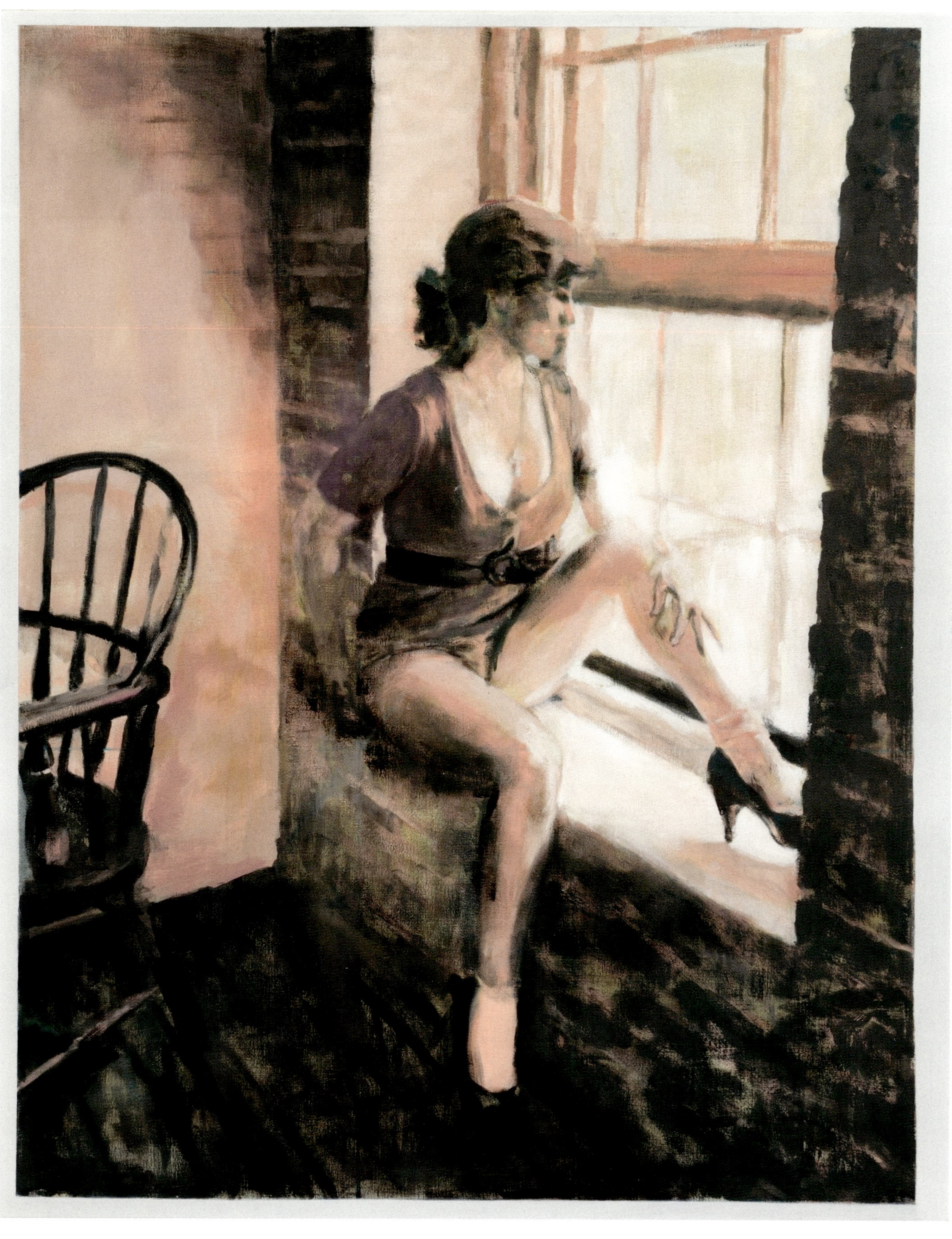

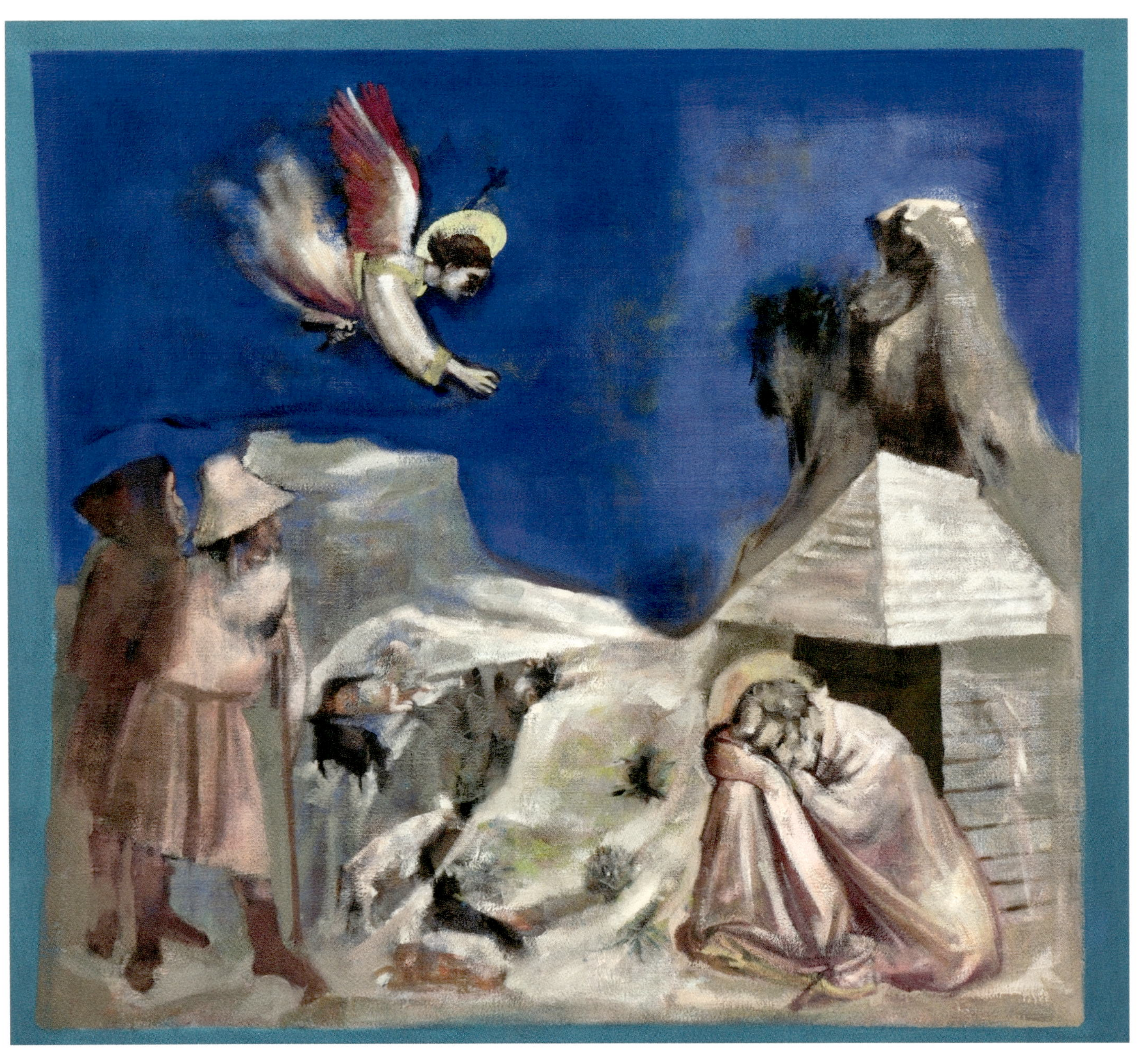

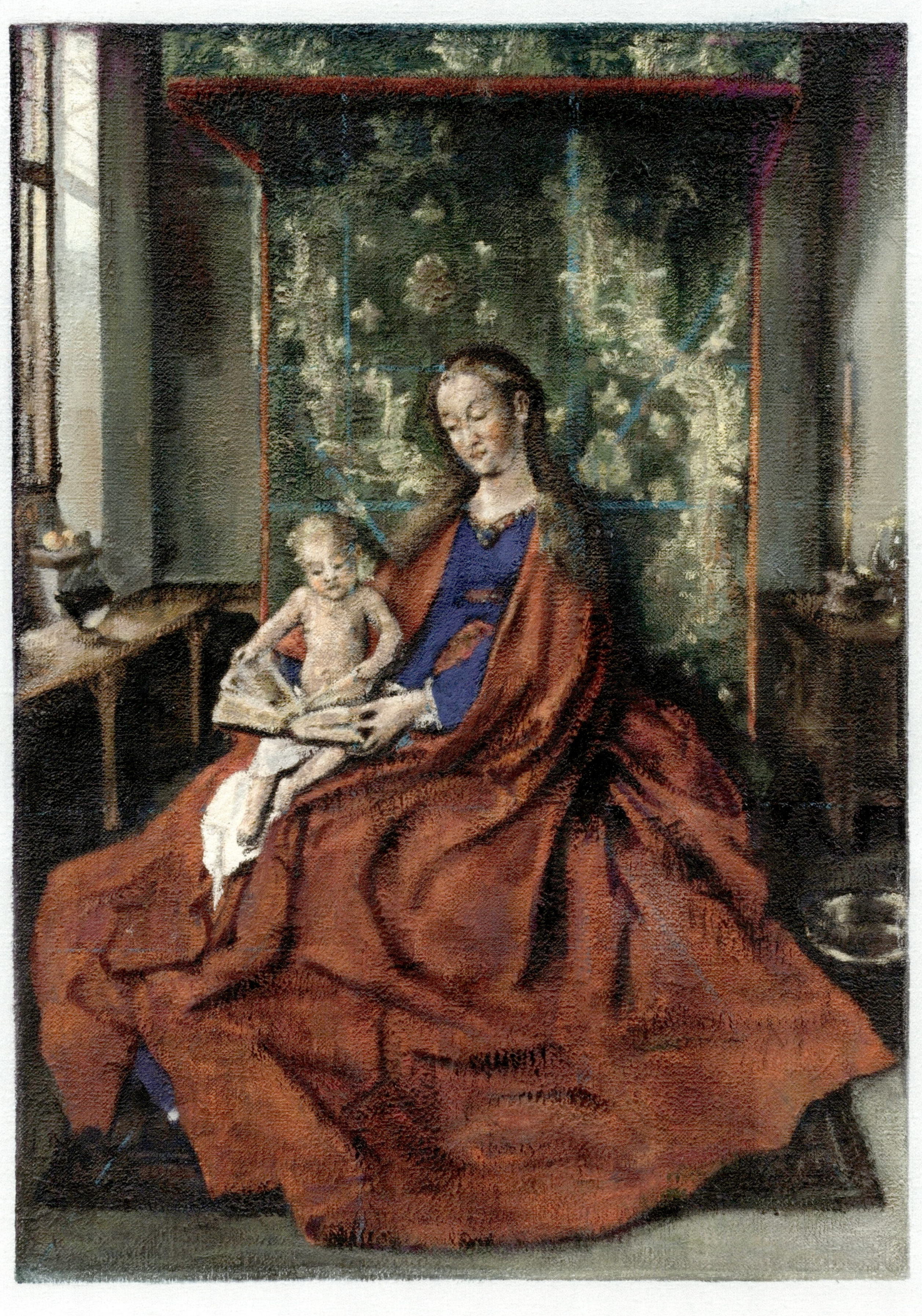

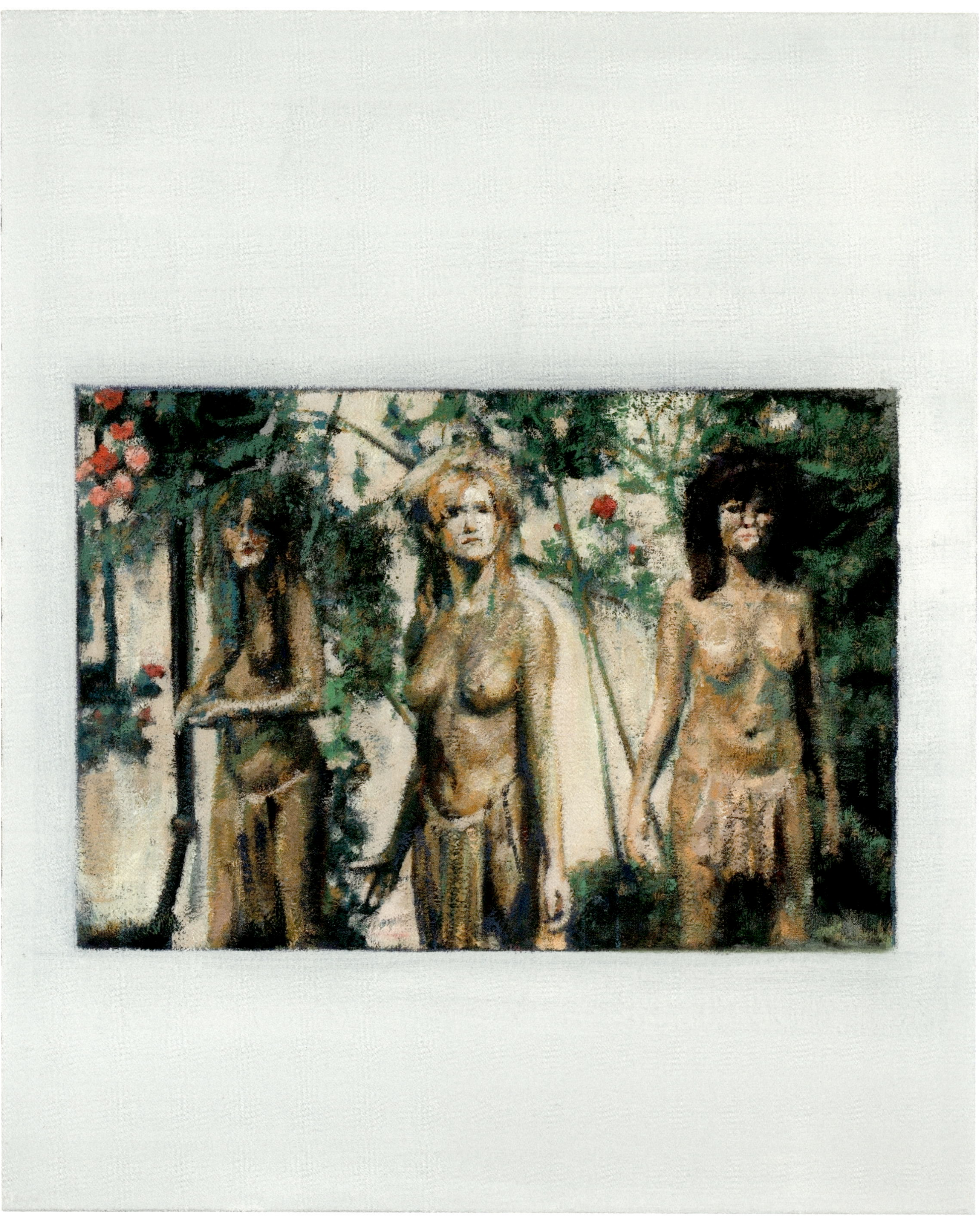

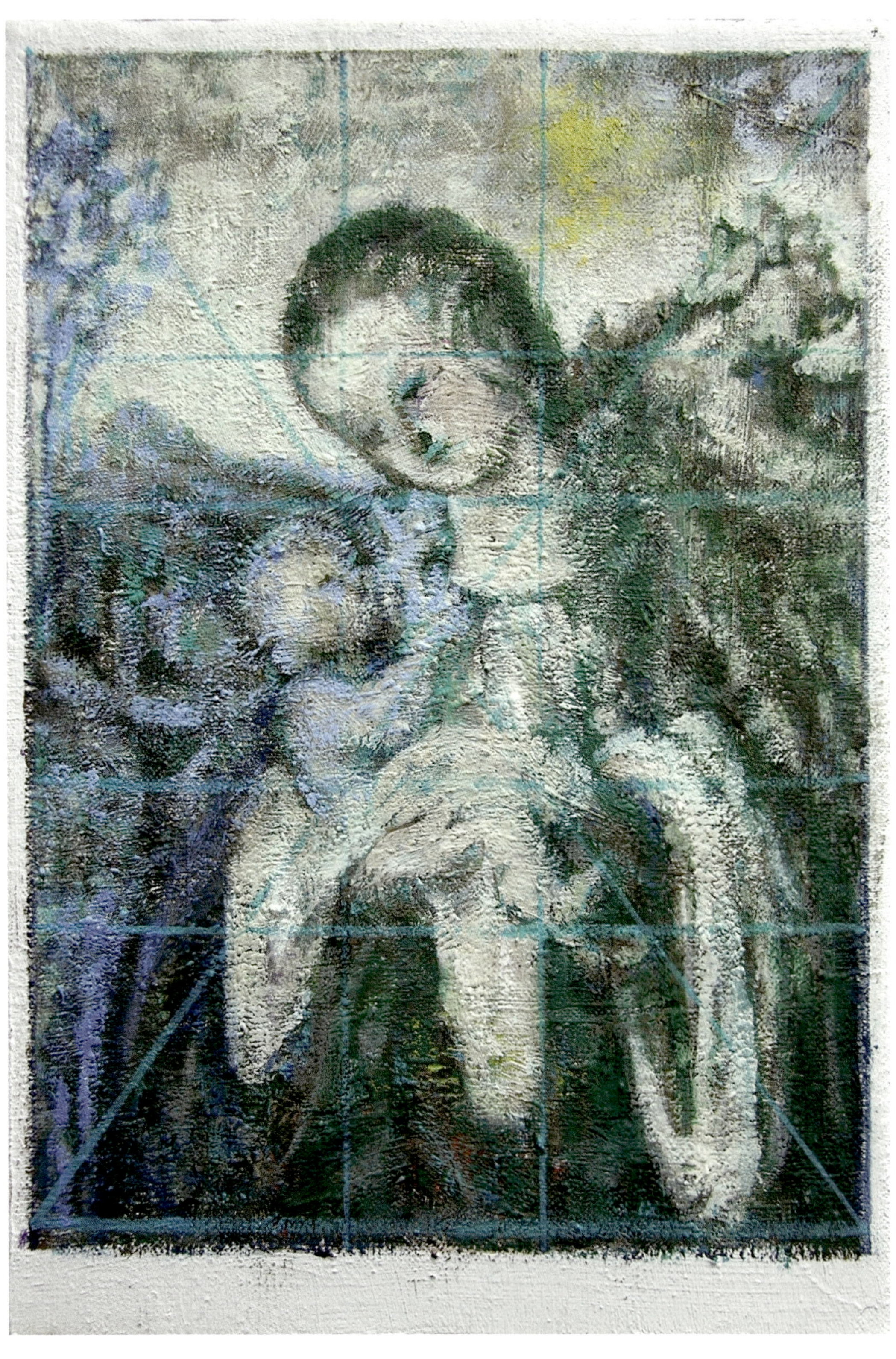

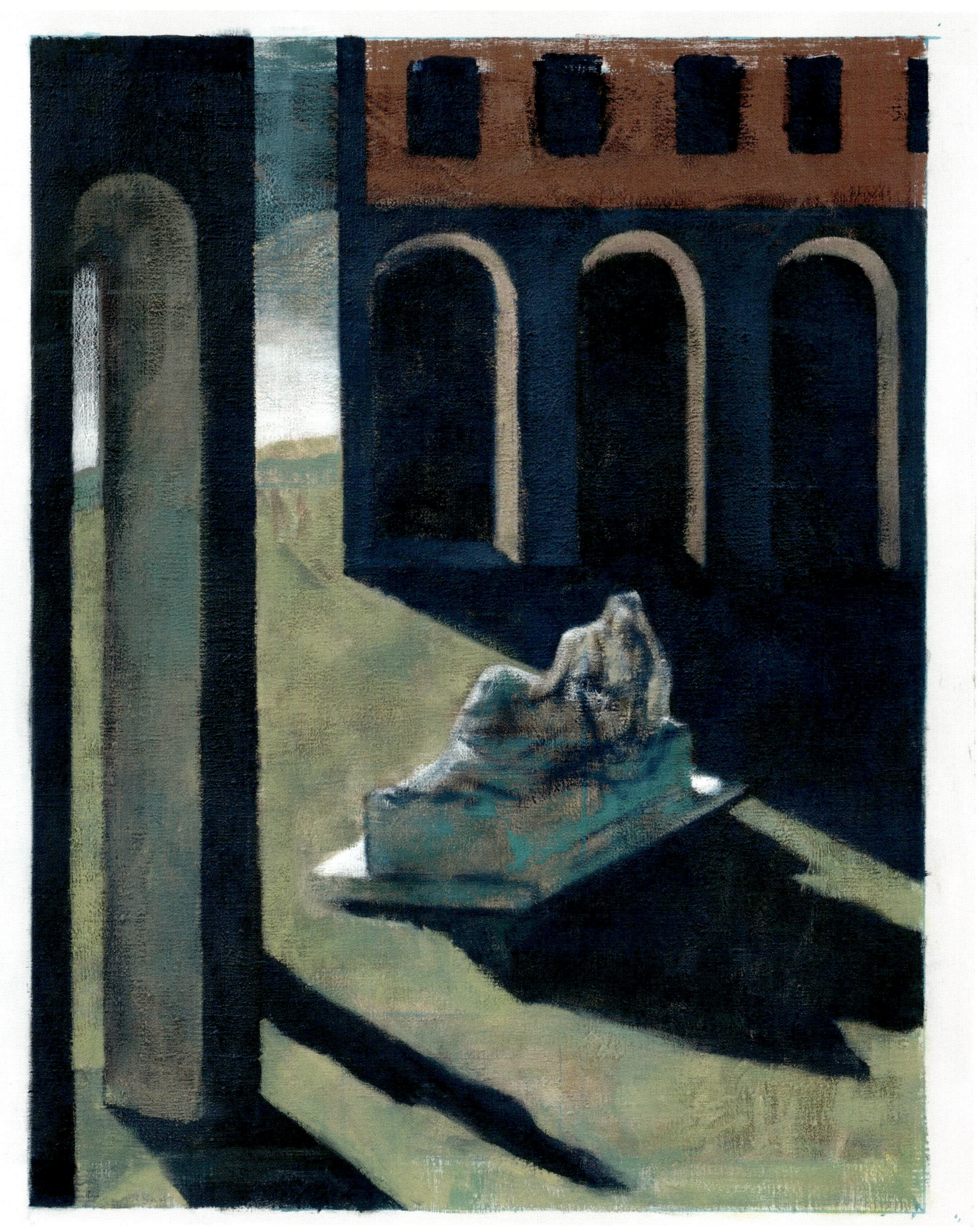

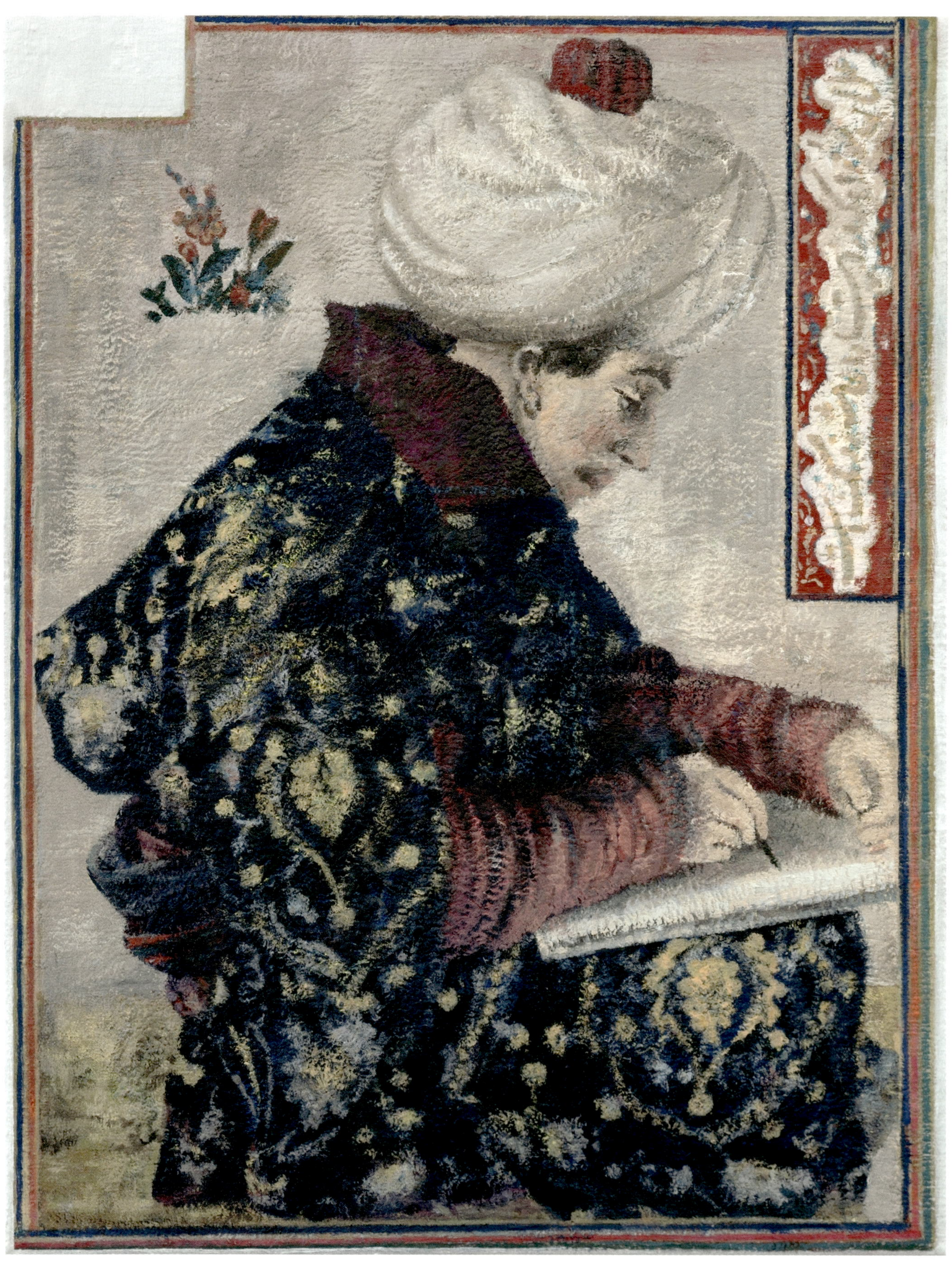

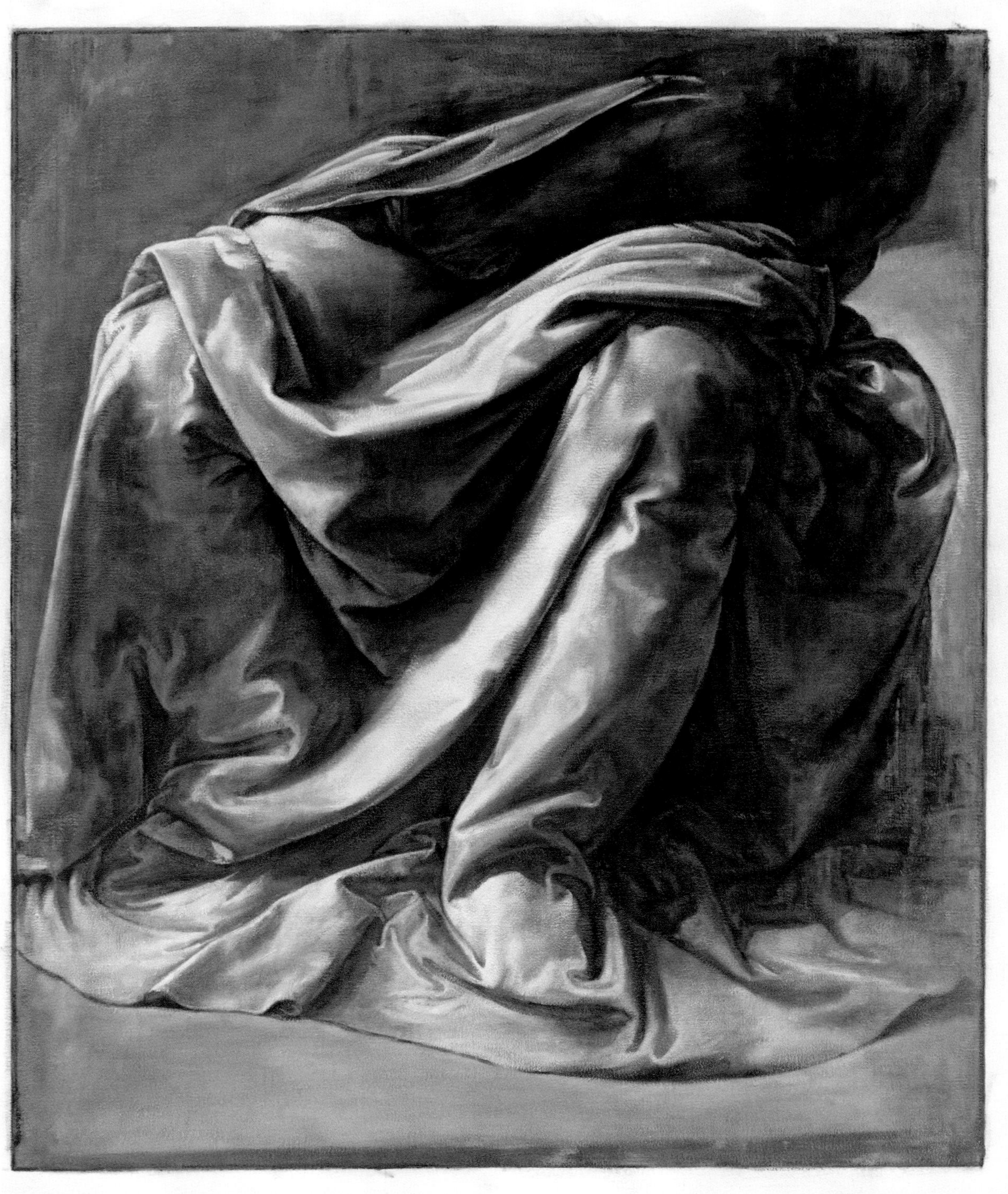

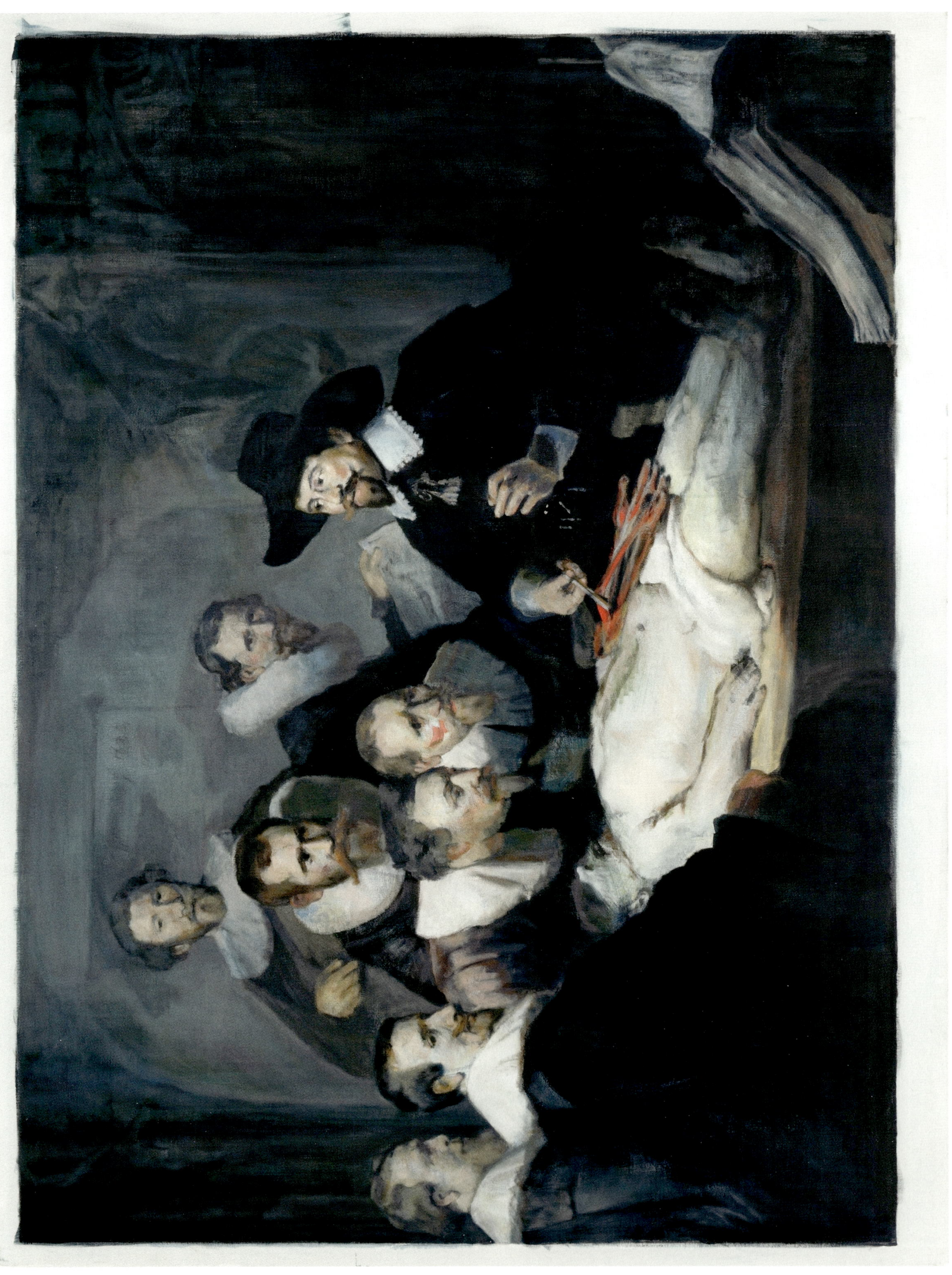

I am in love 1

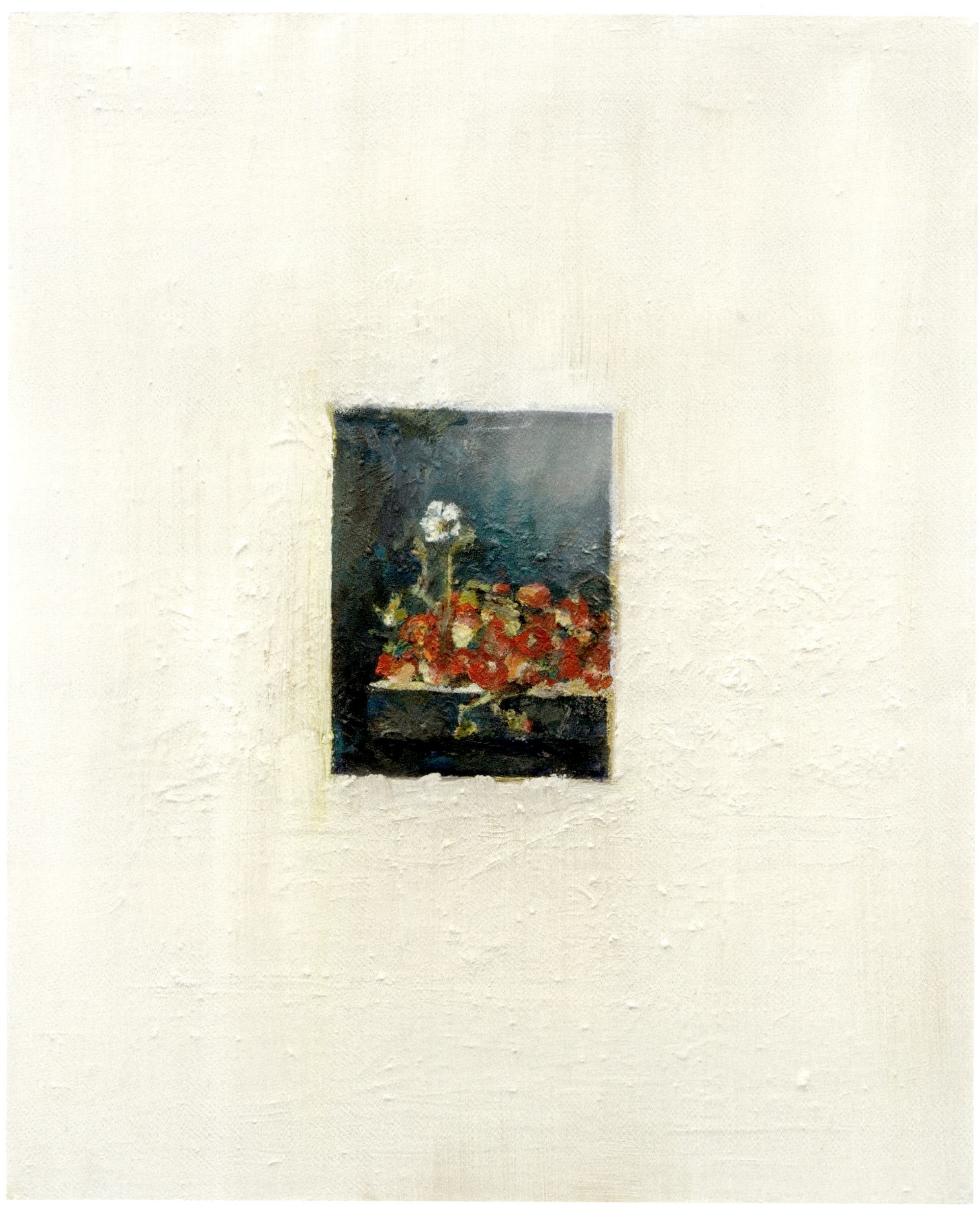

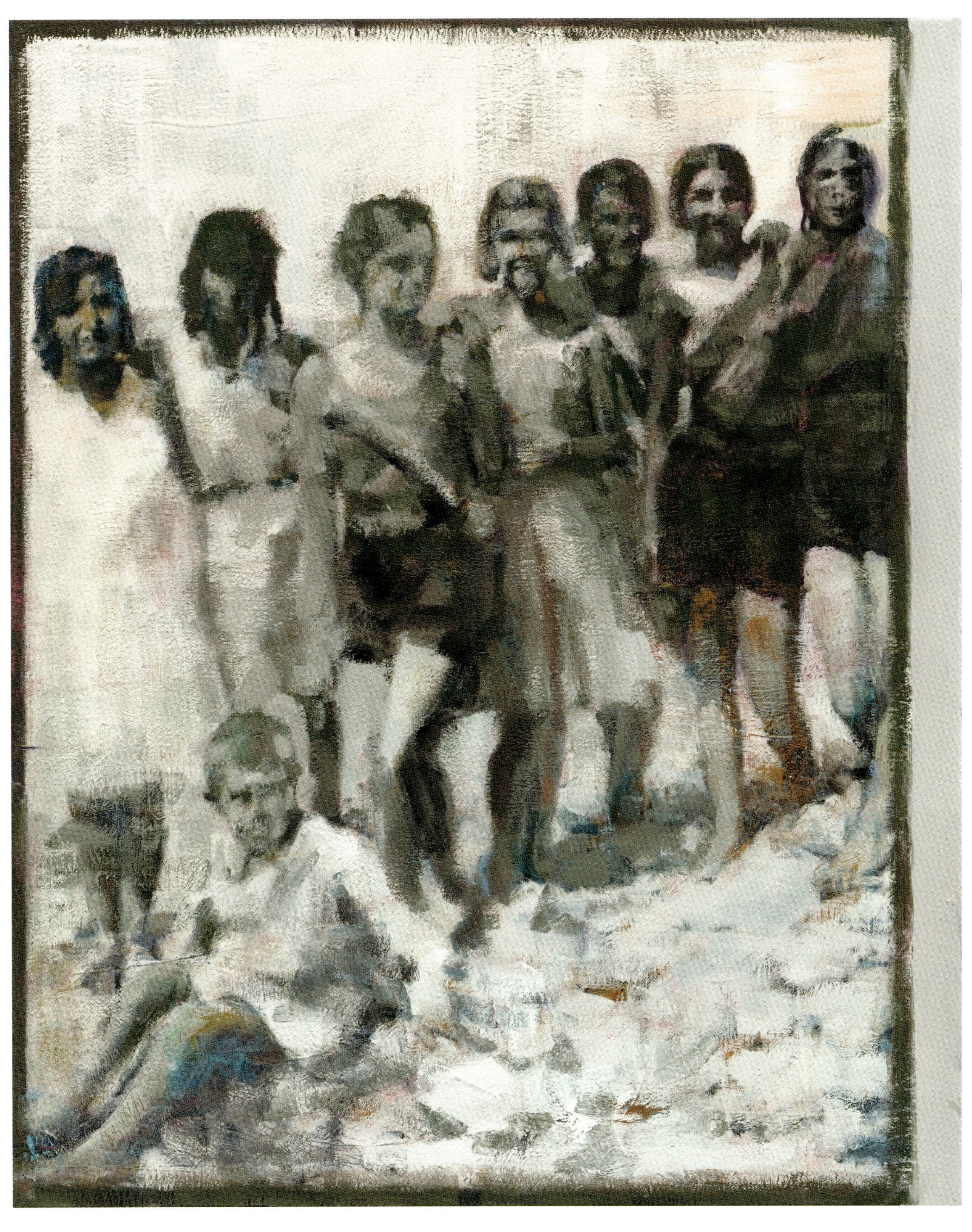

I am in love 3

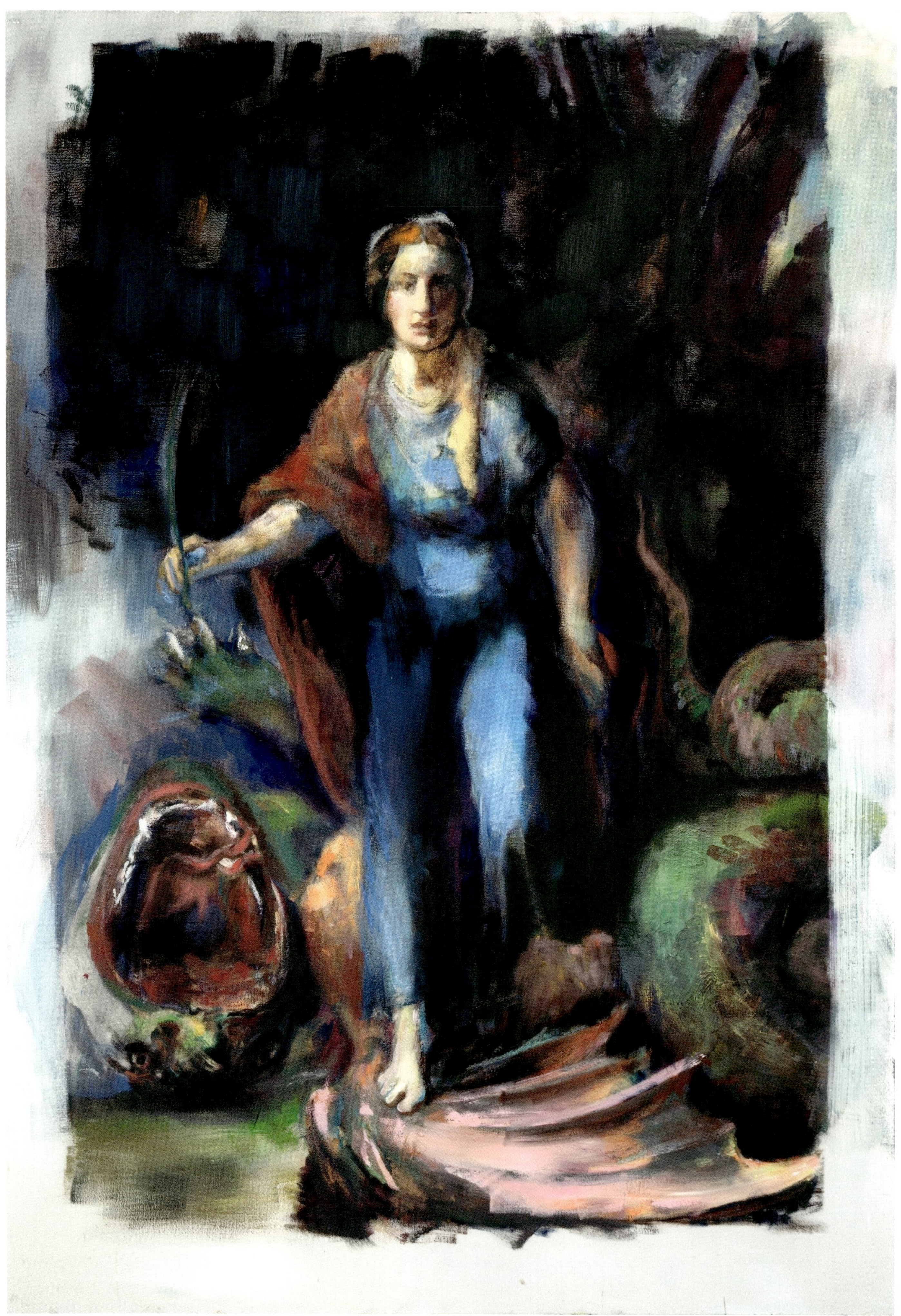

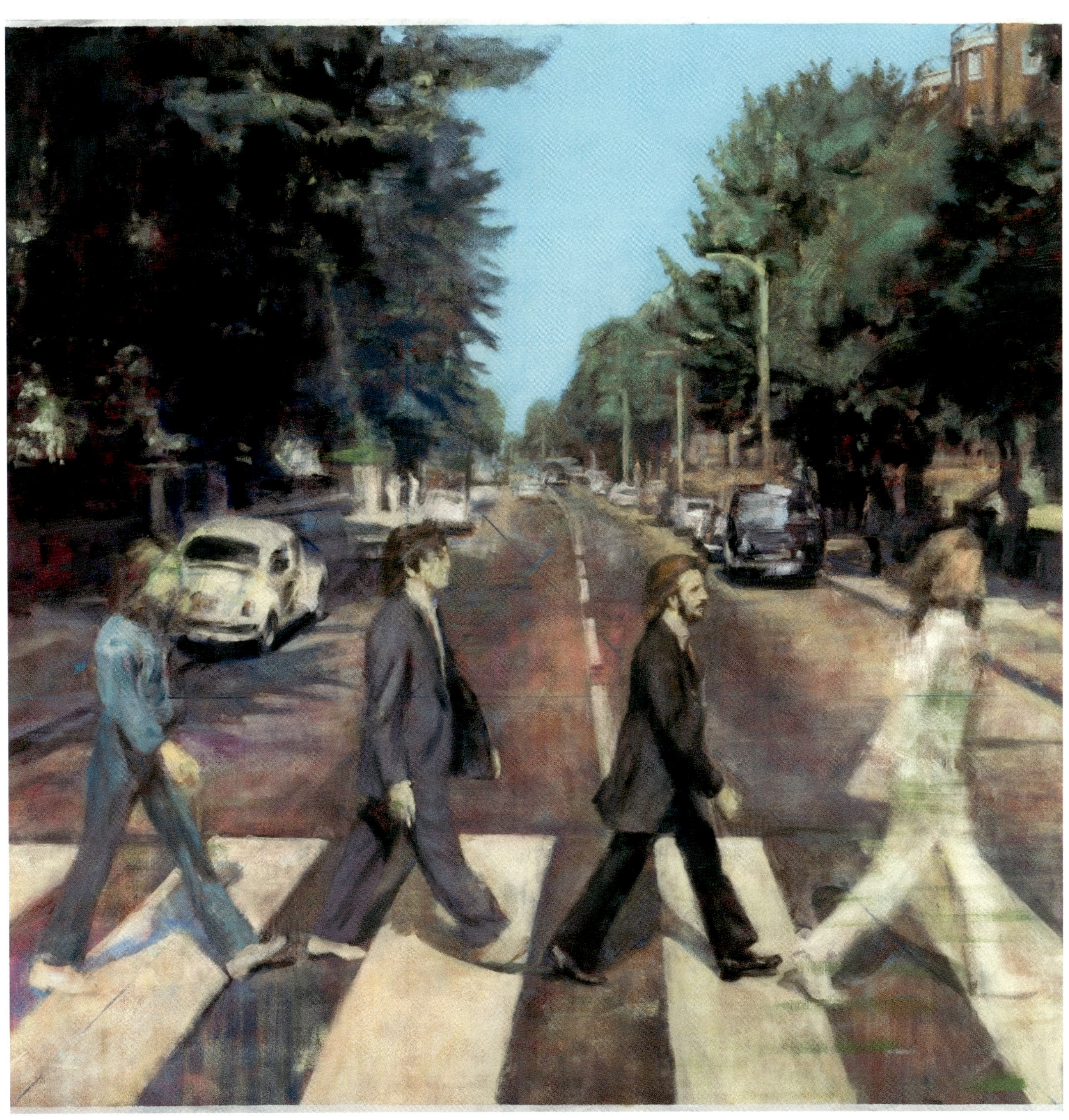

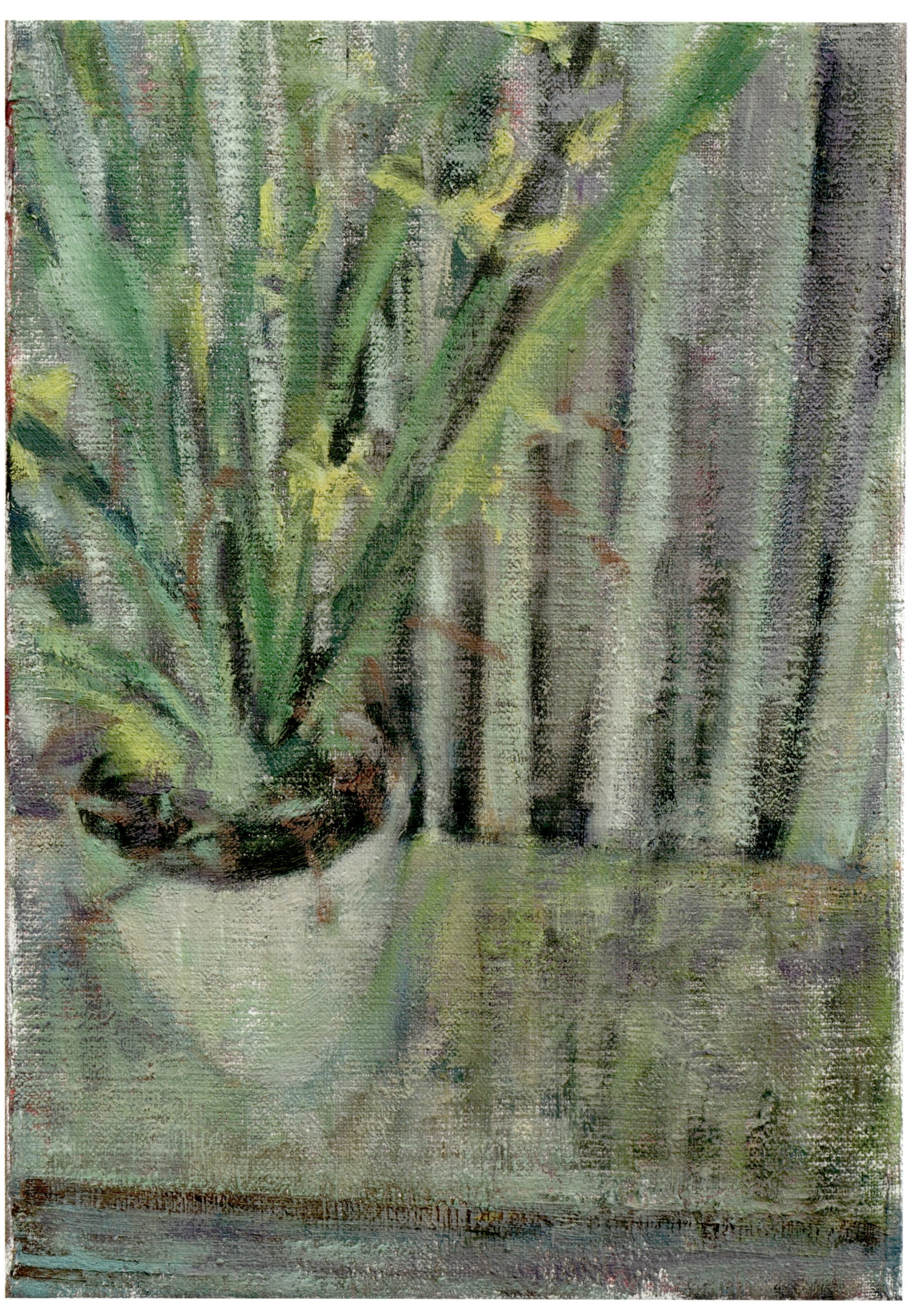

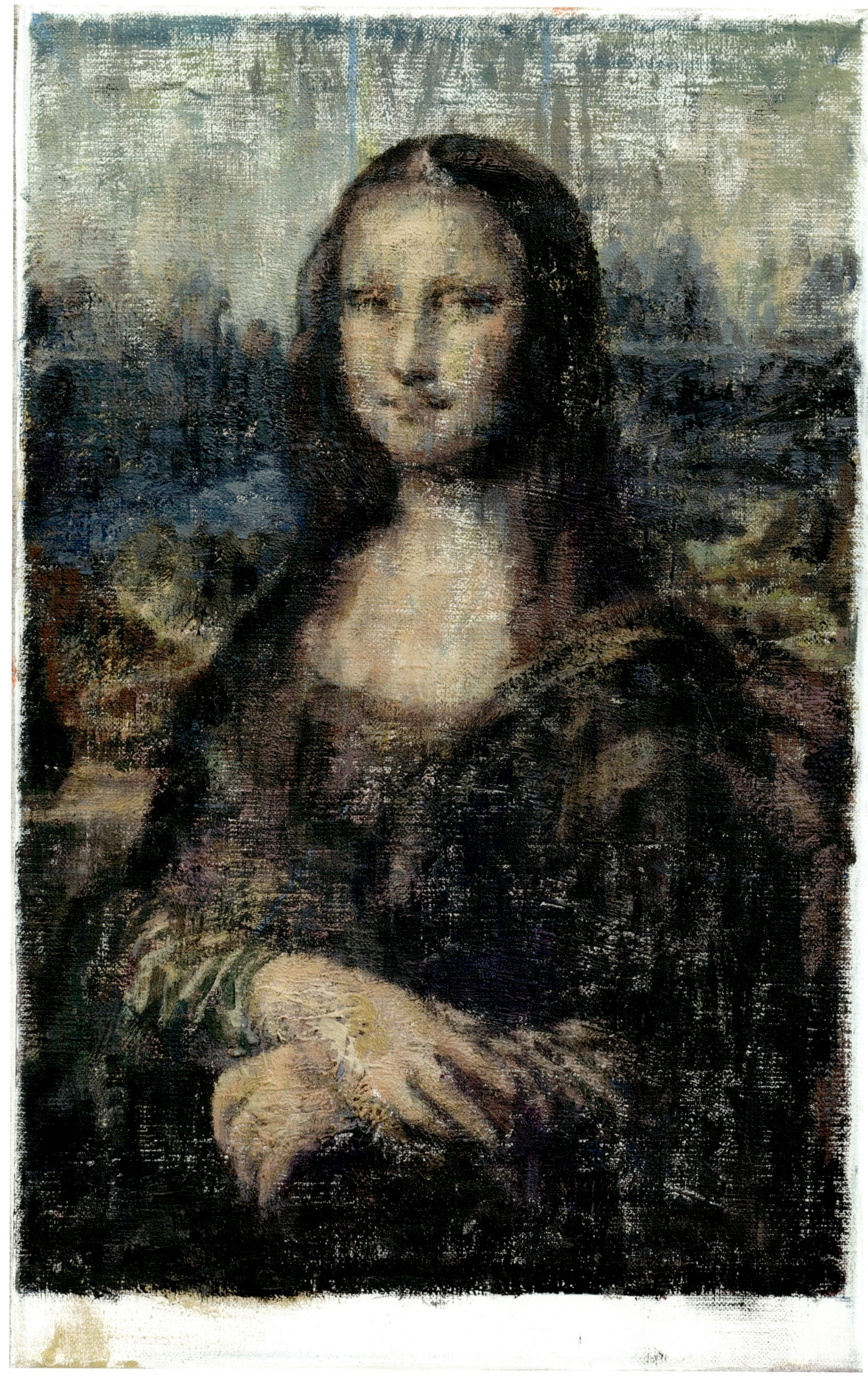

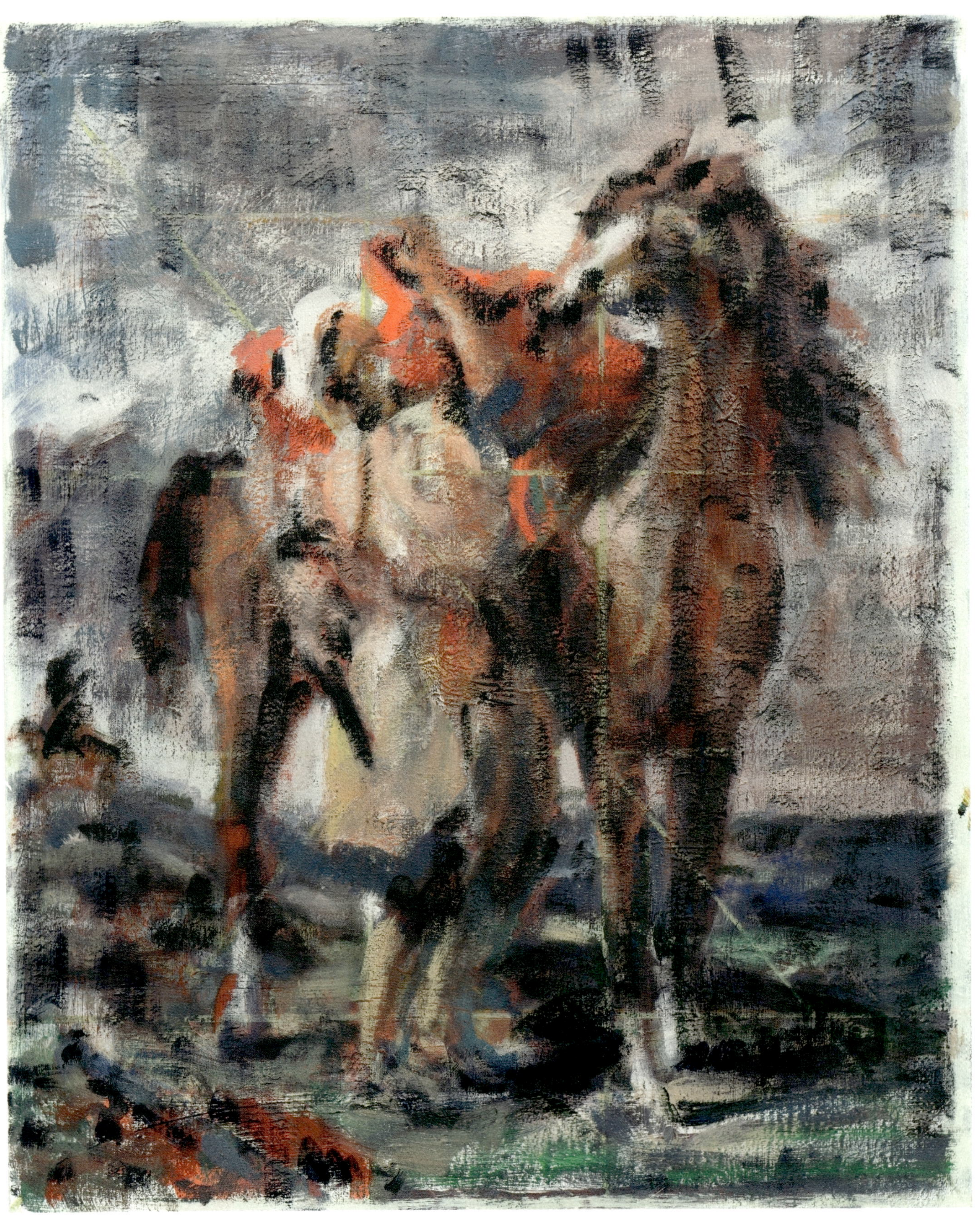

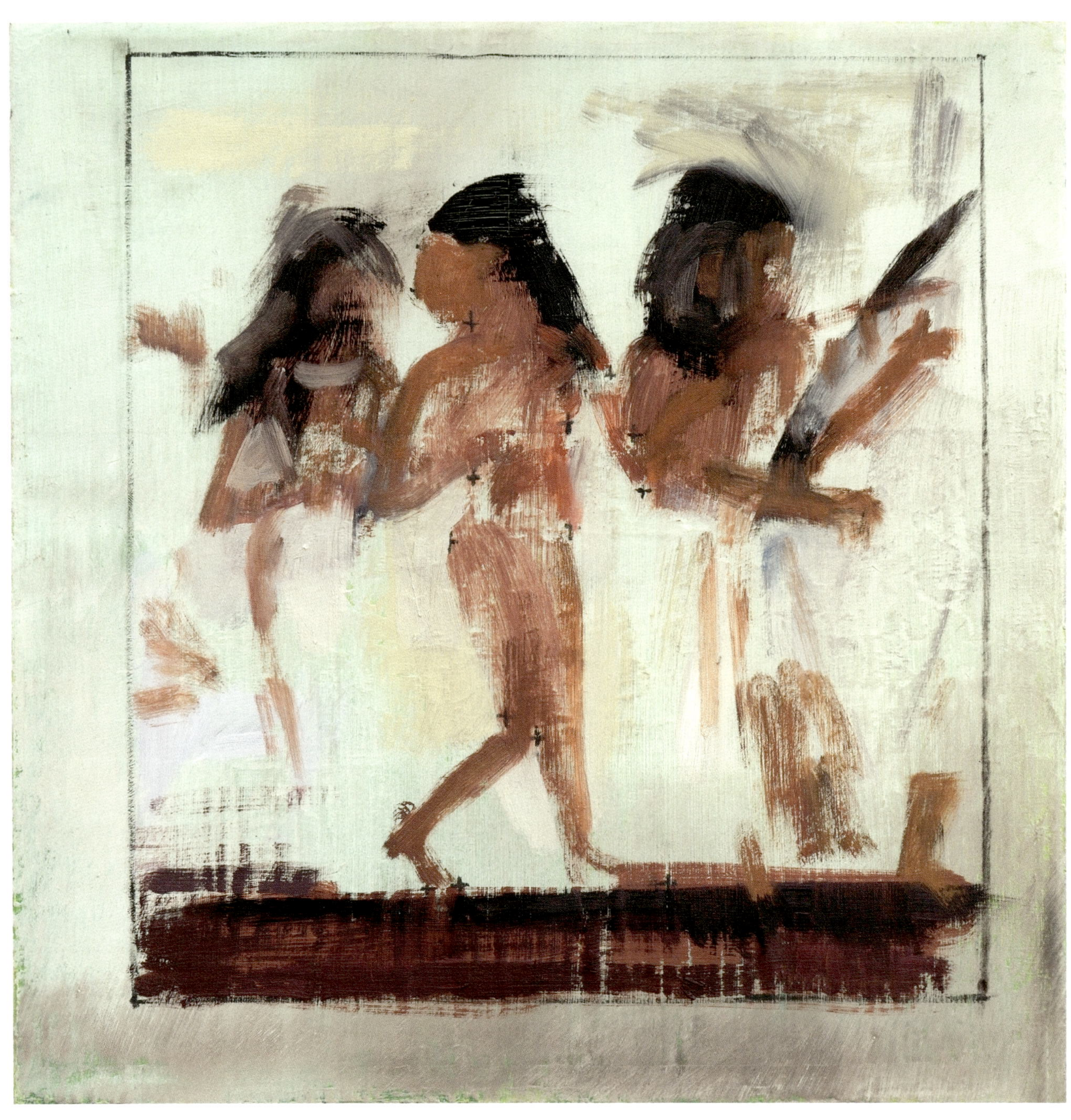

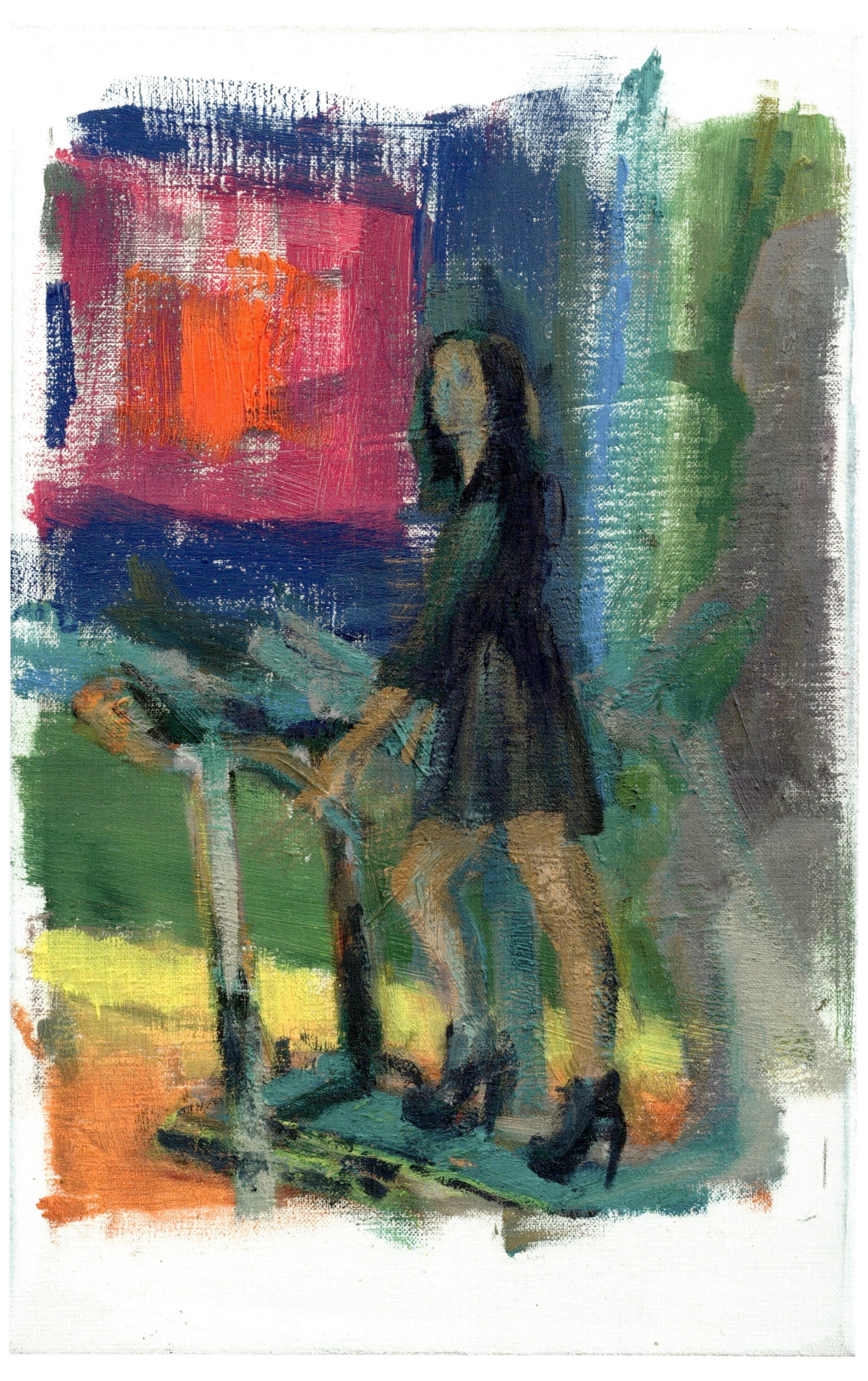

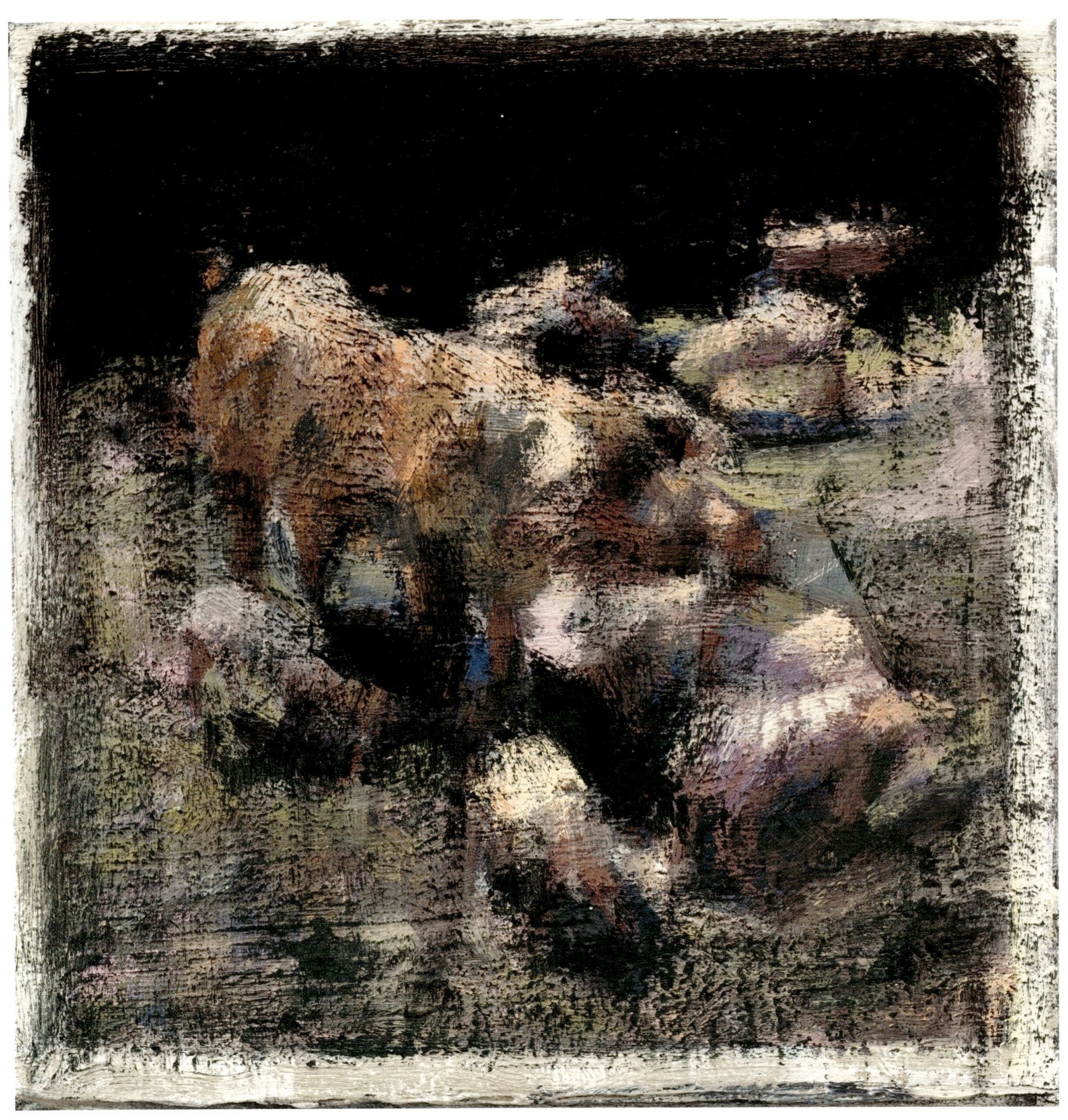

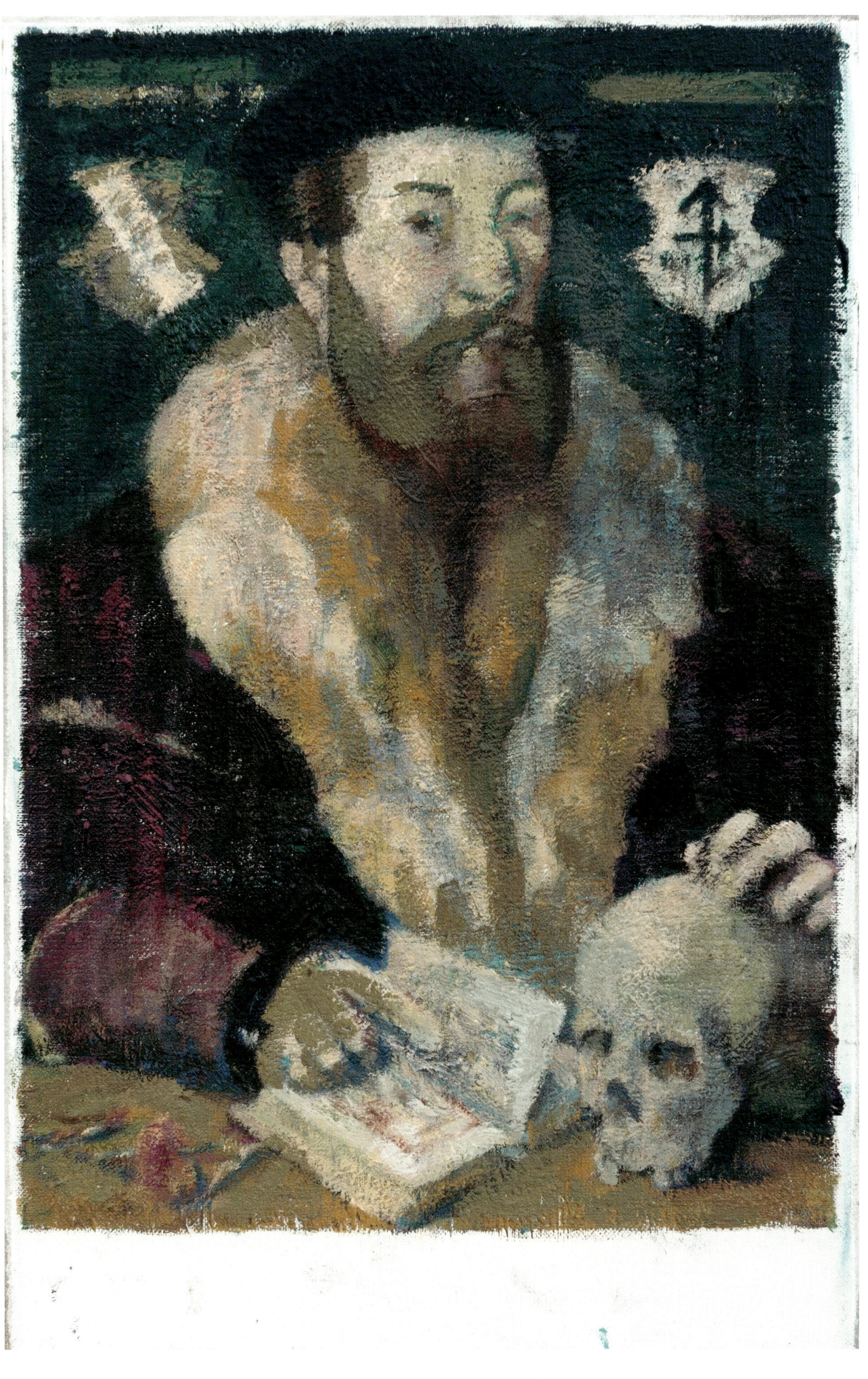

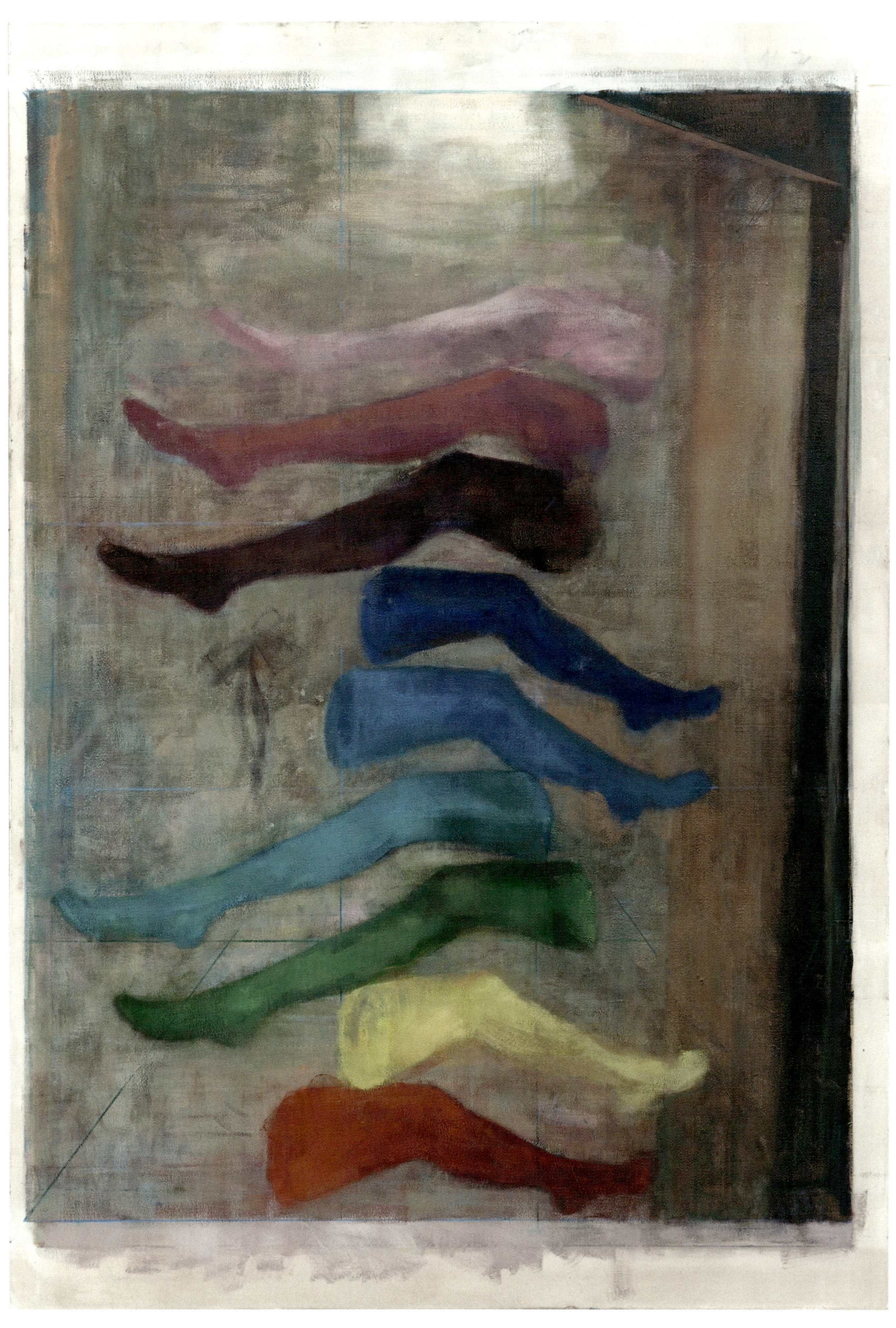

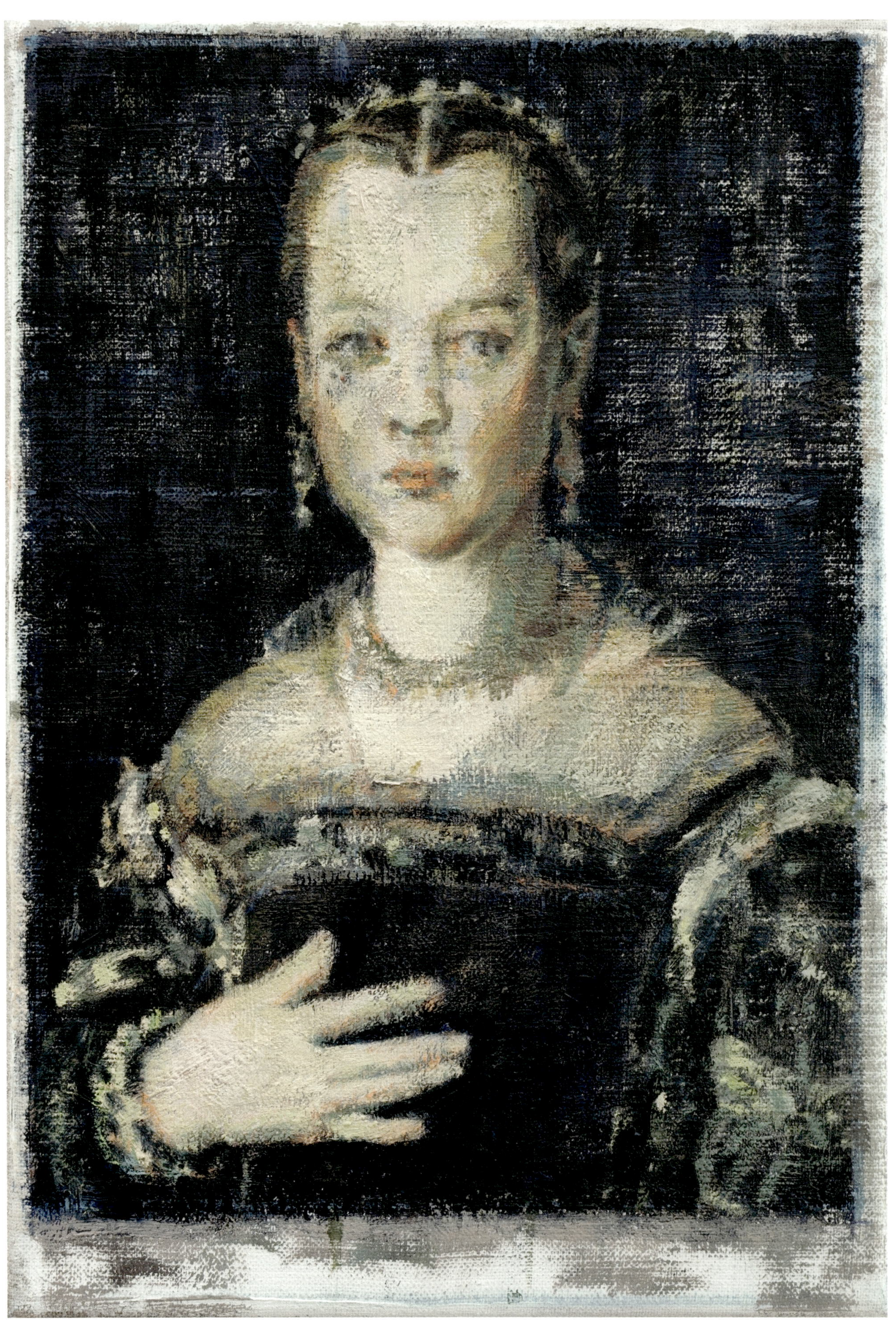

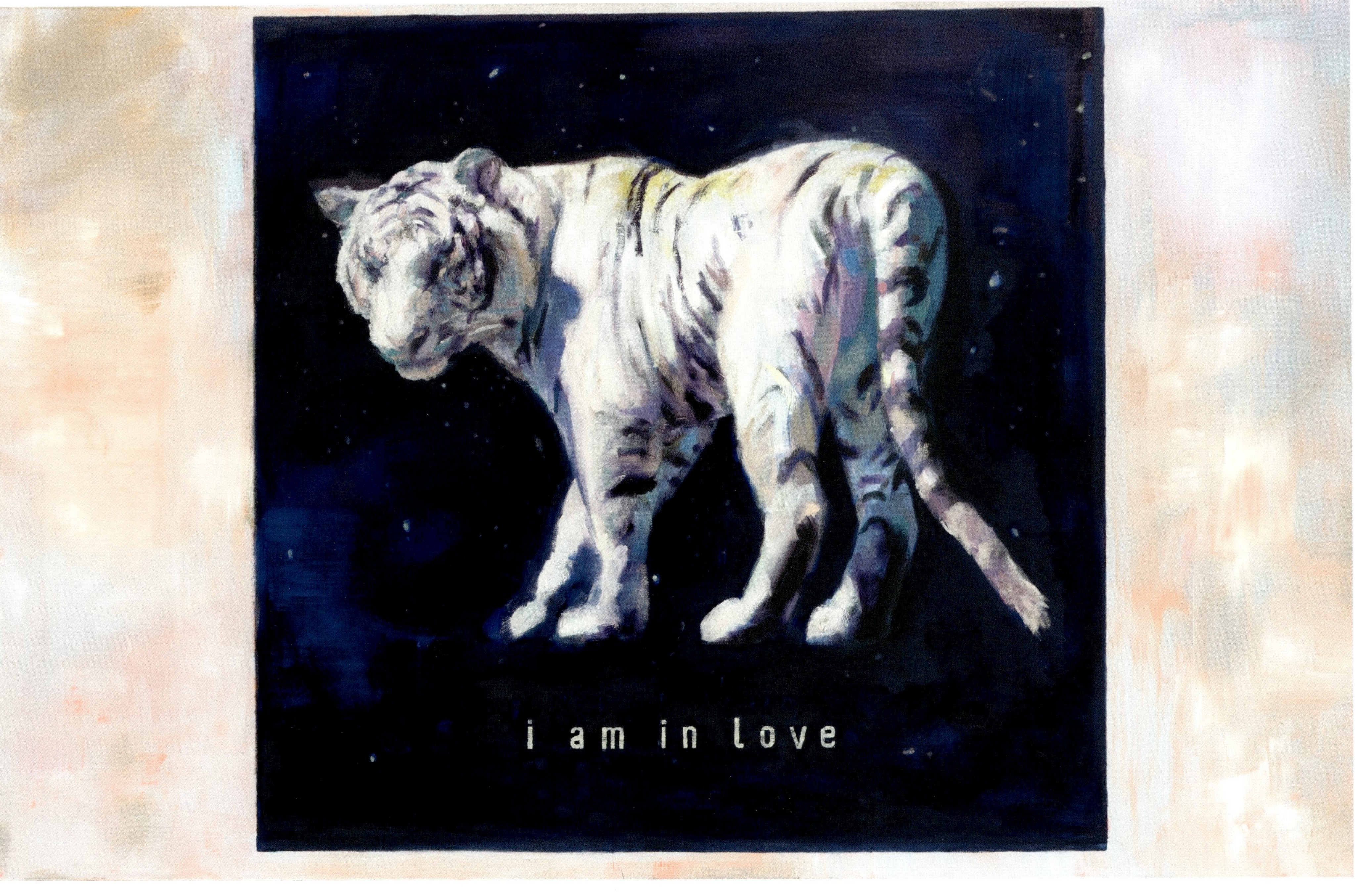

i am in love

2012

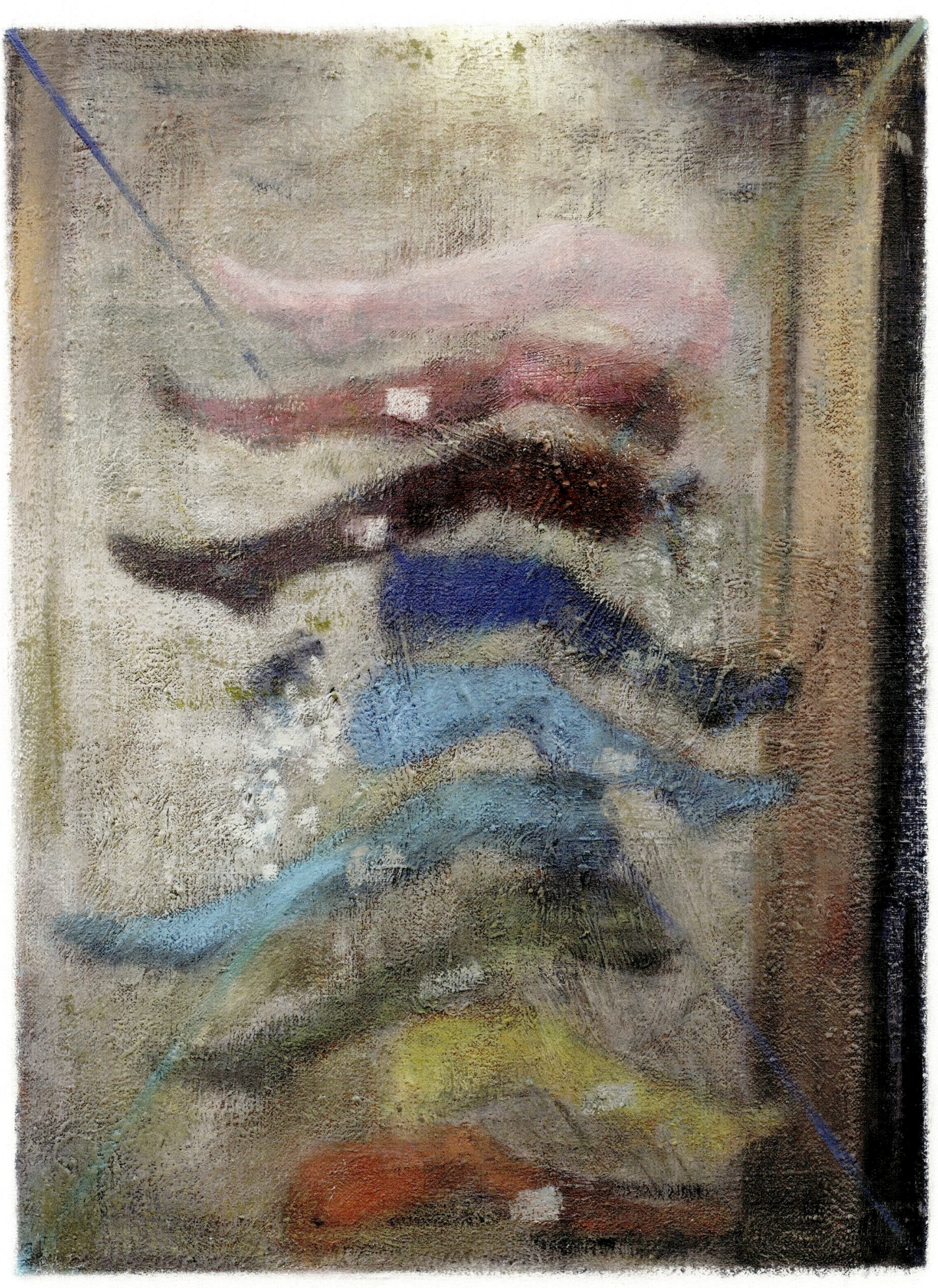

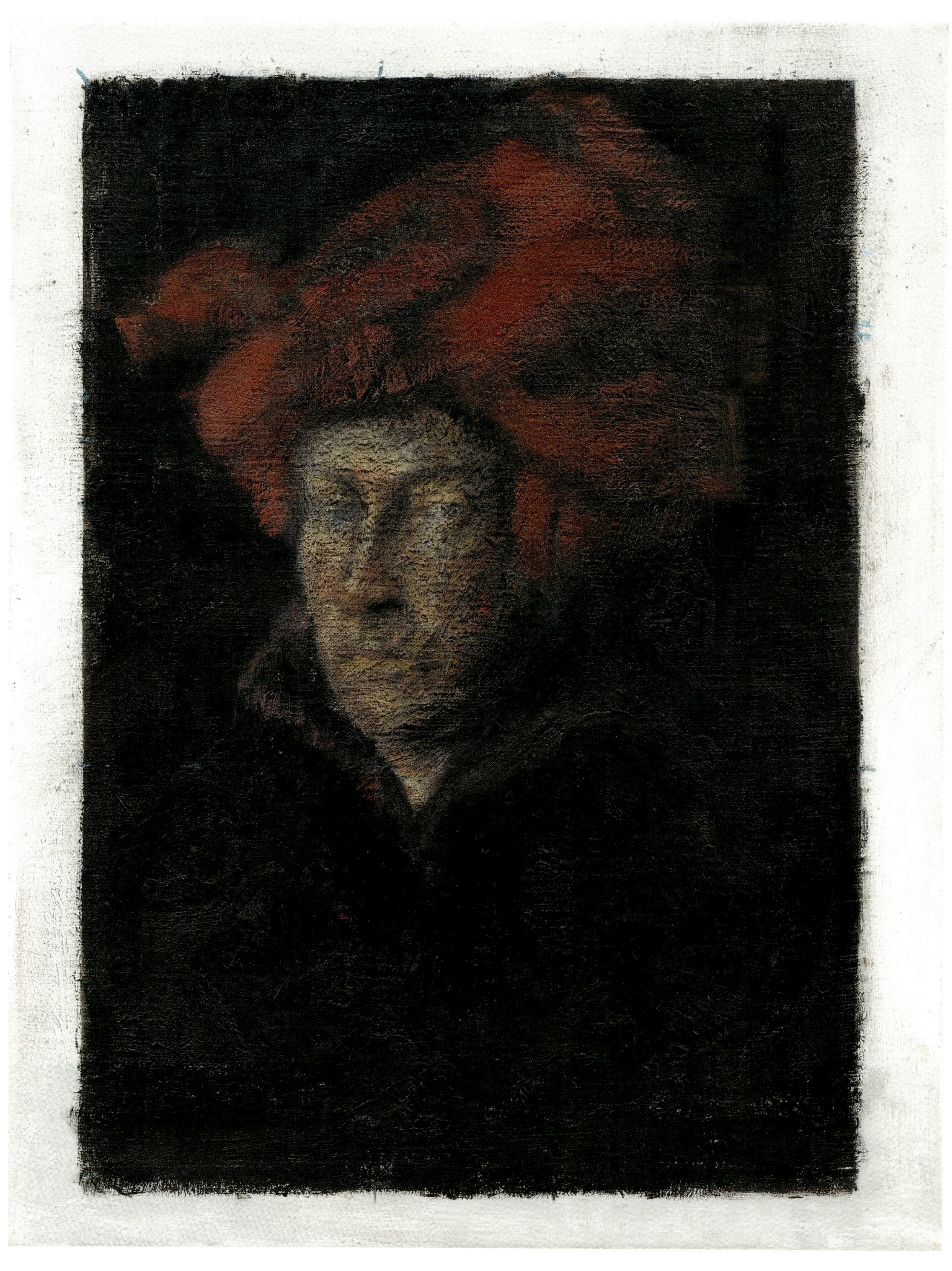

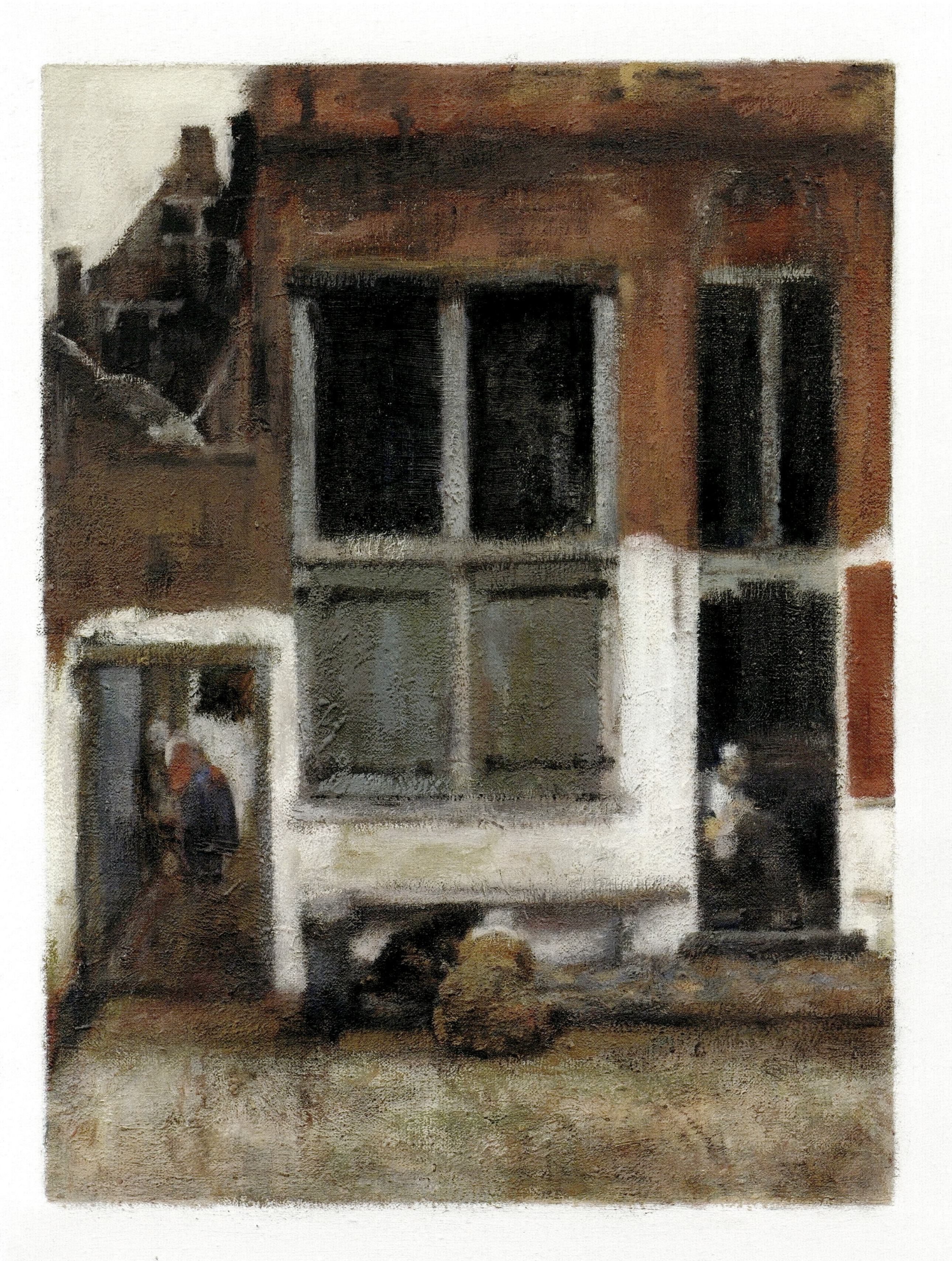

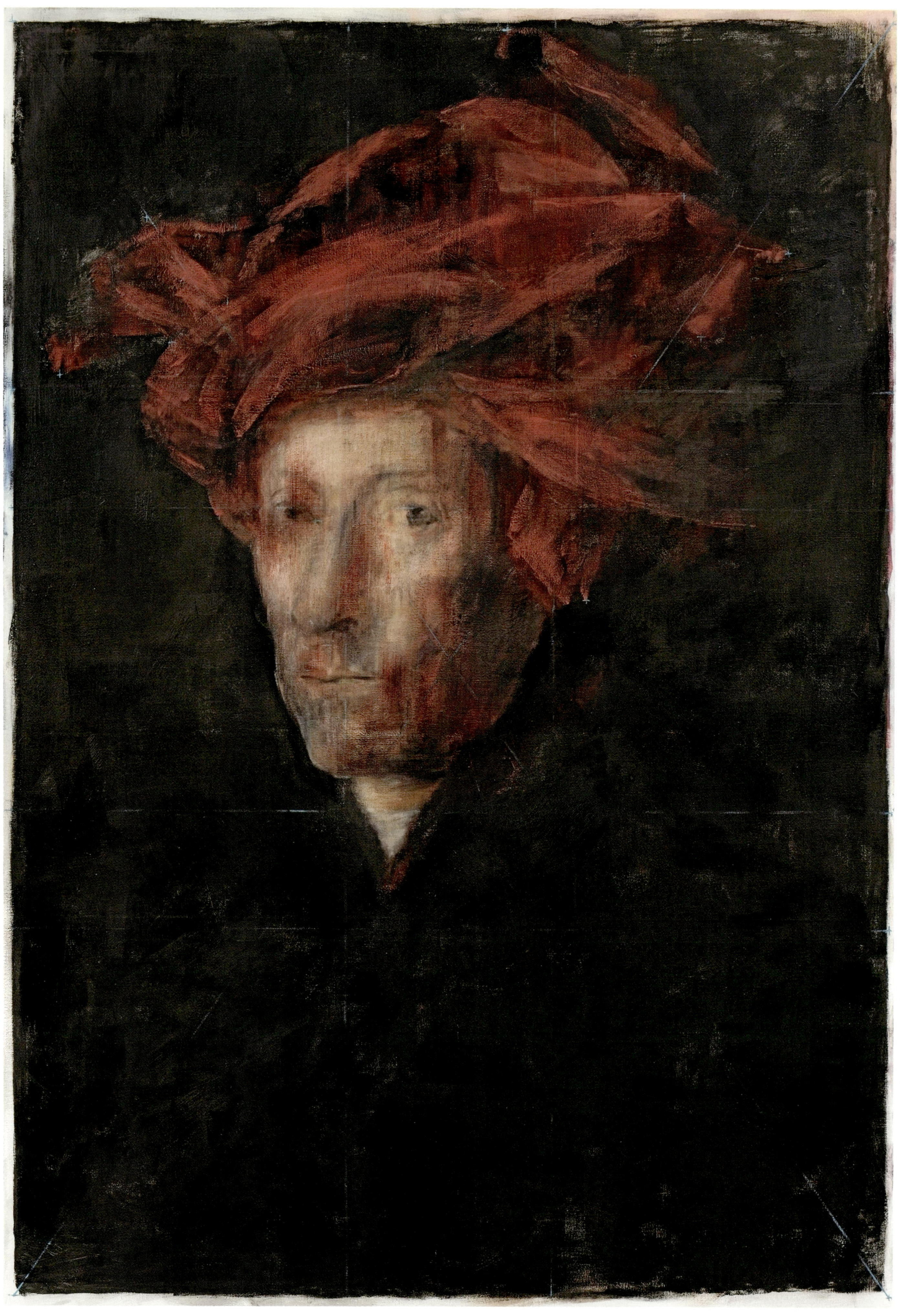

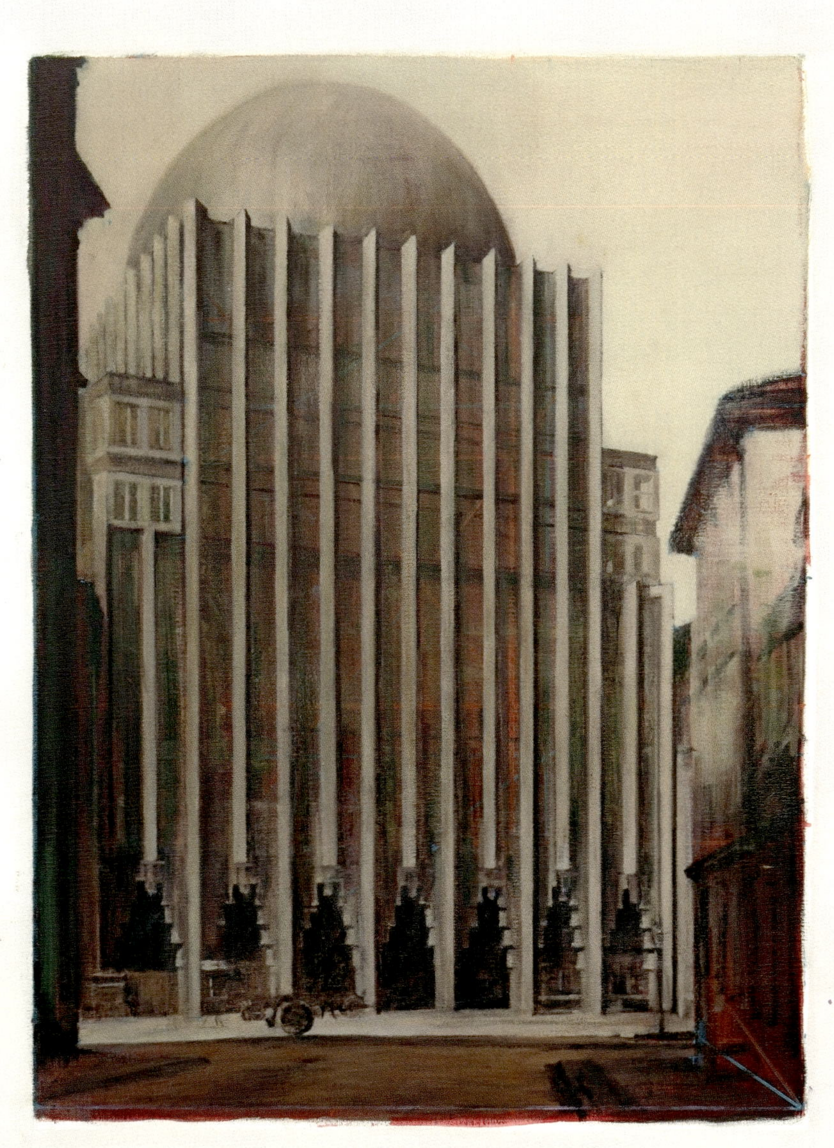

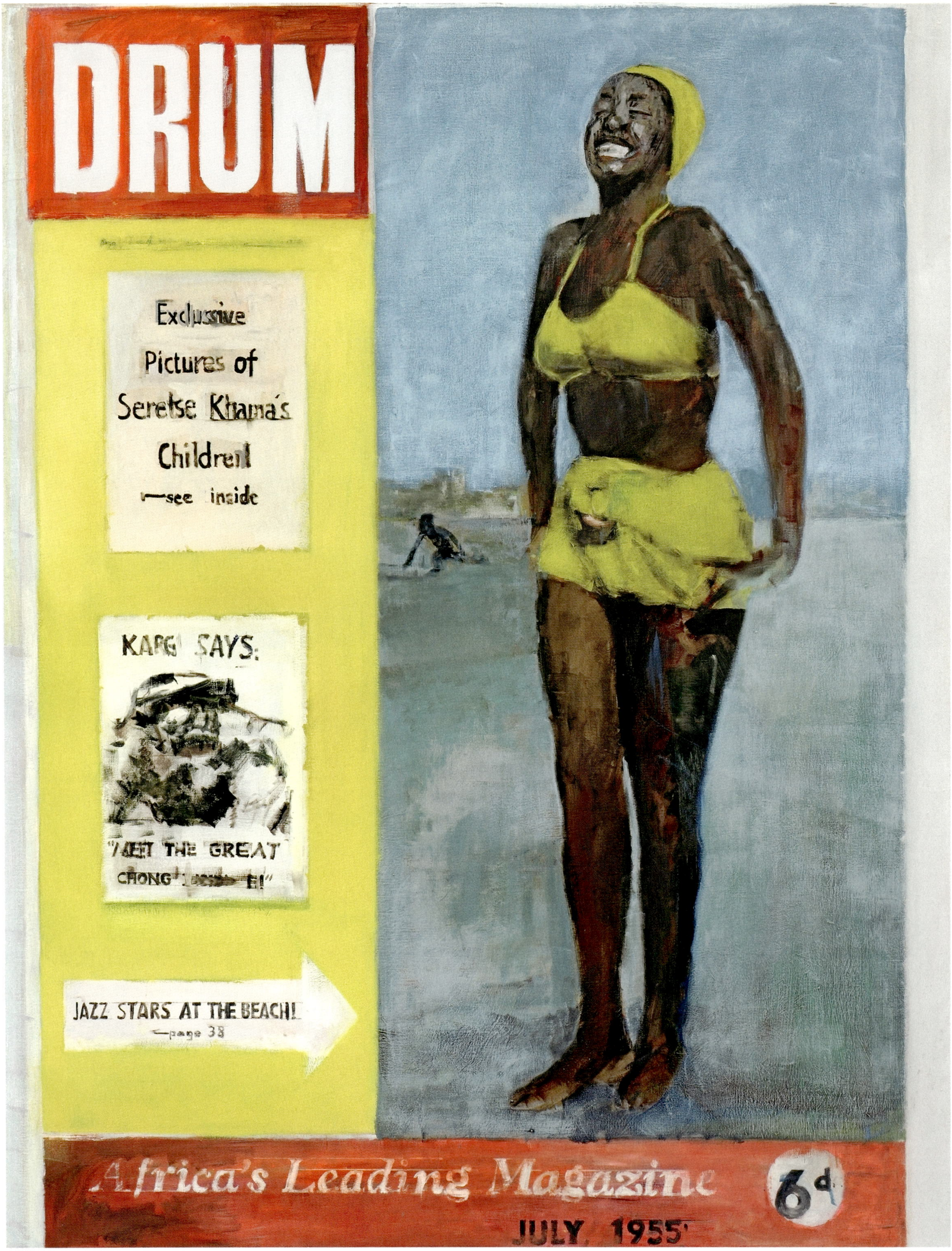

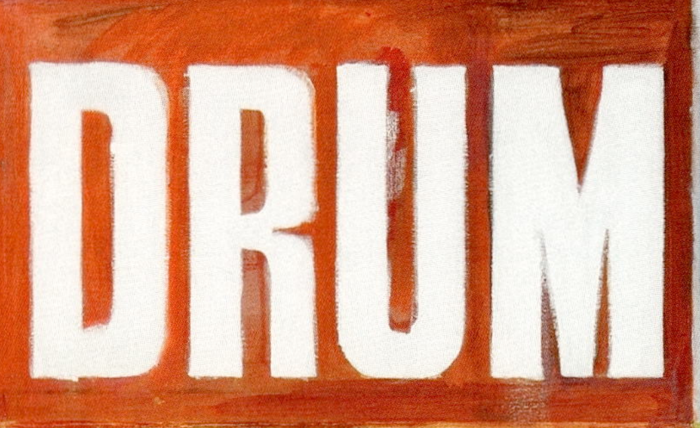

DRUM

Exclusive
Pictures of
Seretse Khama's
Children
—see inside

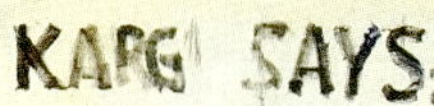

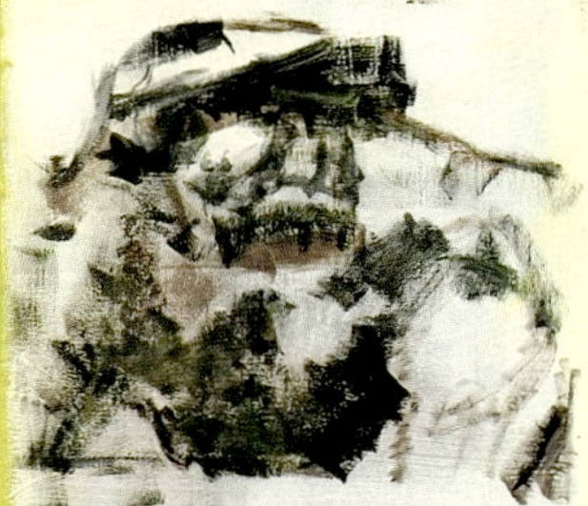

KAPO SAYS:
"MEET THE GREAT
CHONG LOSSOM EI"

JAZZ STARS AT THE BEACH!
—page 38

Africa's Leading Magazine

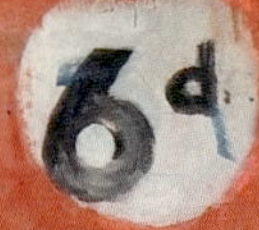

6d

JULY 1955

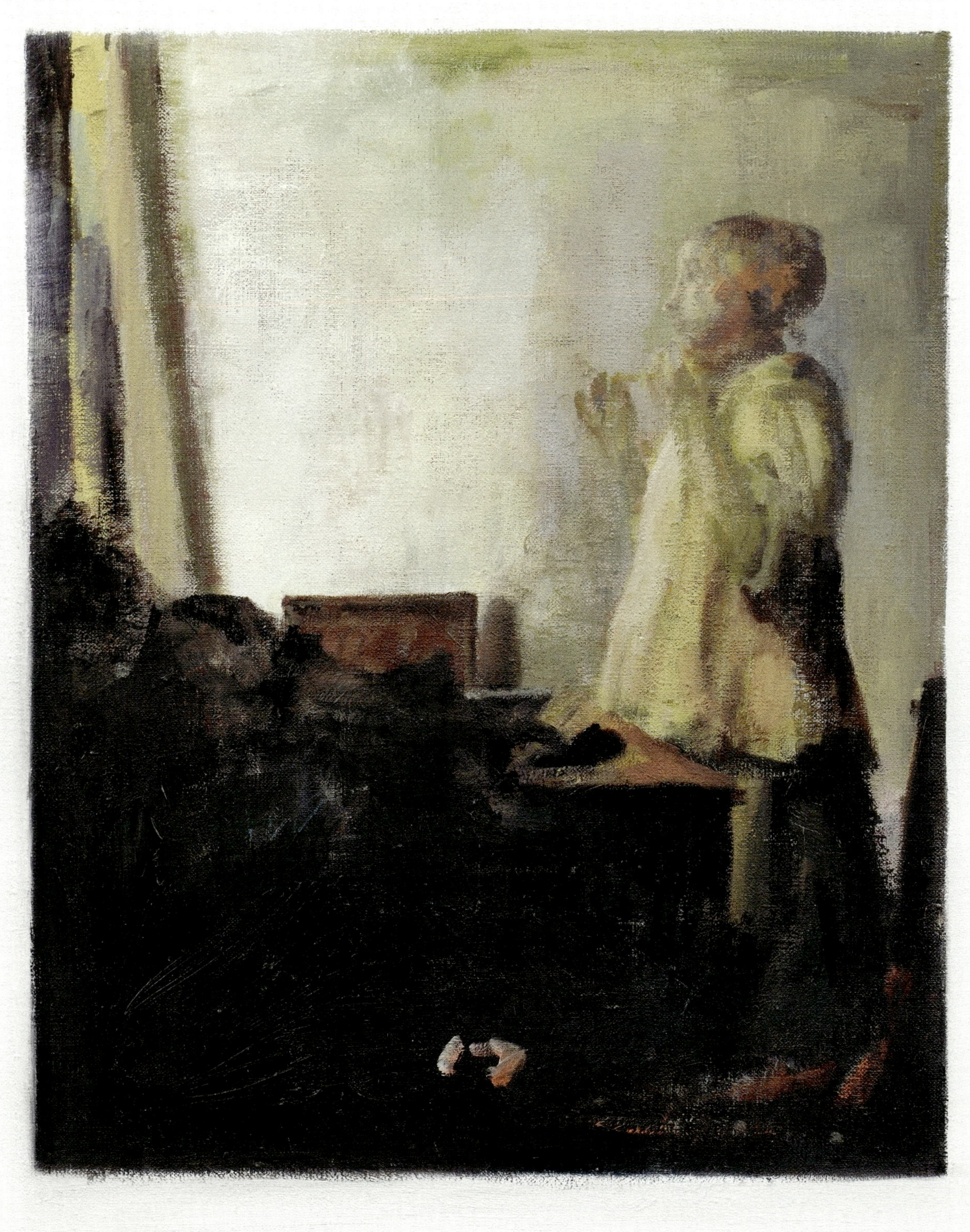

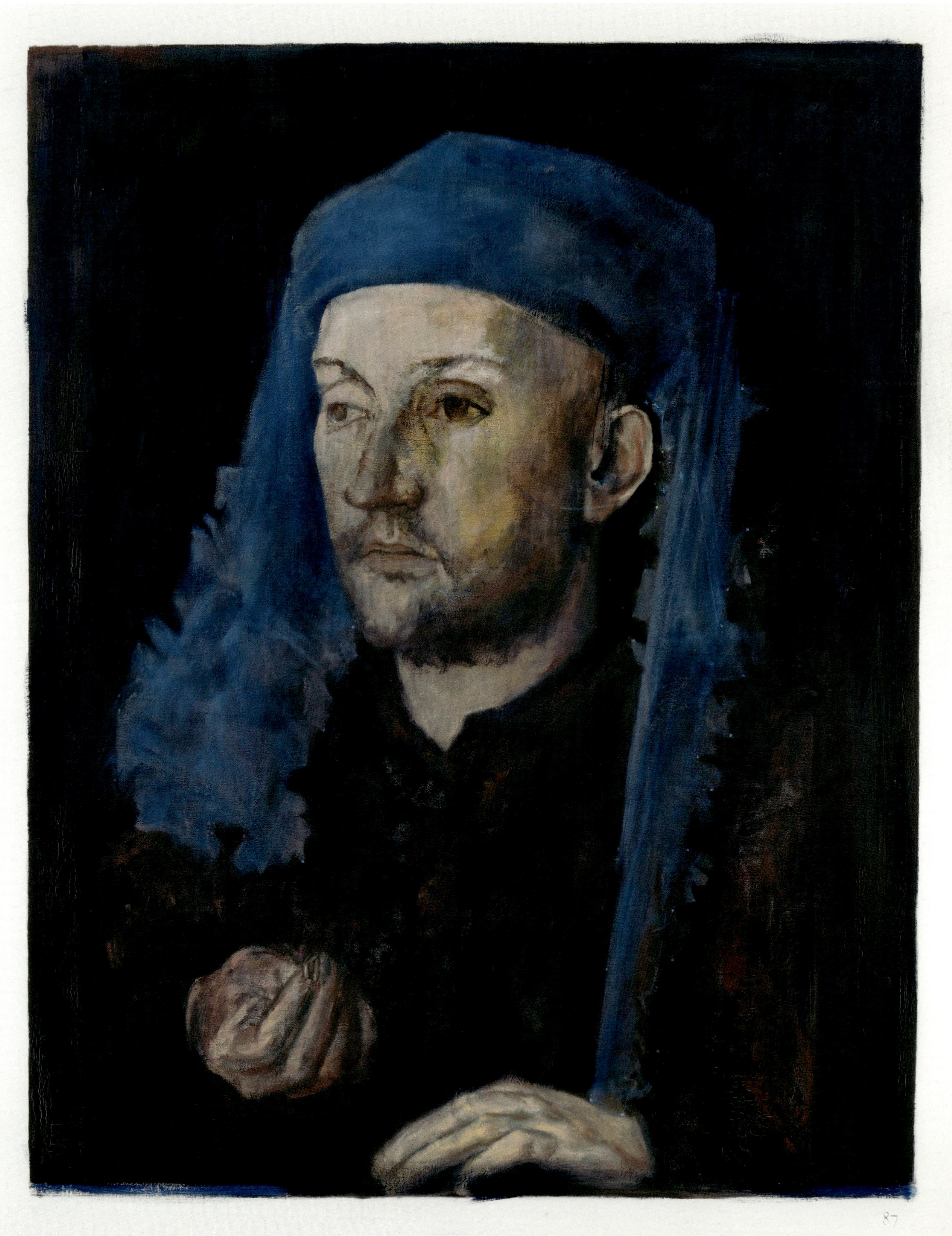

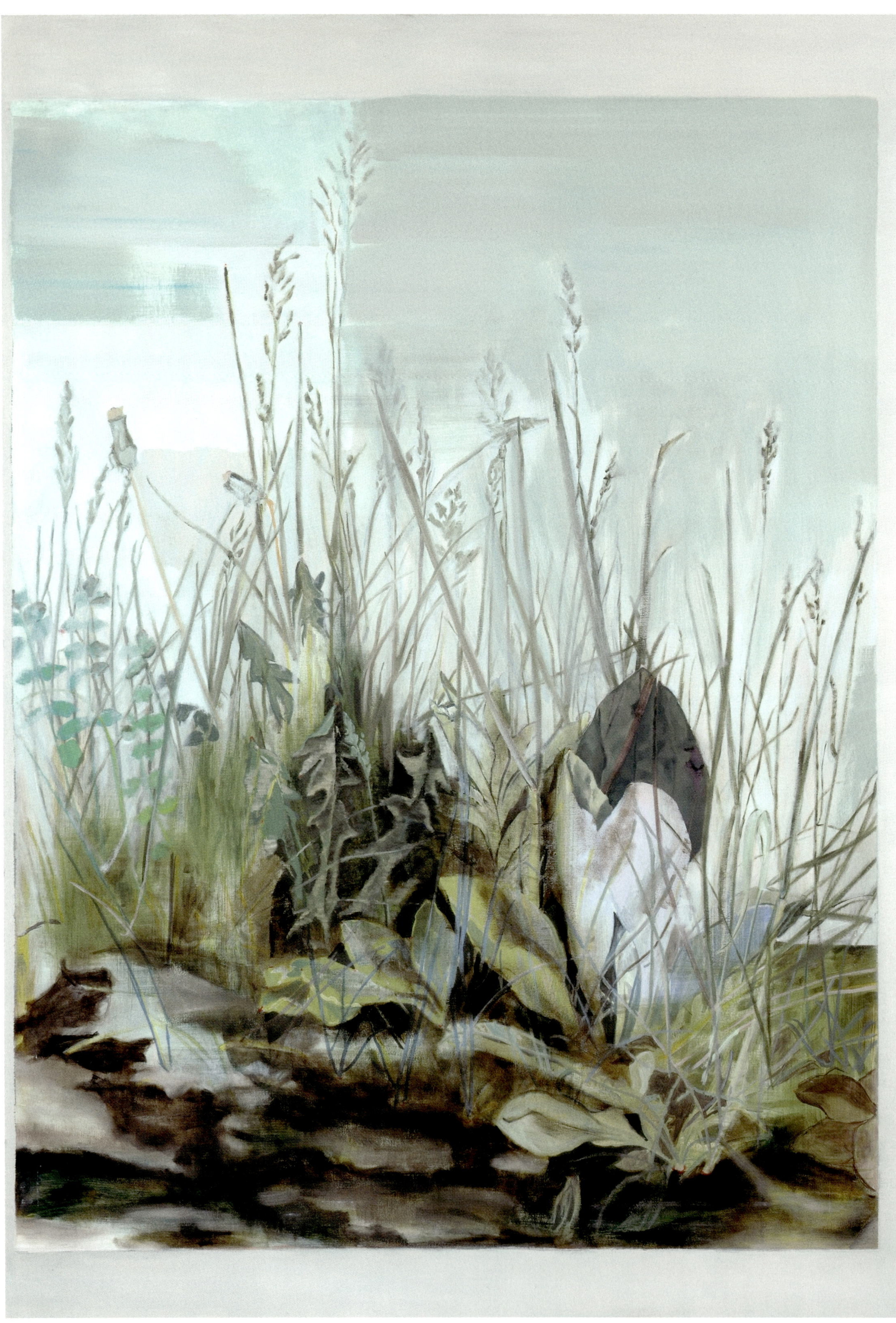

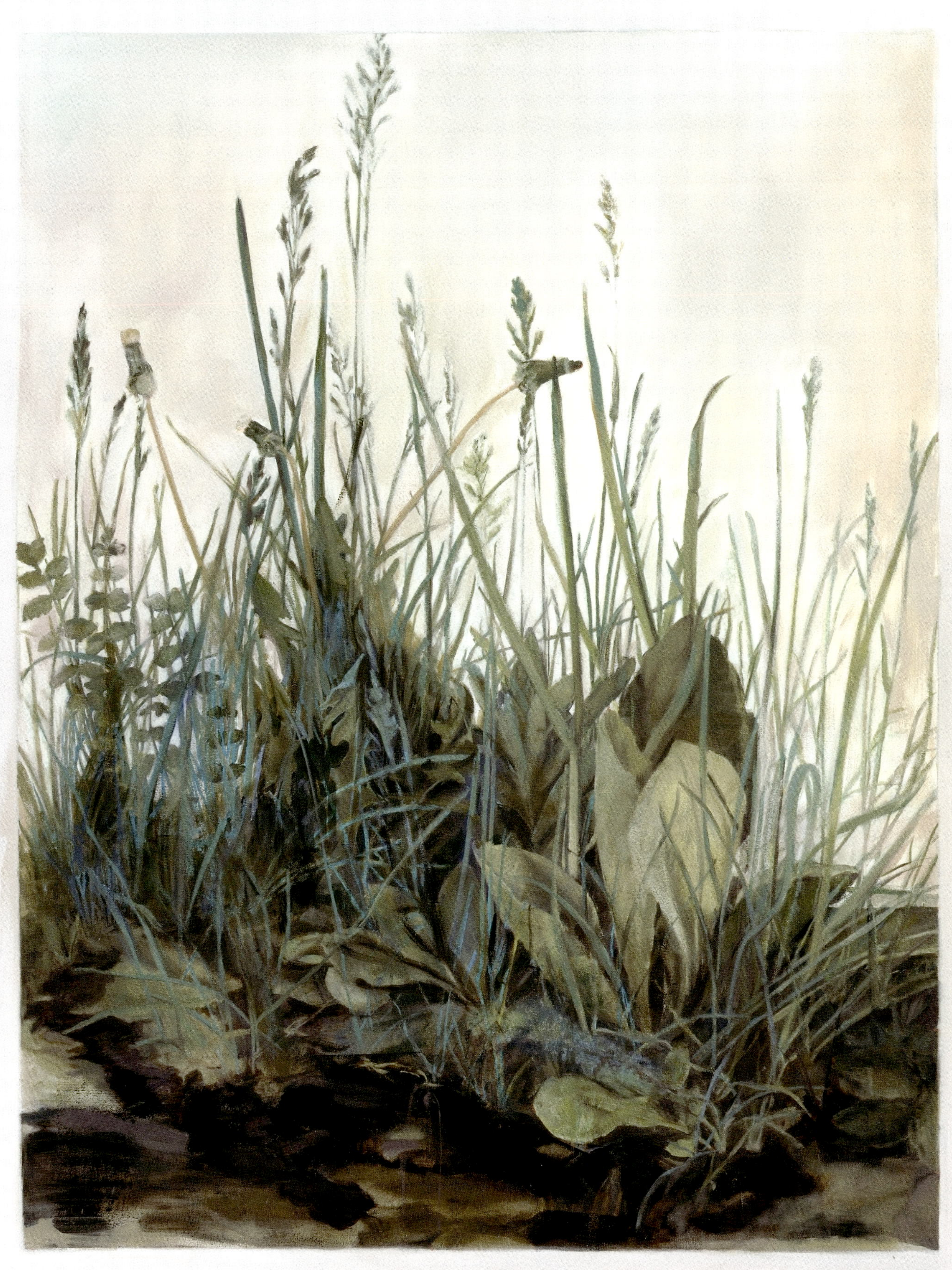

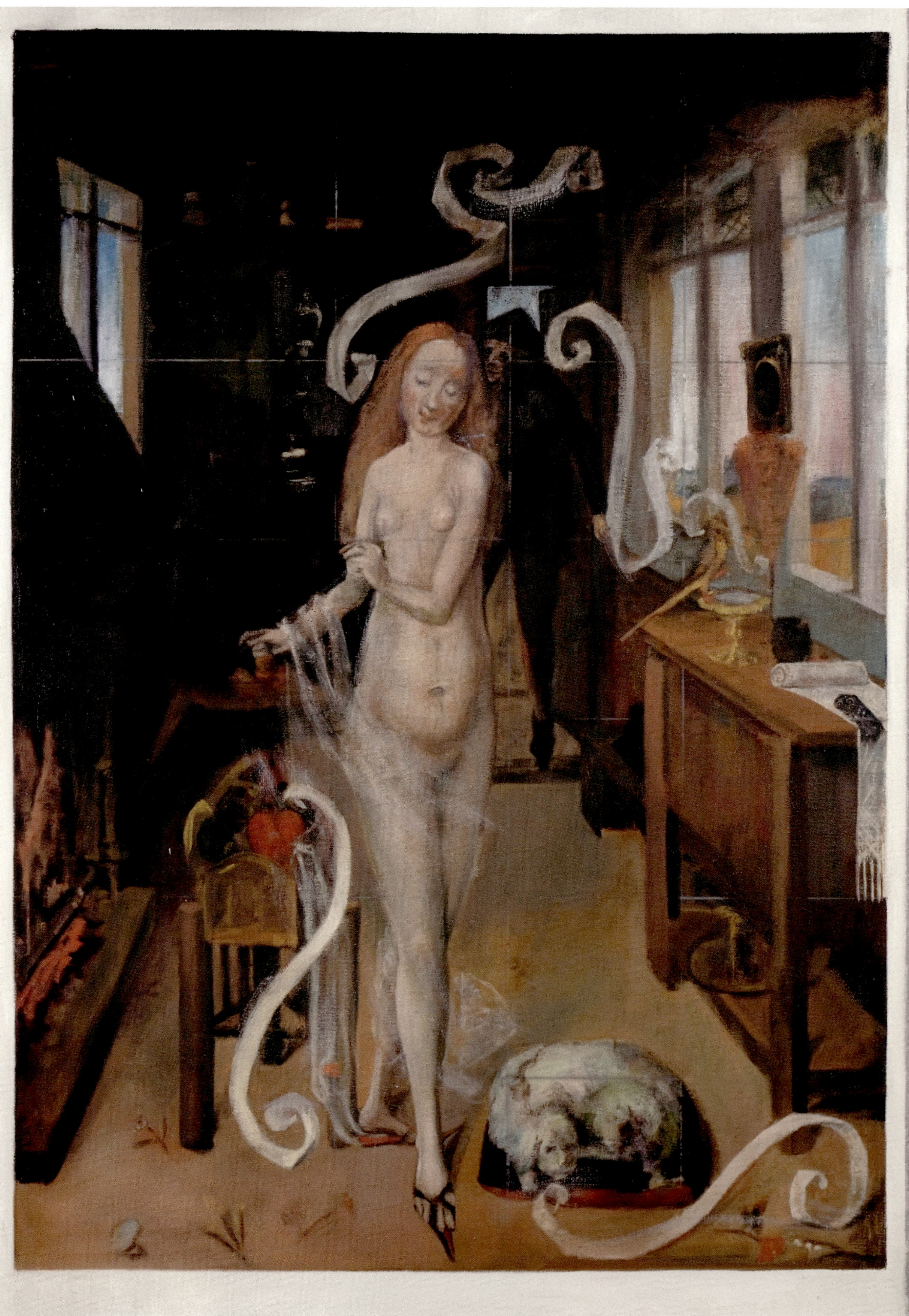

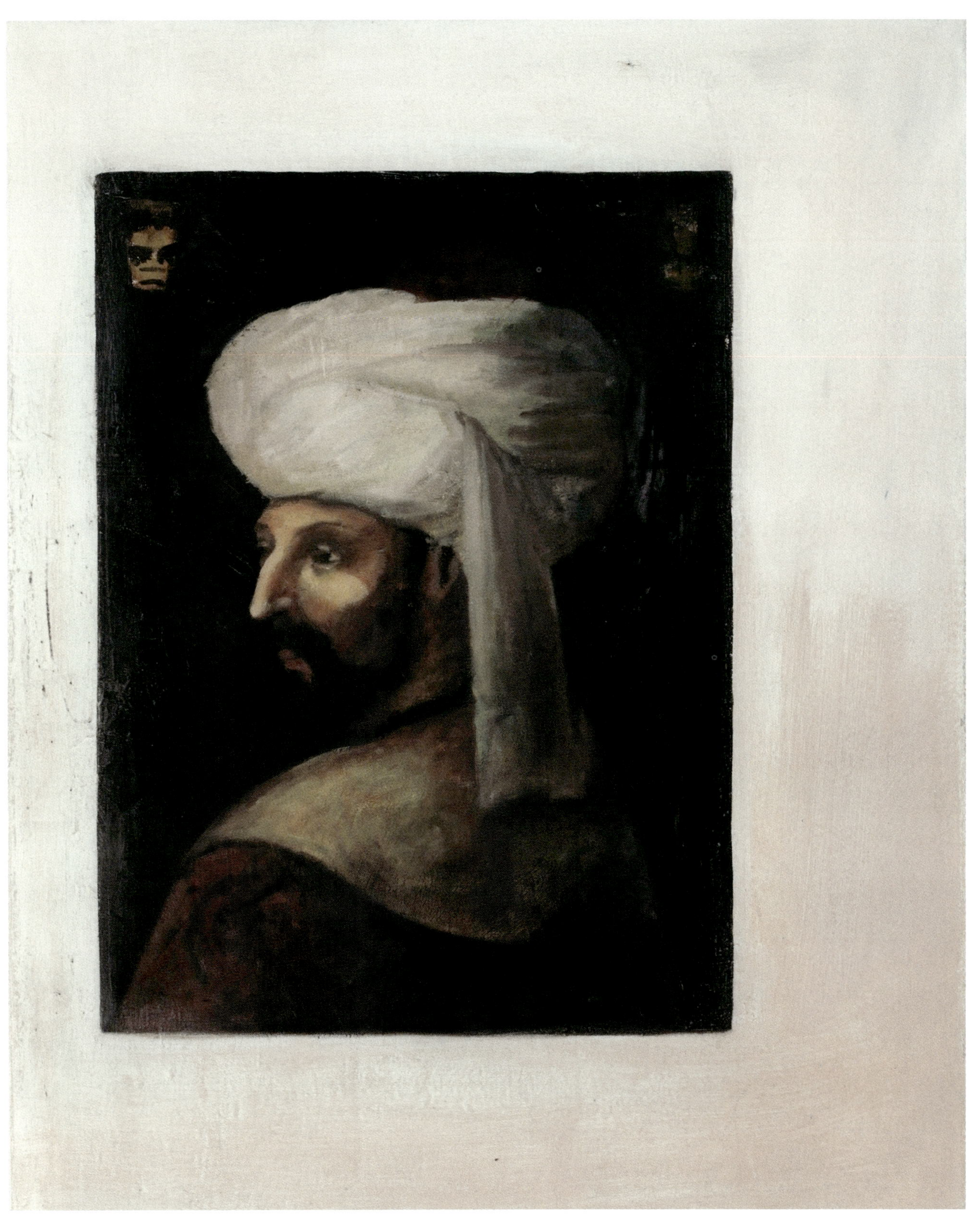

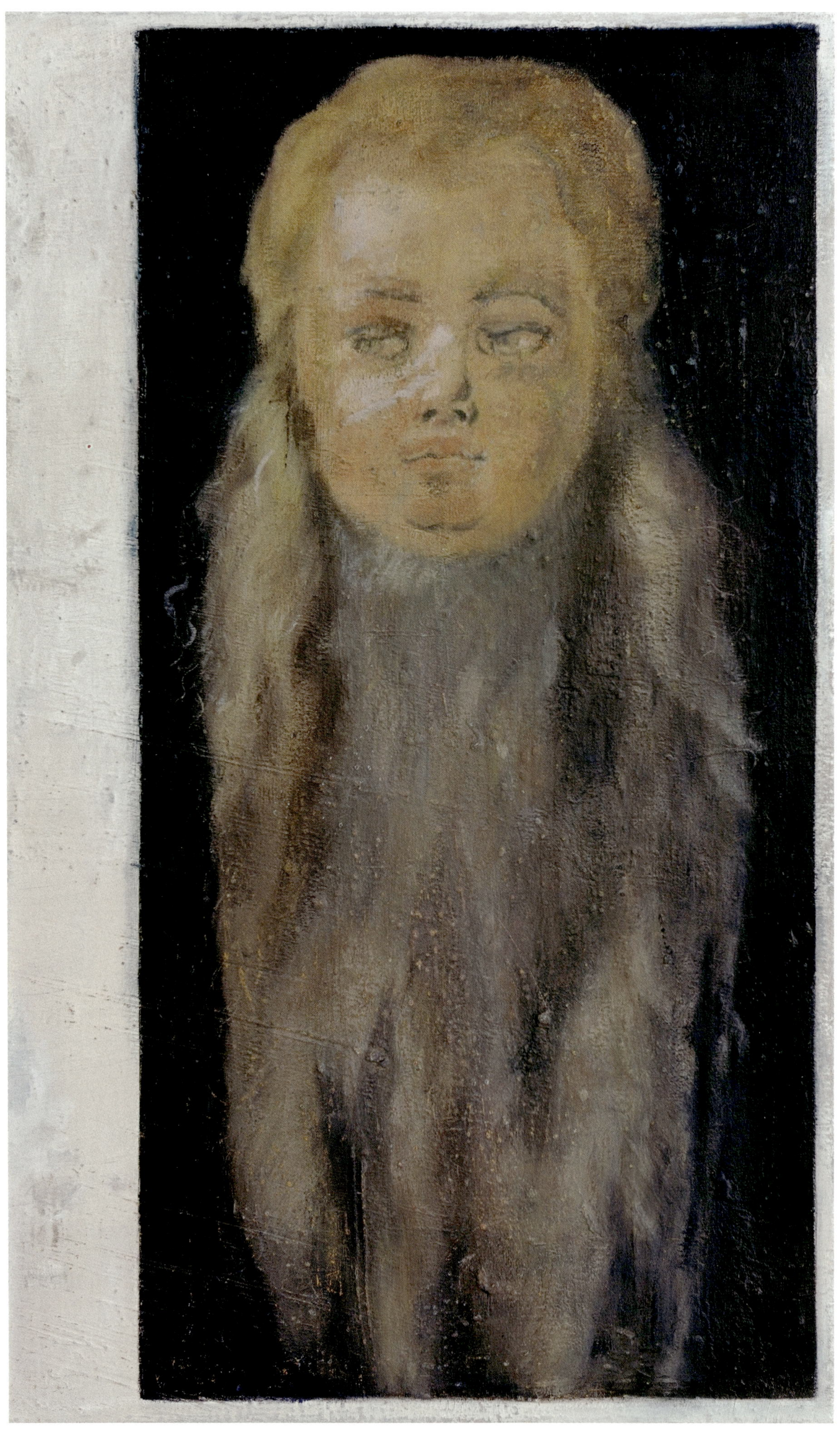

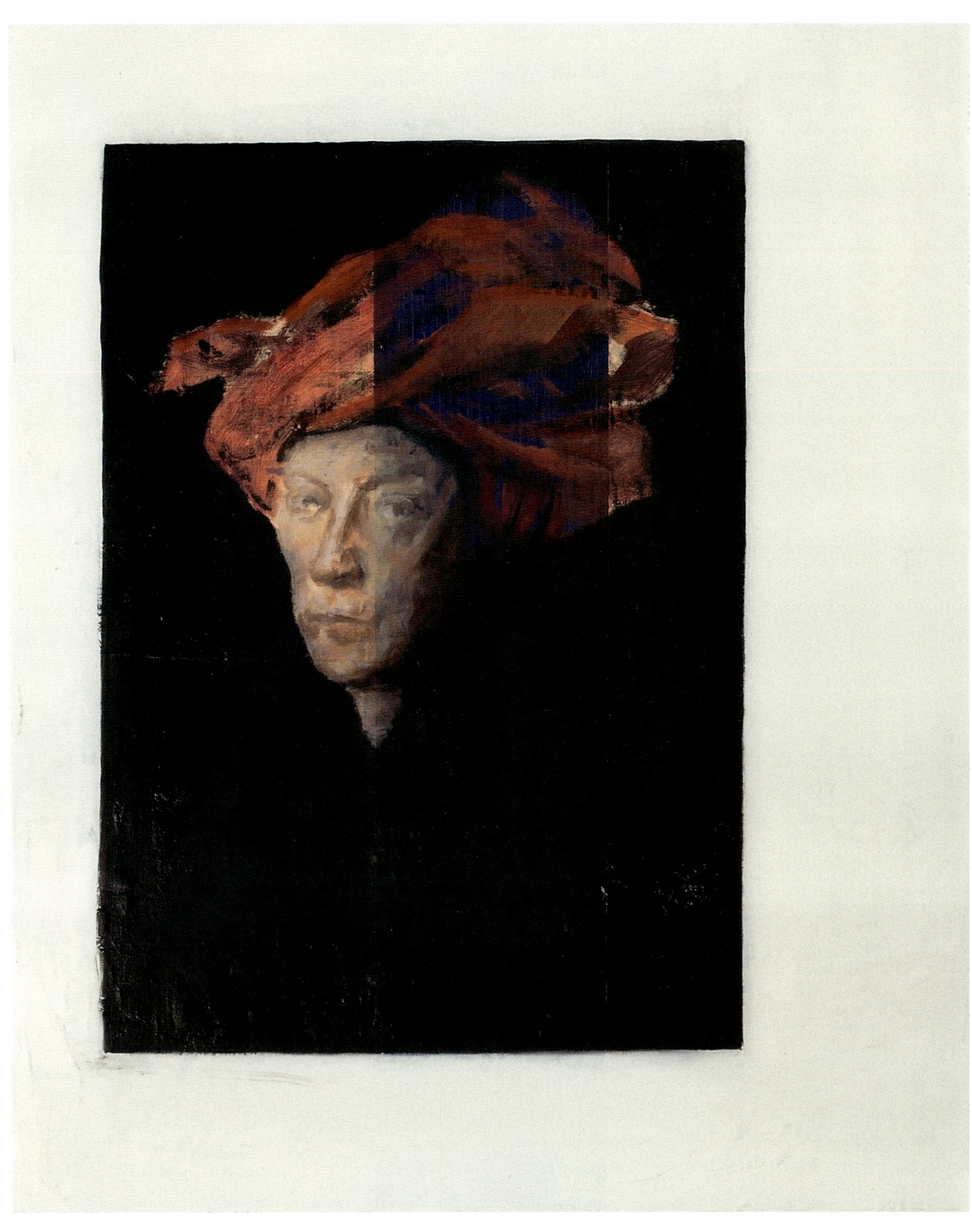

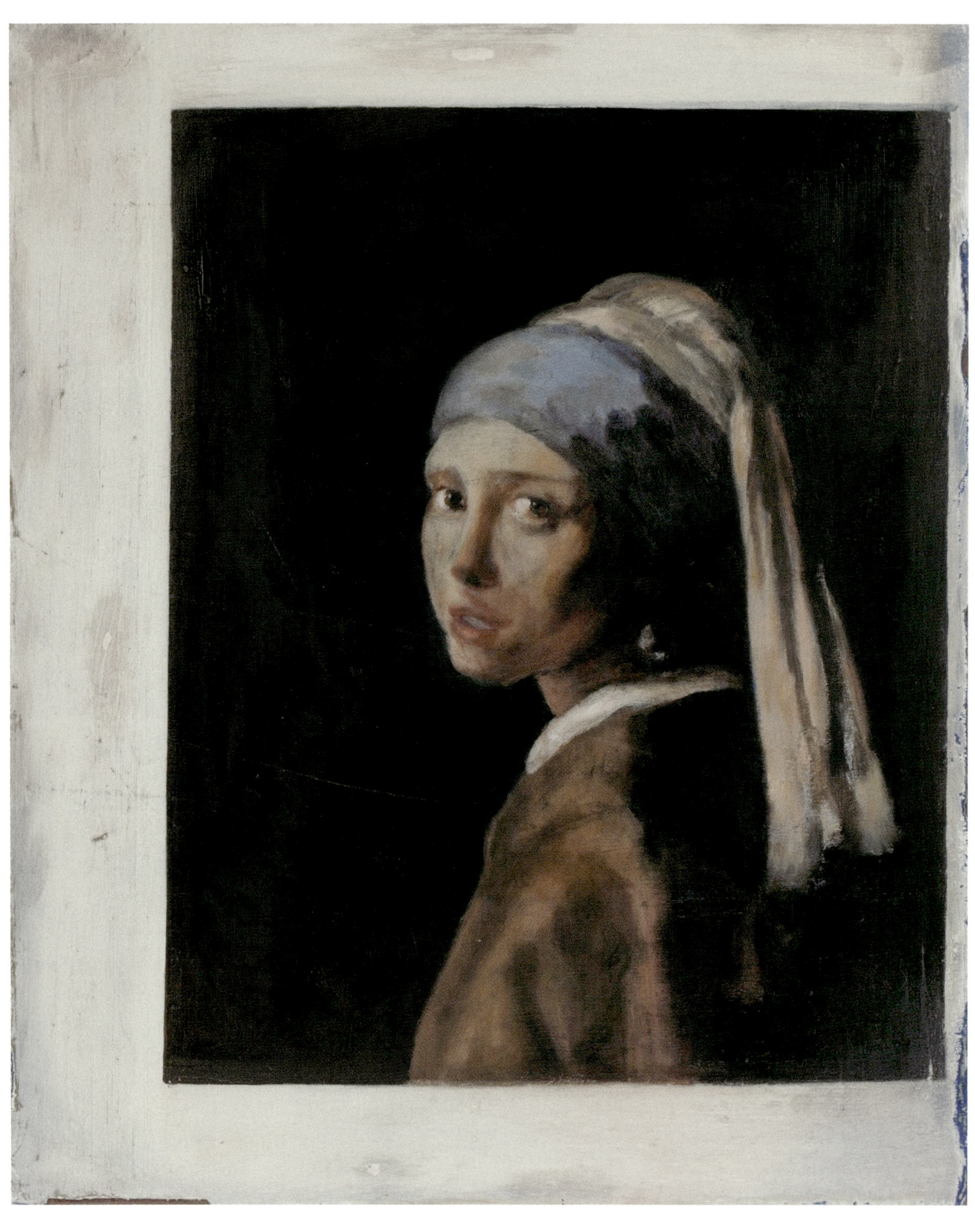

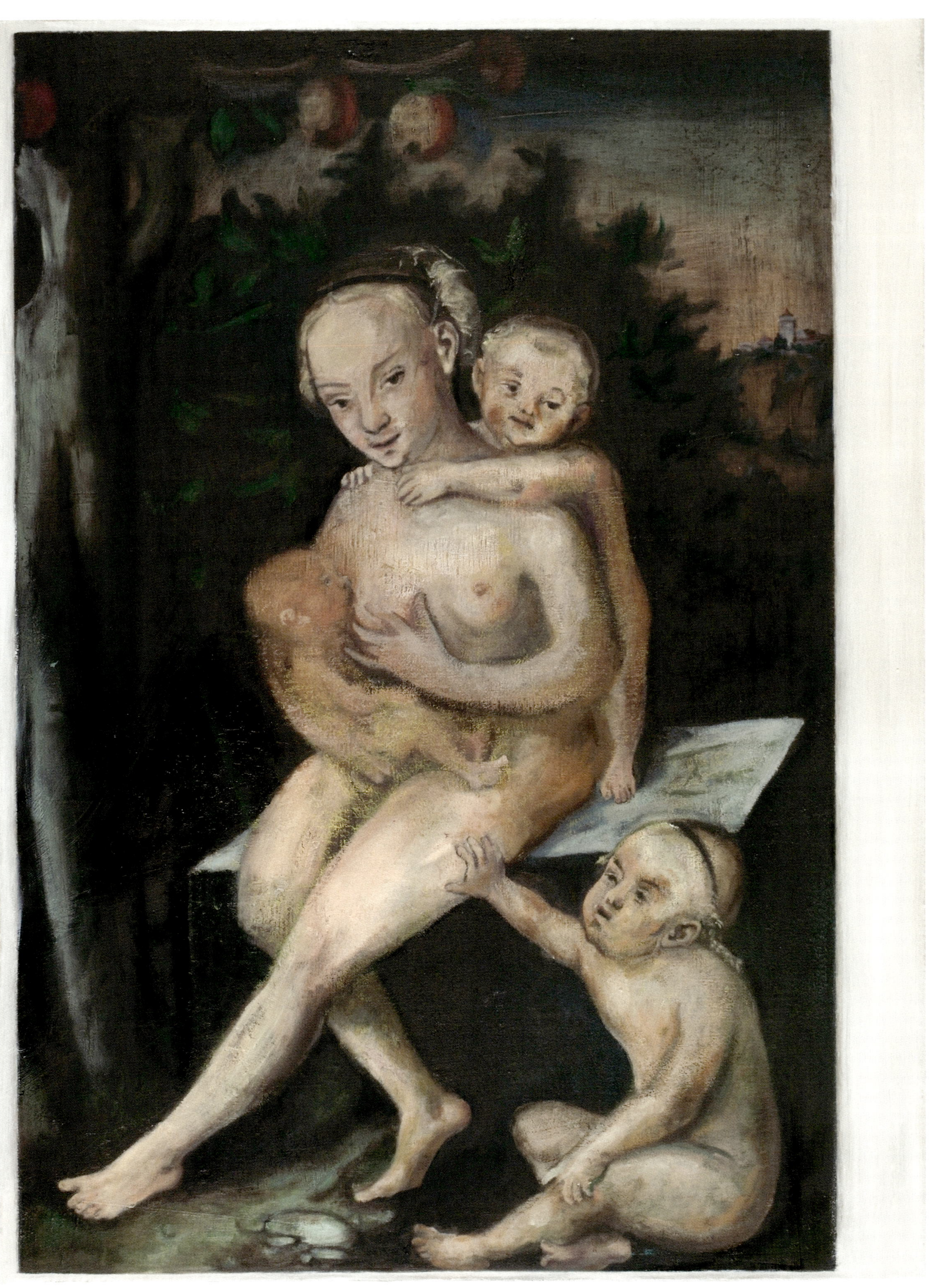

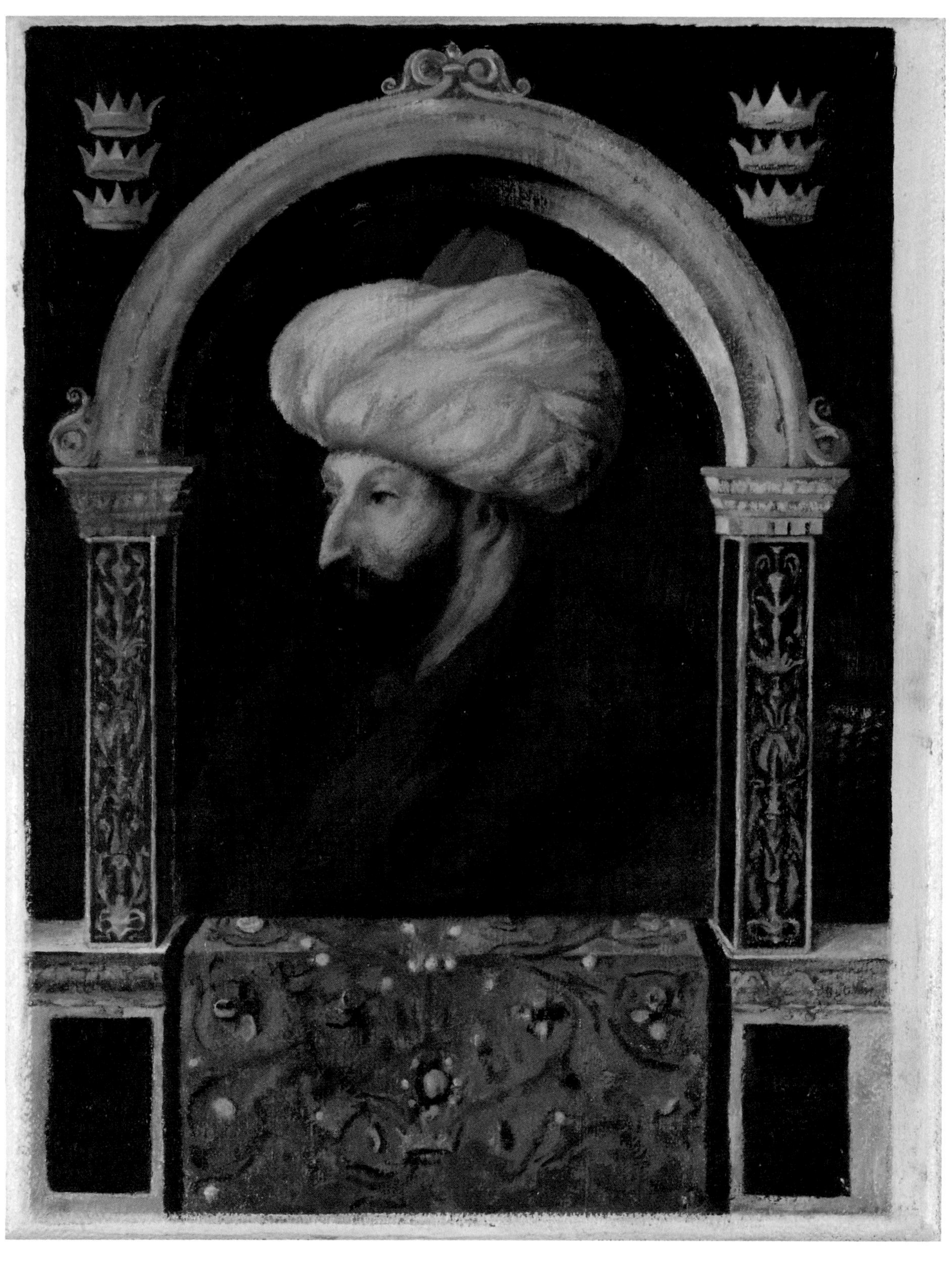

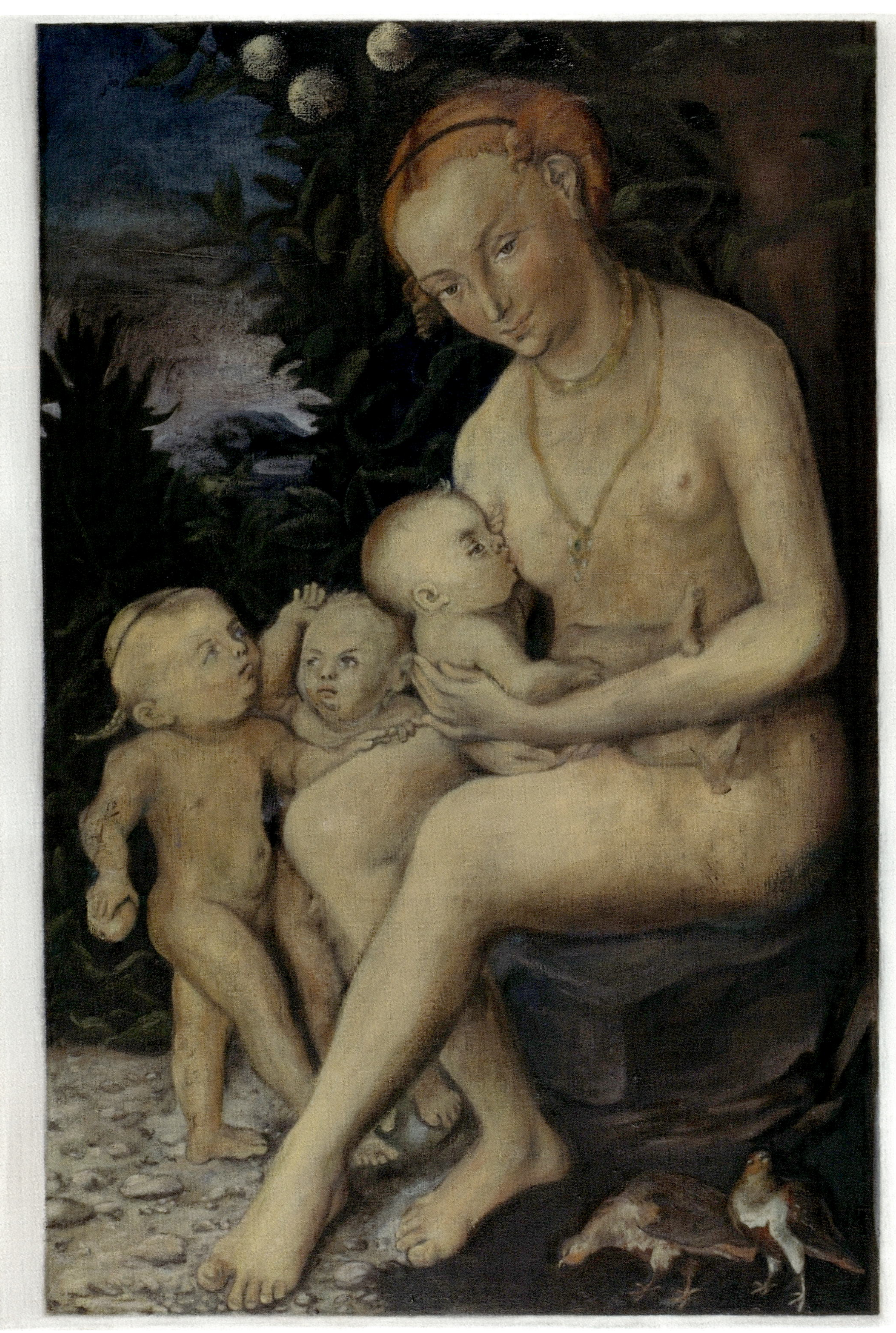

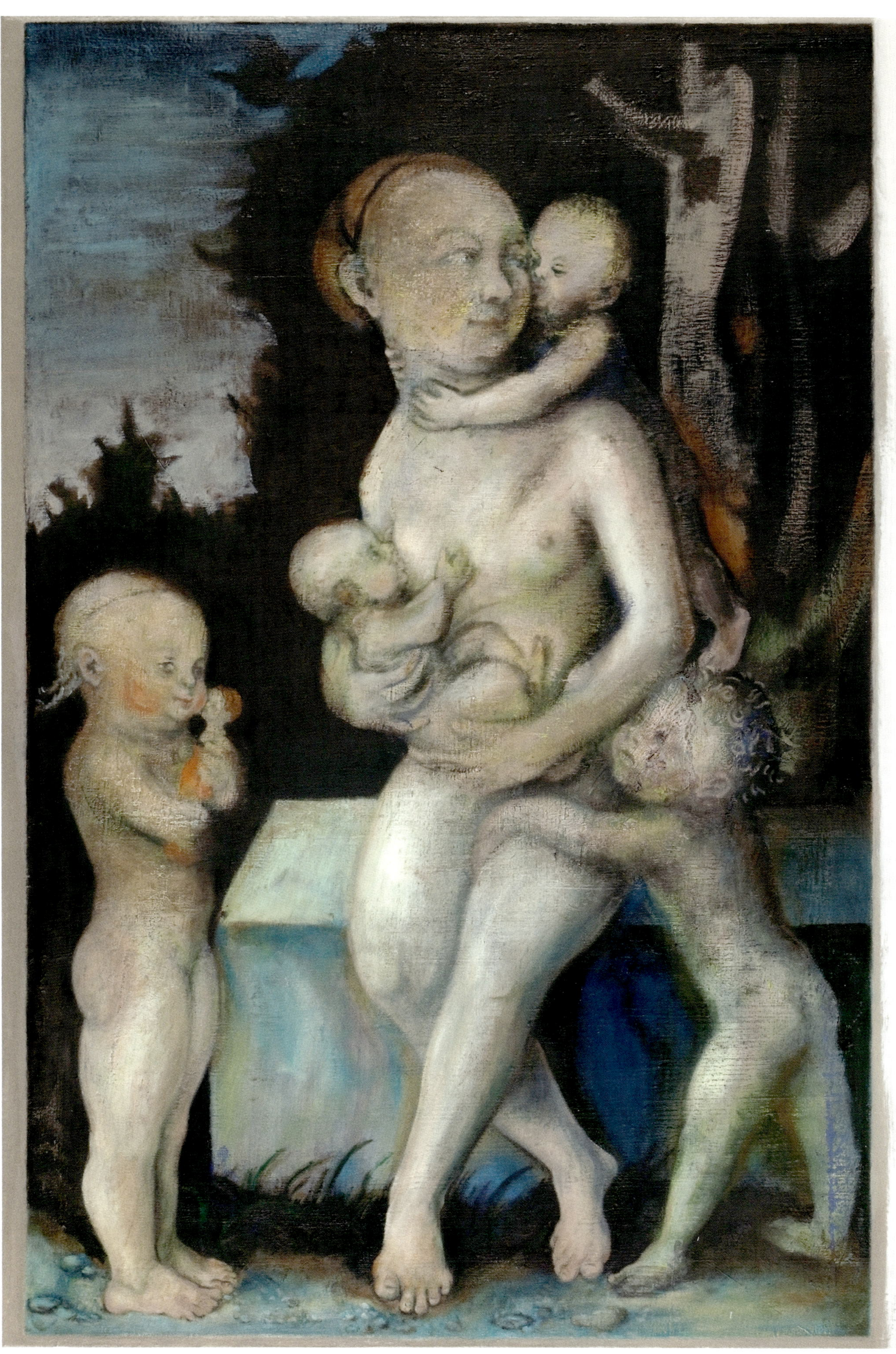

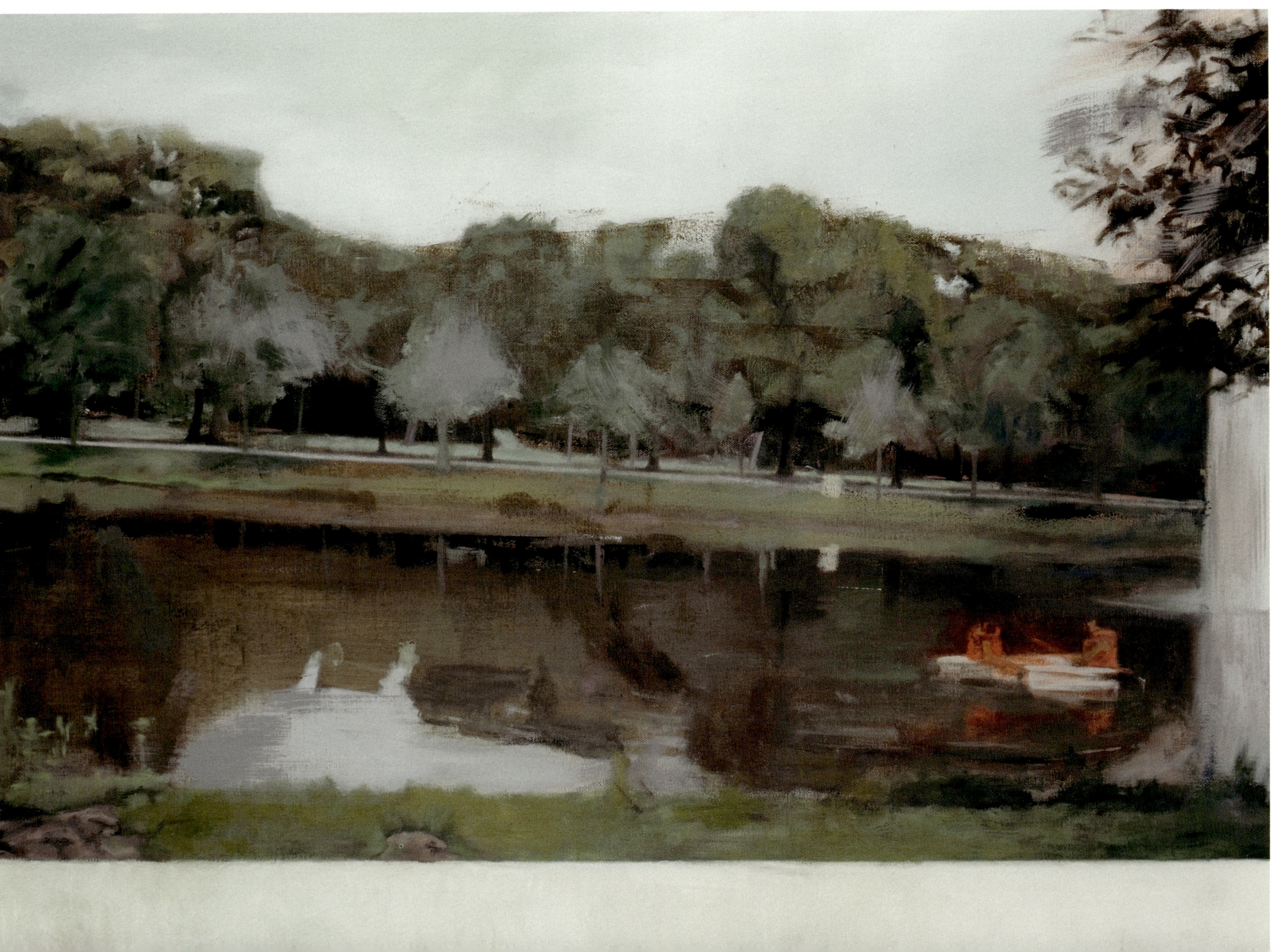

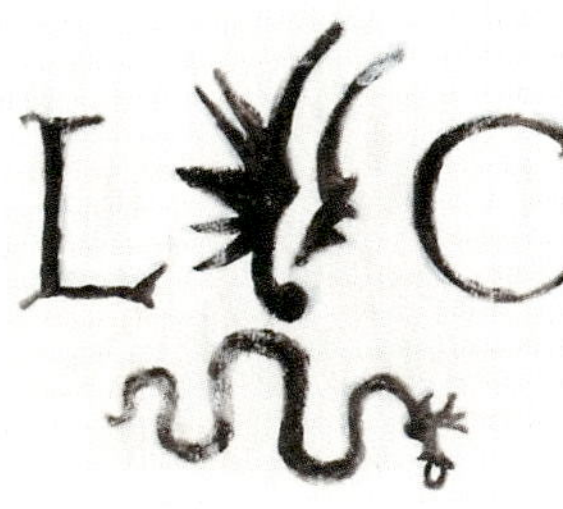

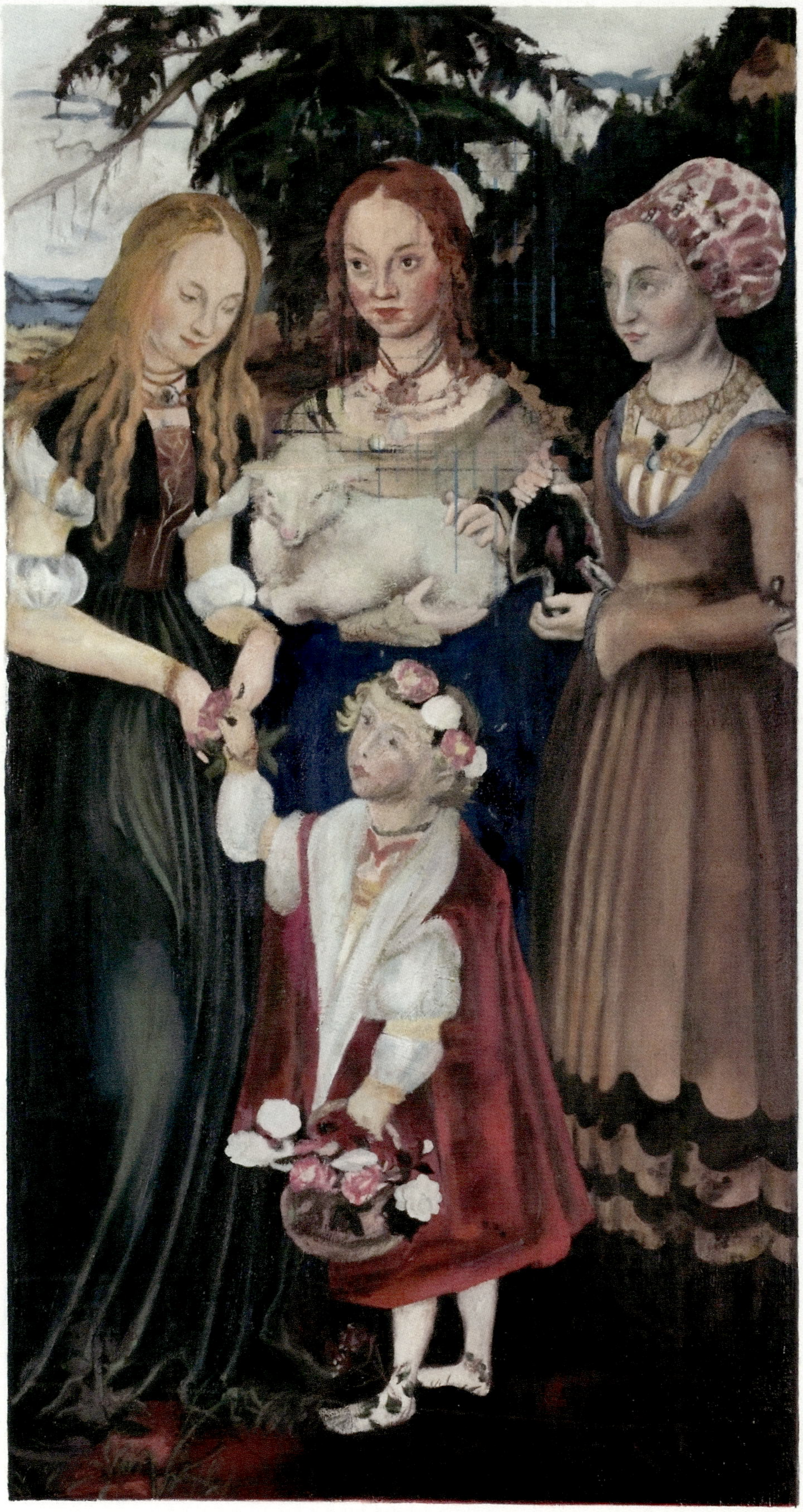

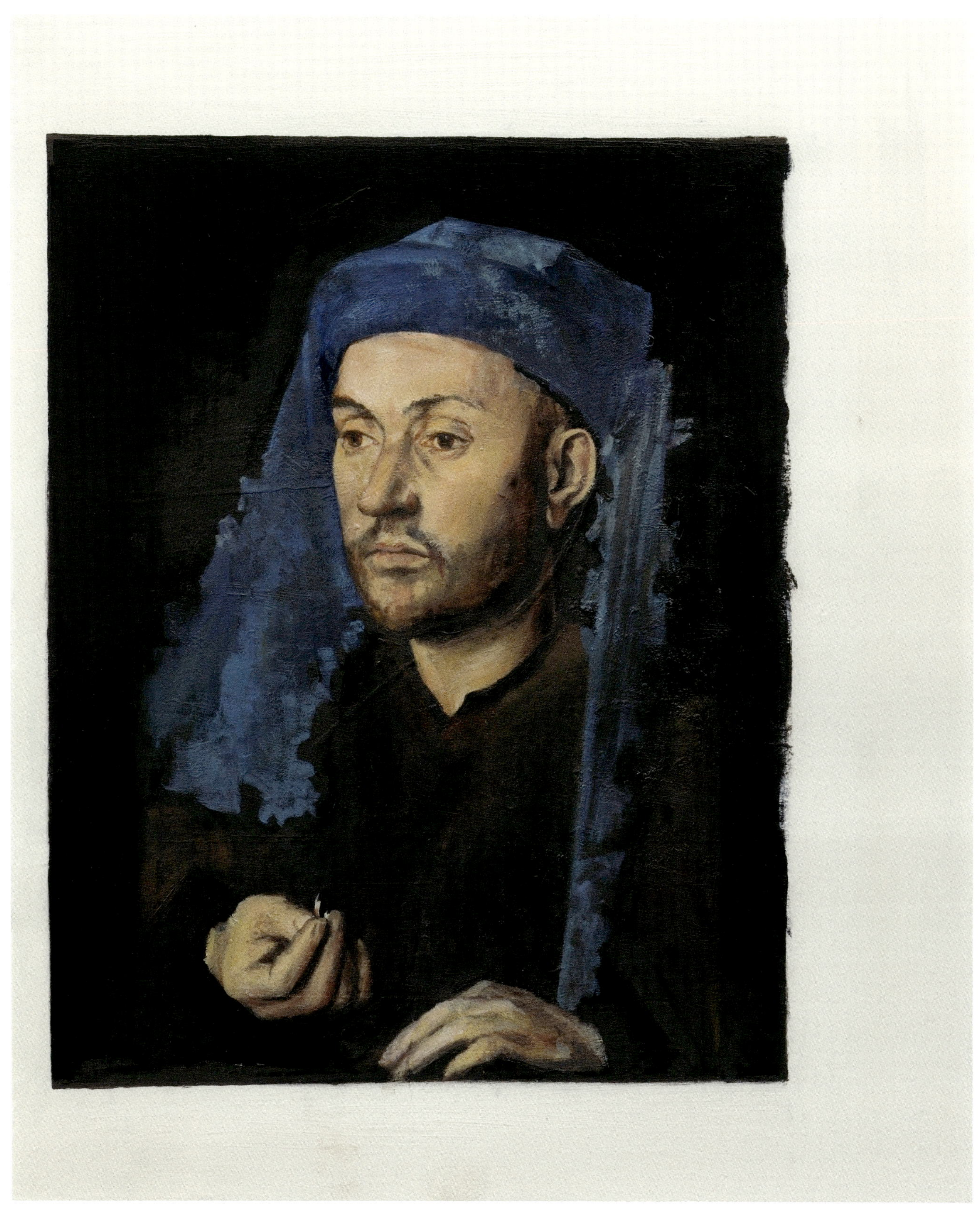

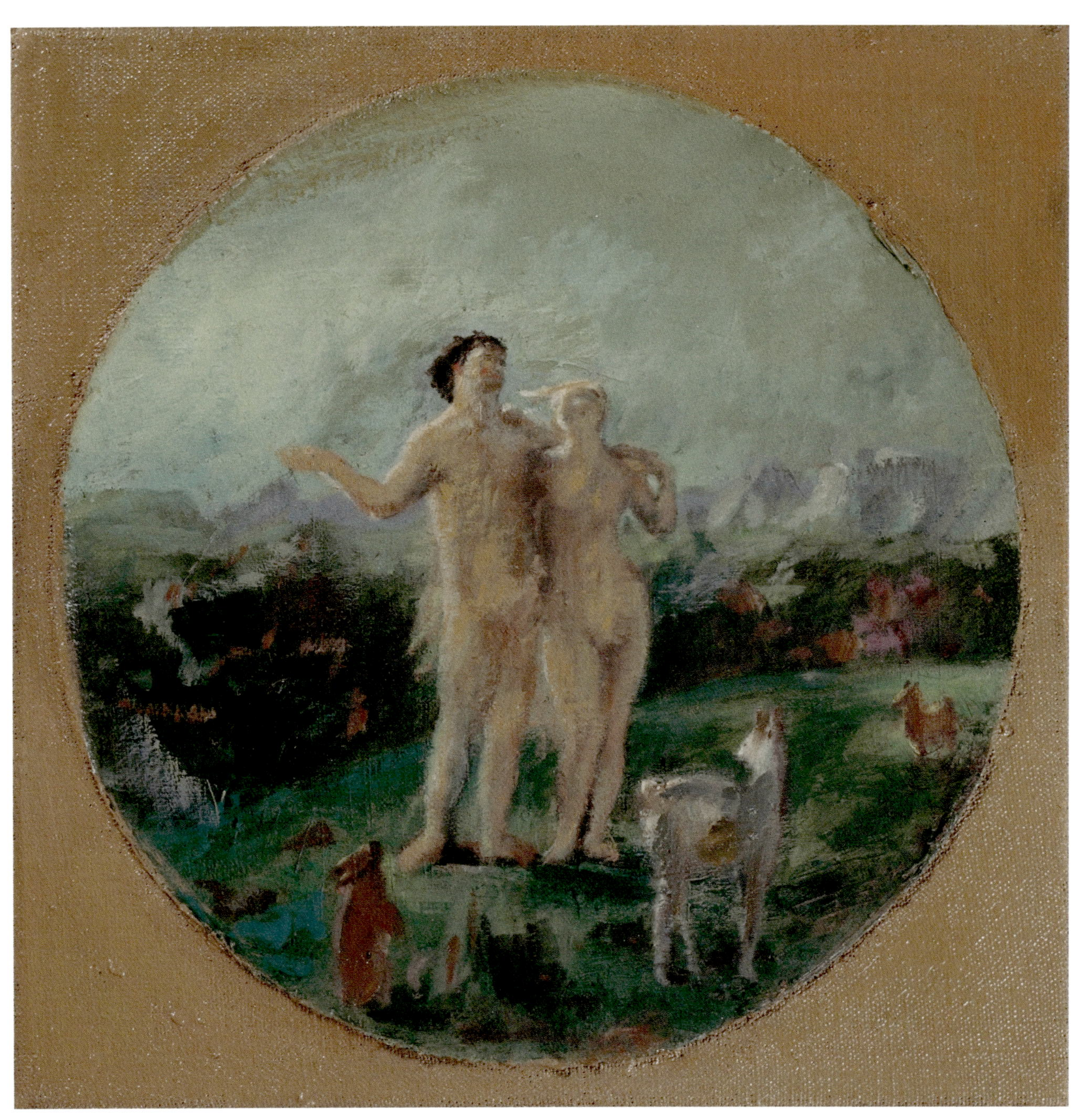

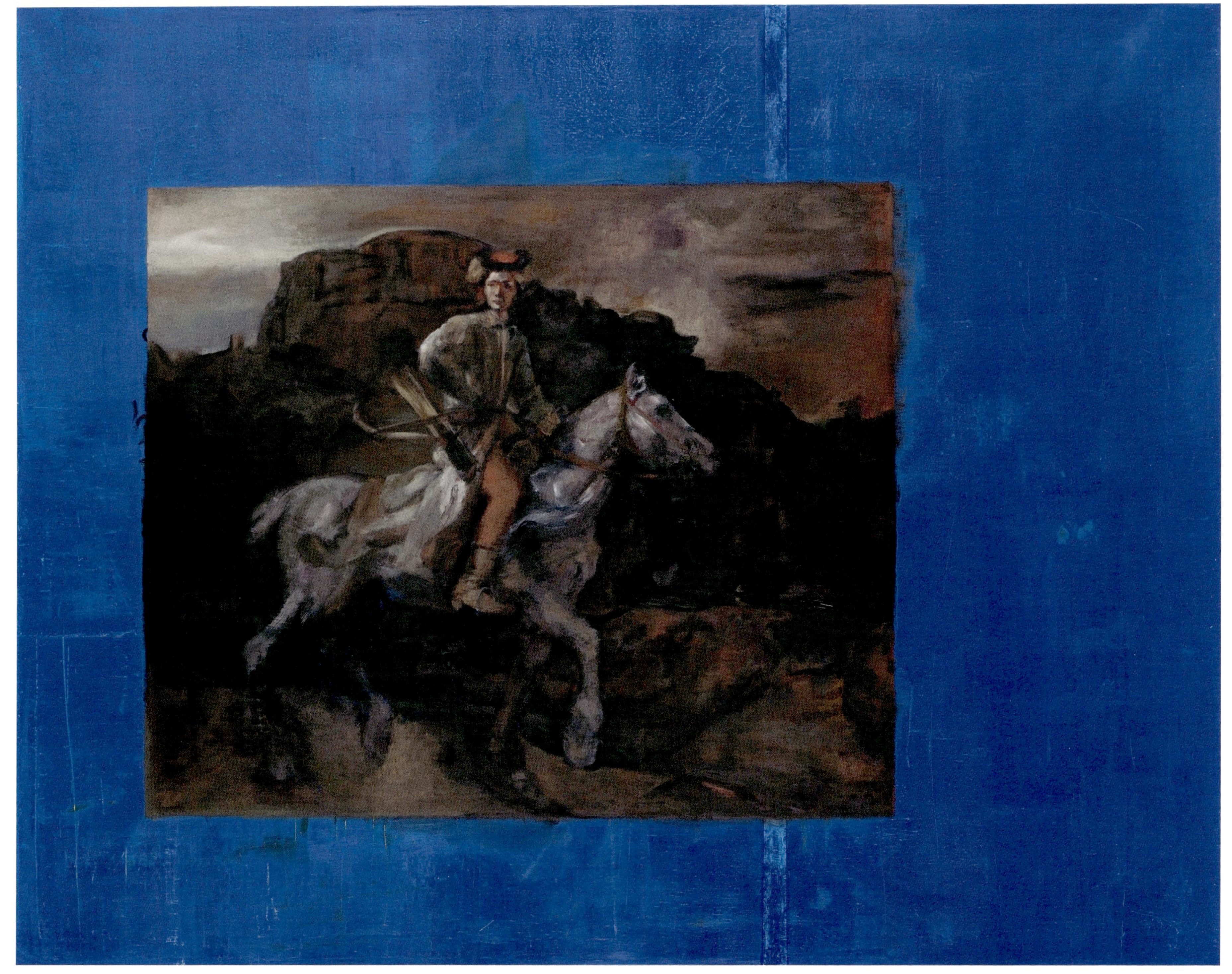

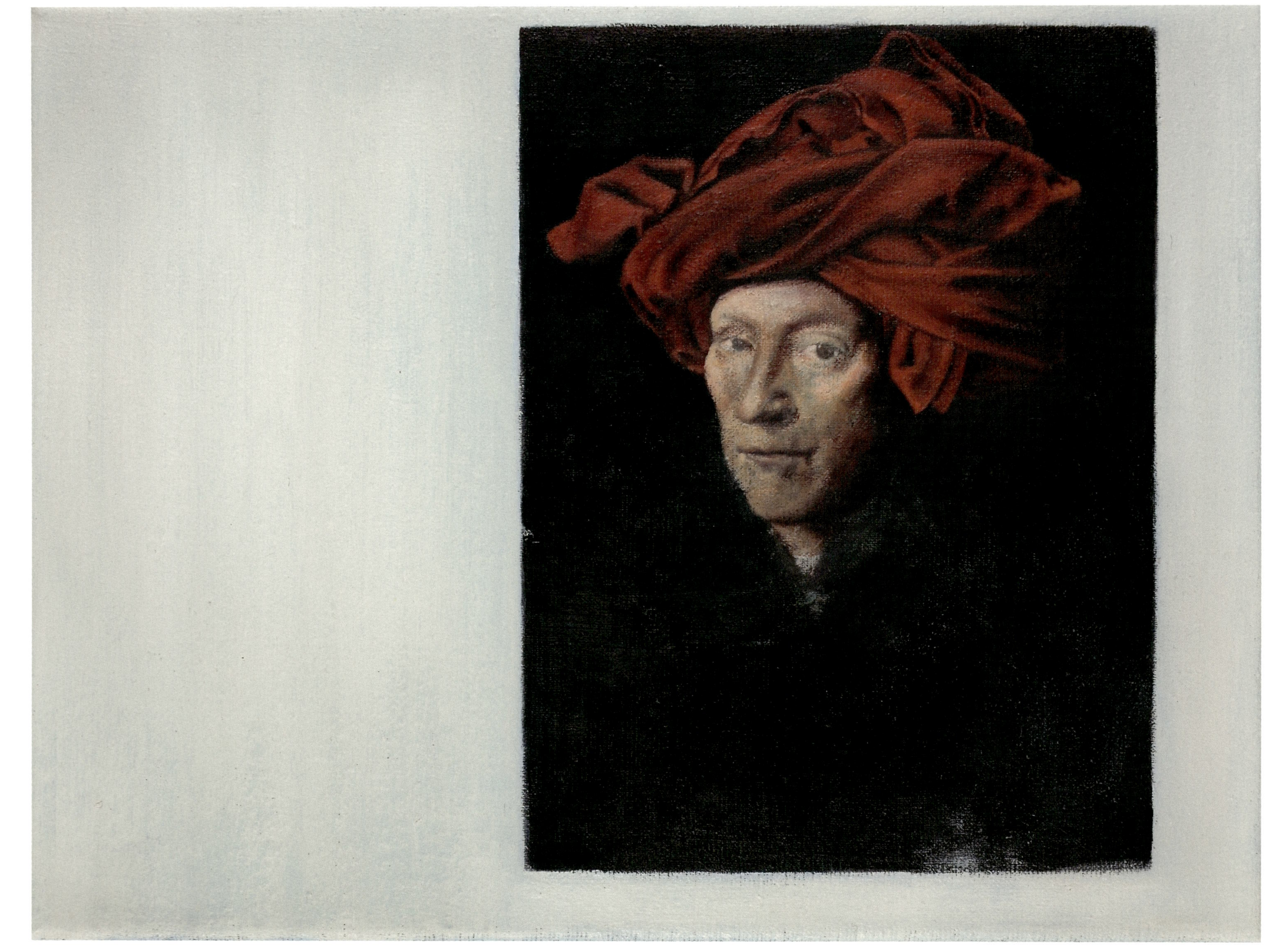

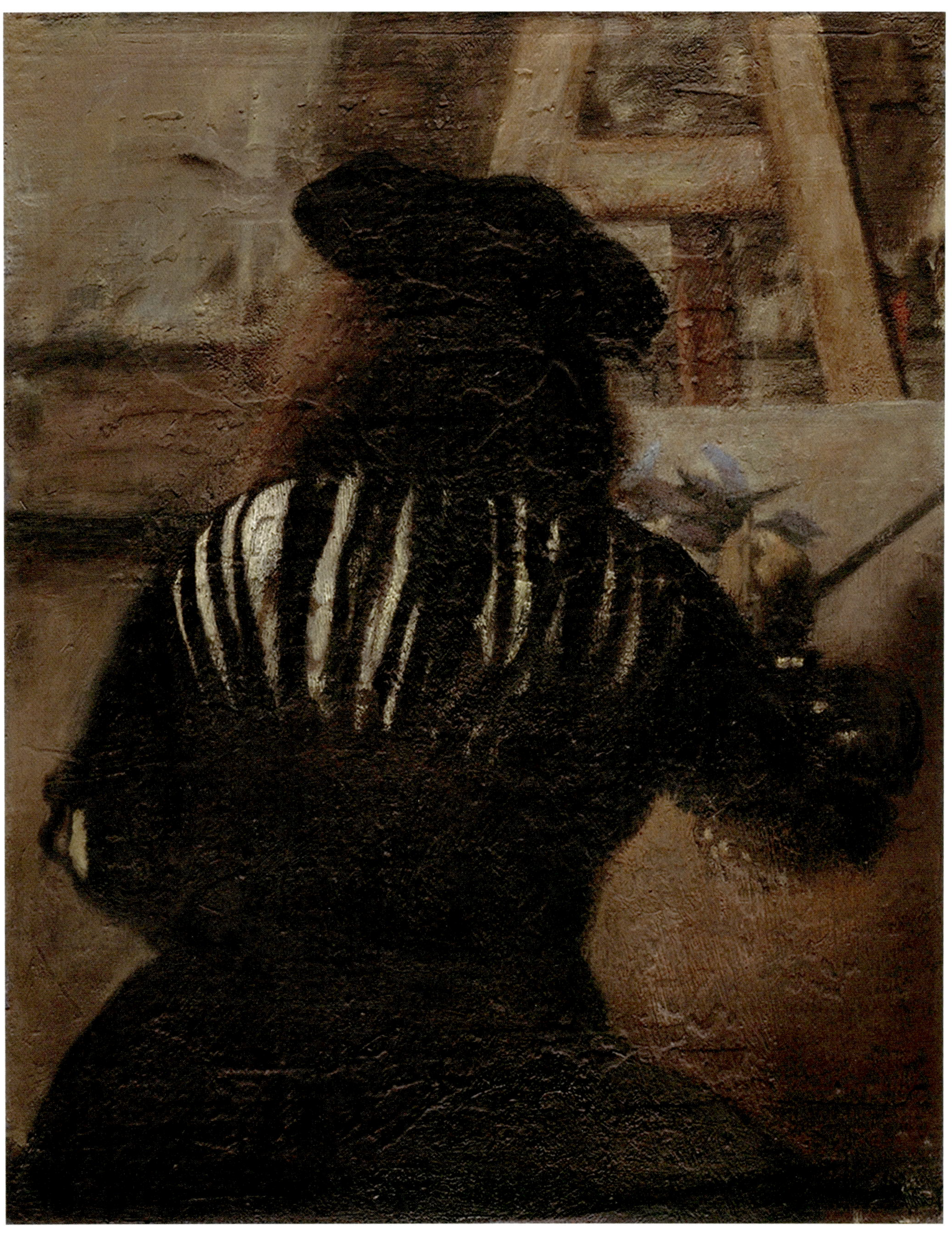

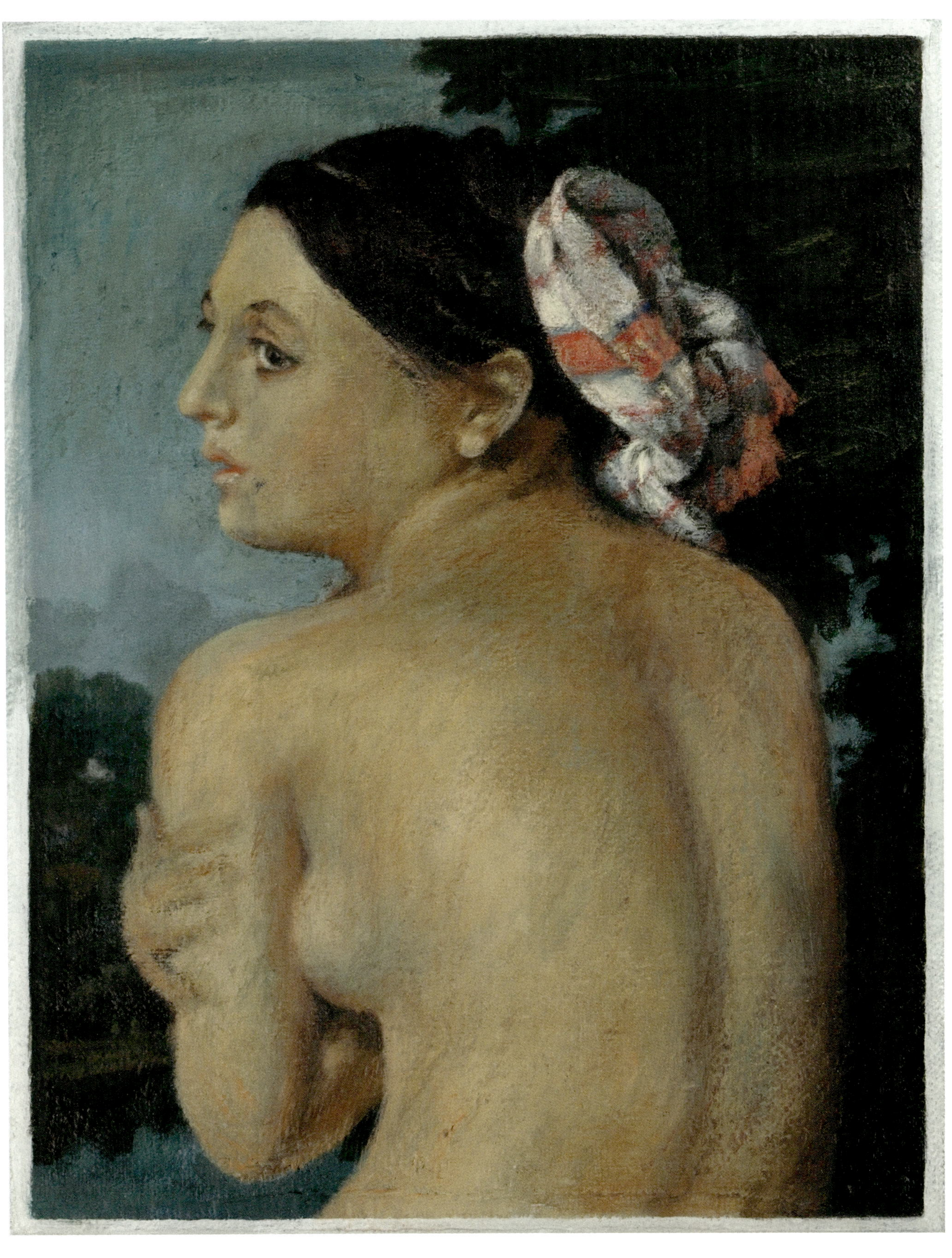

2010

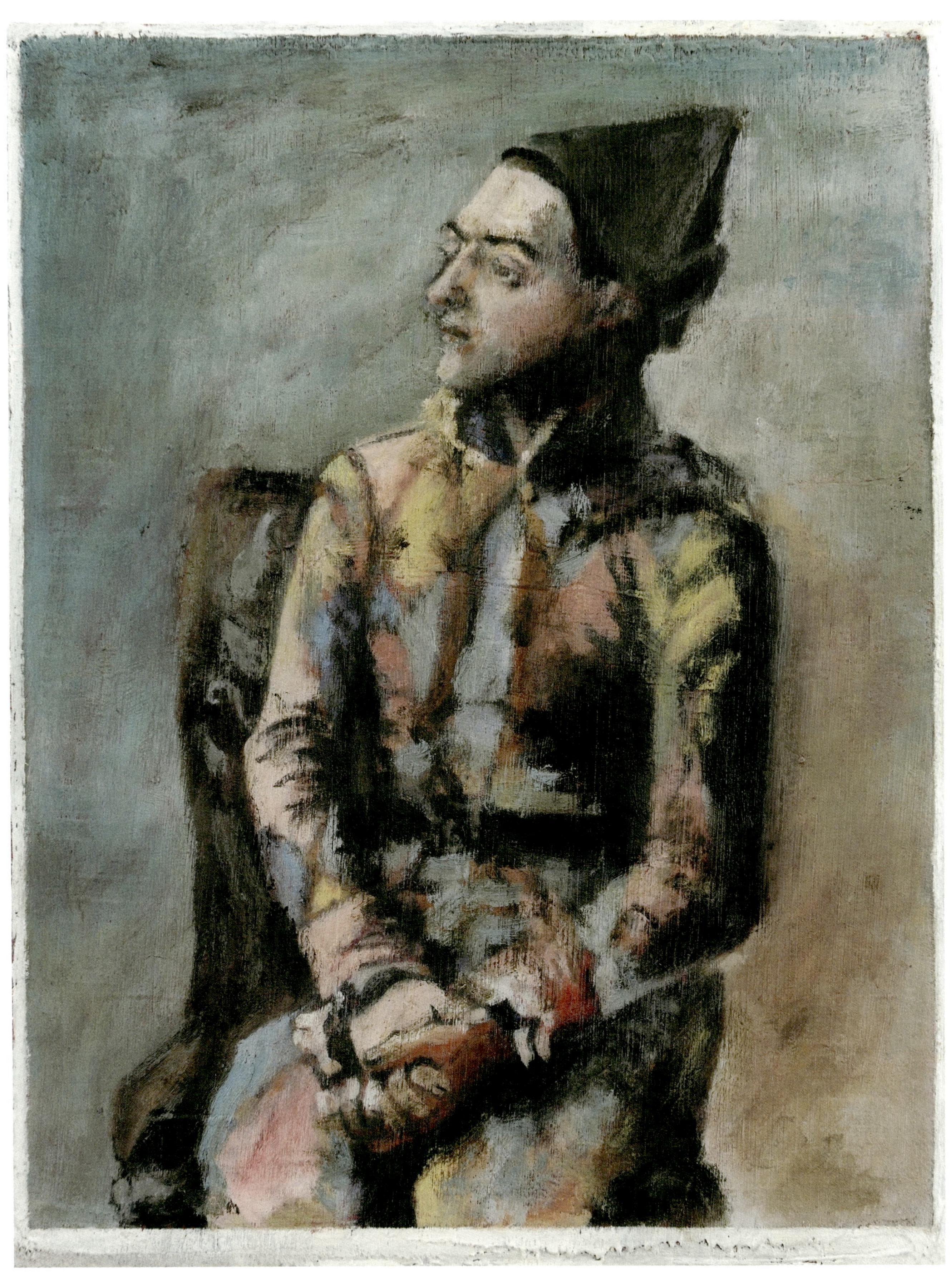

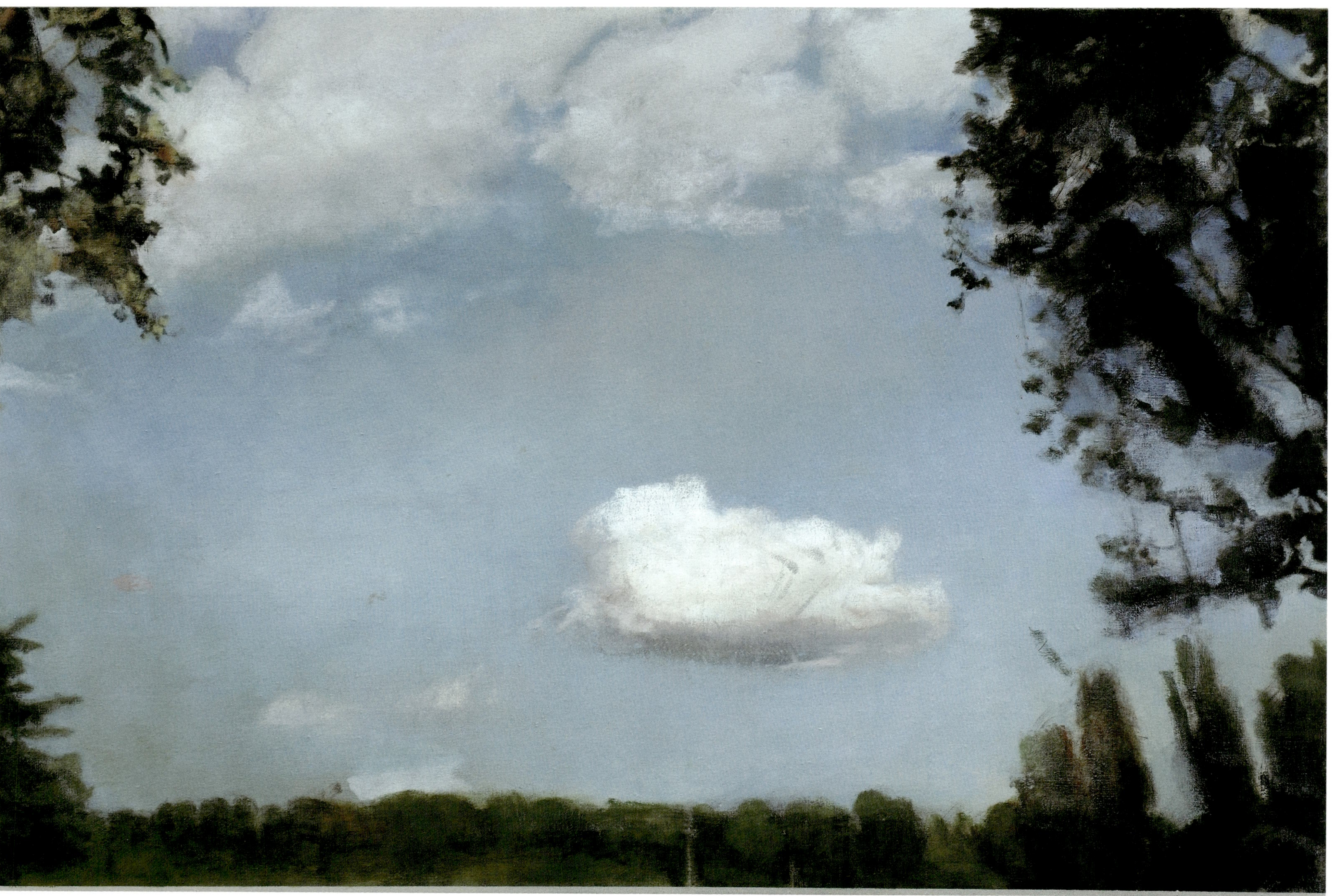

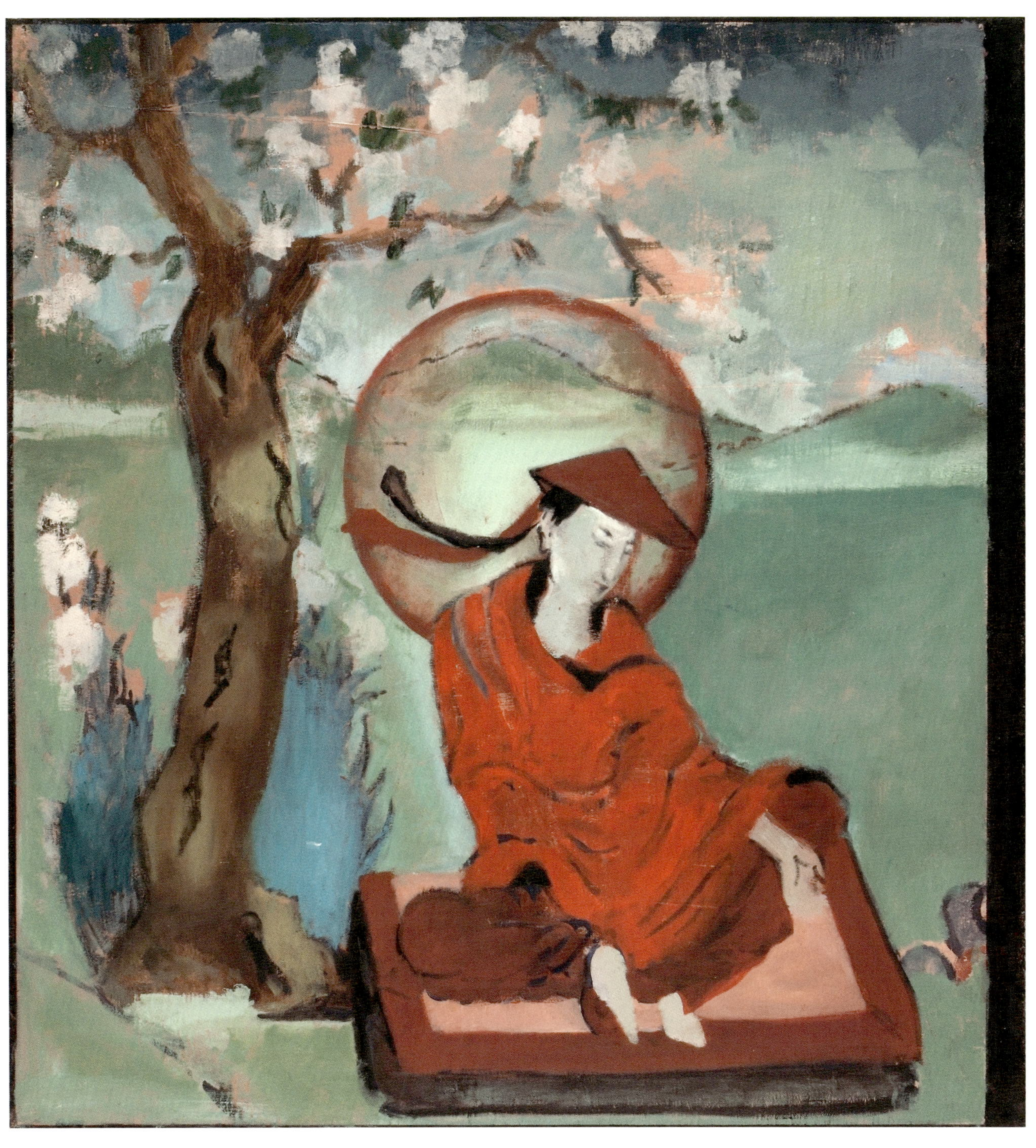

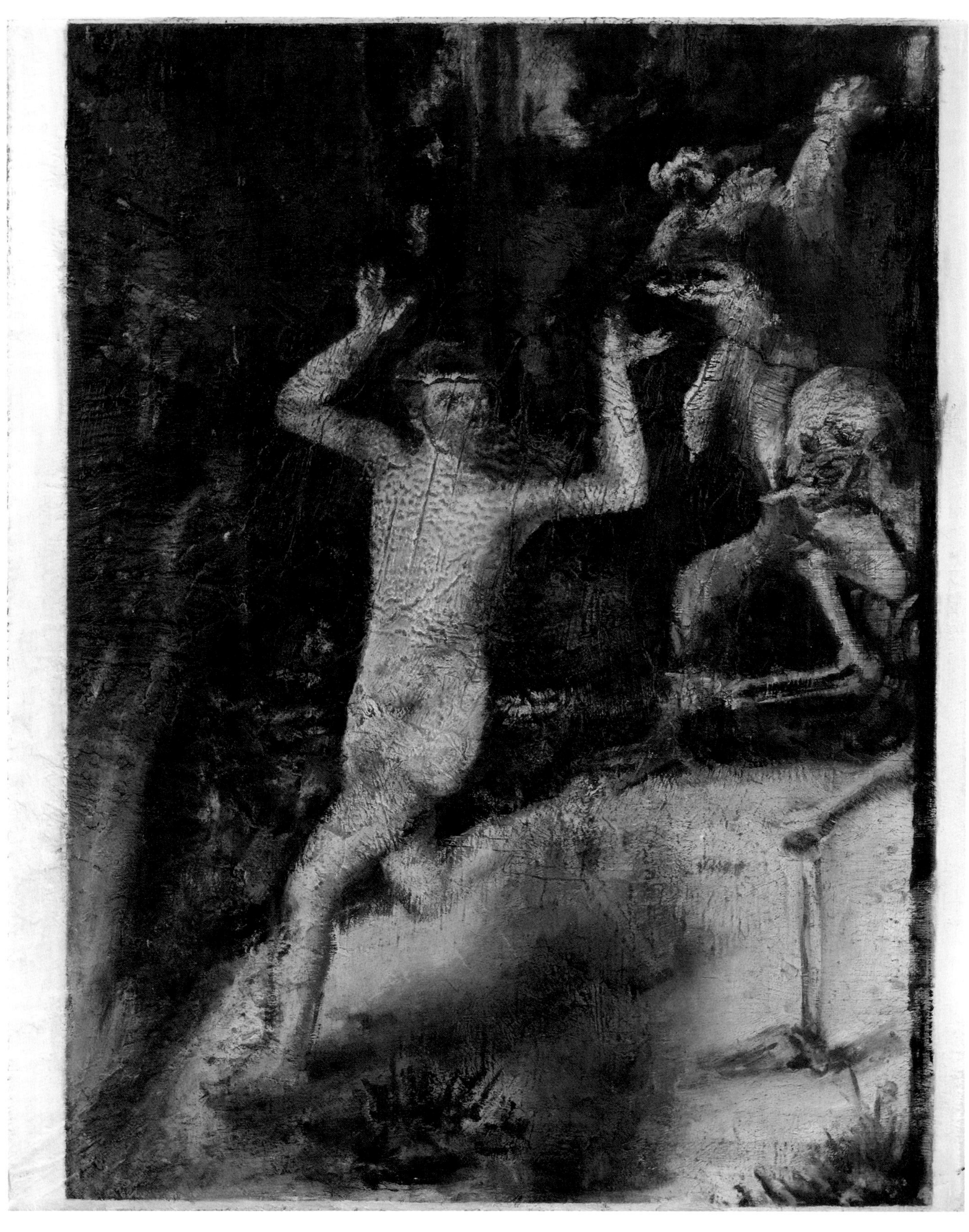

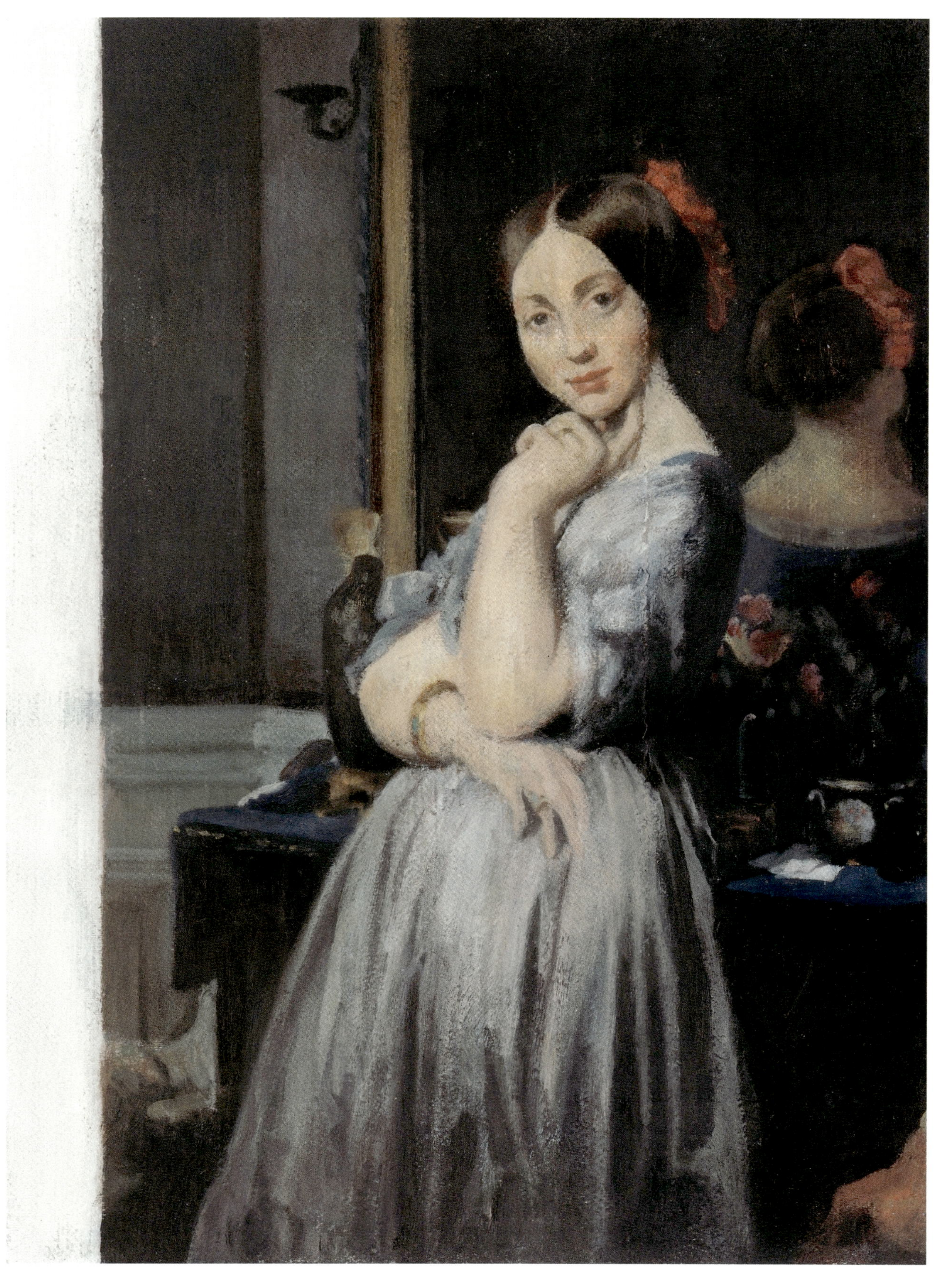

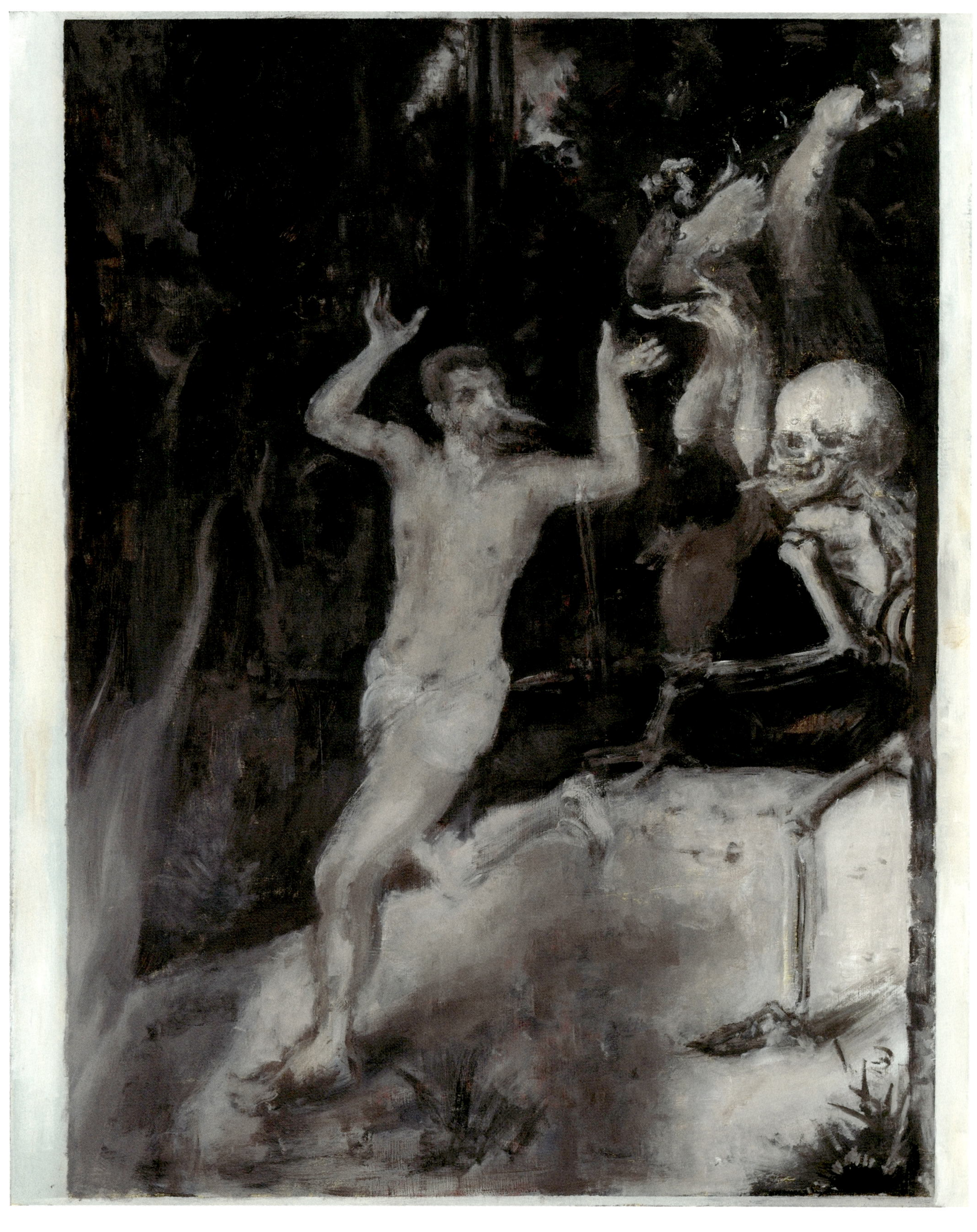

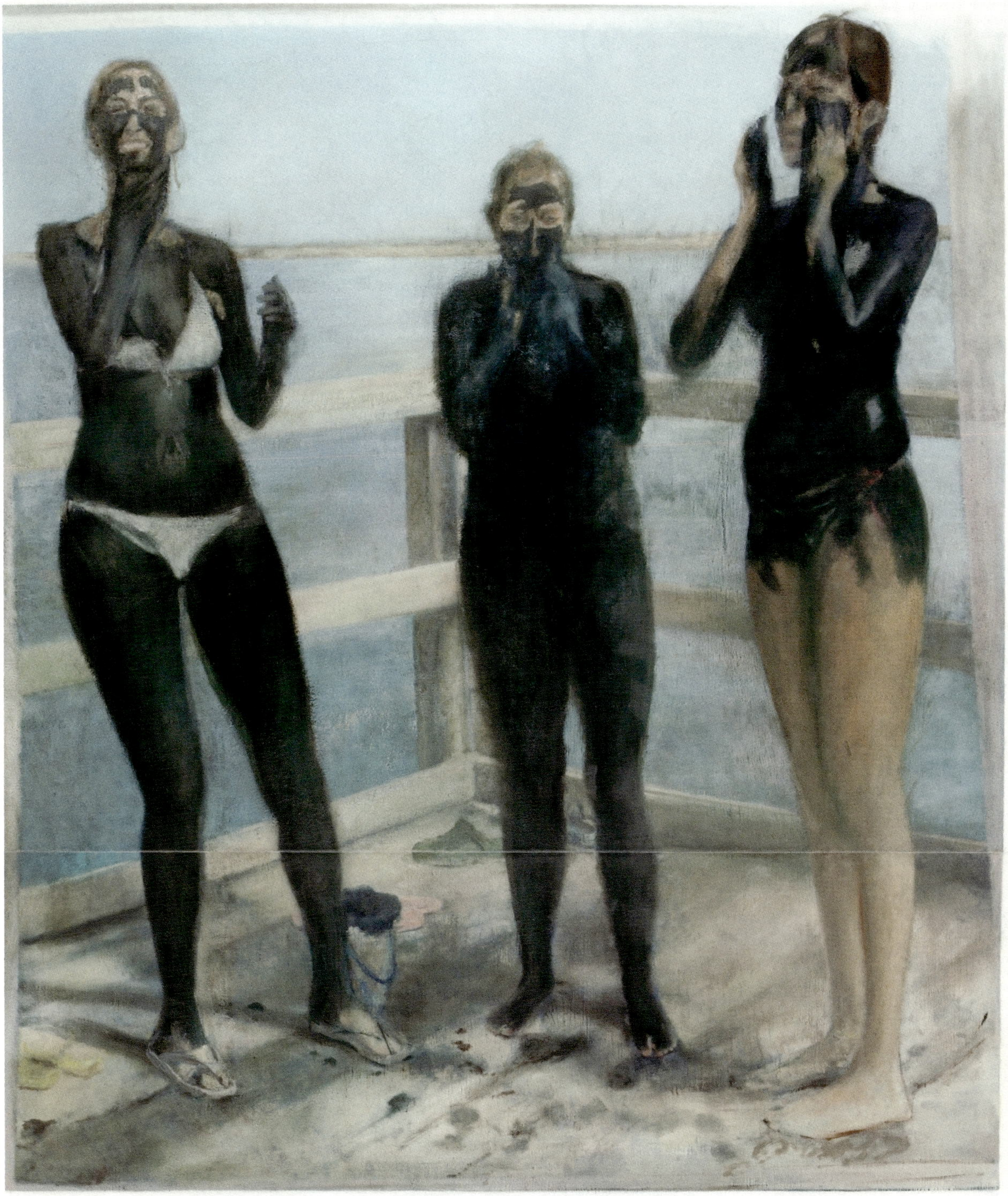

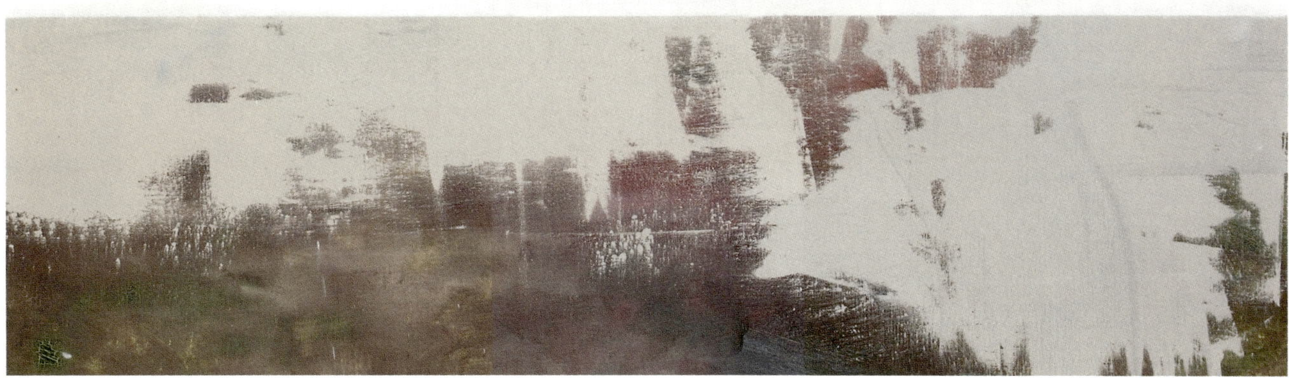

_14 = 2014
_13 = 2013
_12 = 2012
_11 = 2011
_10 = 2010

Alle Bilder Öl auf Leinen
All works oil on canvas

Courtesy ASPN Galerie,
Leipzig

28 _ 14
(BILDNIS EINER JUNGEN FRAU
IM PROFIL / PORTRAIT OF A YOUNG
LADY IN PROFILE)
270 × 190 cm
NACH/AFTER: Piero del Pollaiuolo, Bildnis
einer jungen Frau im Profil,
52,5 x 36,5 cm, Öl und Tempera auf
Pappelholz, um 1465 / Portrait of a Young
Lady in Profile, 52.5 x 36.5 cm, oil
and tempera on poplar wood, circa 1465,
Staatliche Gemäldegalerie, Berlin.
IN: wikipedia.org/wiki/Piero_del_Pollaiuolo.

27 _ 14
(CECI N'EST PAS UNE PIPE)
46 × 36 cm
NACH/AFTER: René Magritte, La trahison
des images, 59 x 65 cm, Öl auf Leinwand /
oil on canvas, 1929, County Museum,
Los Angeles.
IN: wikipedia.org/wiki/La_trahison_des_
images.

26 _ 14
(CECI N'EST PAS UNE PIPE)
110 × 90 cm
NACH/AFTER: René Magritte, La trahison
des images, 59 x 65 cm, Öl auf Leinwand /
oil on canvas, 1929, County Museum,
Los Angeles.
IN: wikipedia.org/wiki/La_trahison_des_
images.

25 _ 14
(CATHY IN GELB / CATHY IN YELLOW)
110 × 90 cm
NACH/AFTER: Wayne Lawrence, Cathy,
93,98 x 76,2 cm, Digital C-print, 2010.
IN: Fundstück / From a photograph,
Frankfurter Allgemeine Zeitung.

24 _ 14
(SOUVENIR DU MAROC / MEMENTO
OF MOROCCO)
41,5 × 60 cm
Sammlung / Collection Thiery, Leipzig
NACH/AFTER: Fundstück, Postkarte /
Found postcard, 12 x 16,9 cm.

23 _ 14
(BIENE AUF KORIANDER /
BEE ON CORIANDER)
60 × 41,5 cm
NACH/AFTER: Amada44, Original file
2,431 x 1,620 pixels, 15. Juni / June 15, 2010.
IN: commons.wikimedia.org/wiki/File:
Biene_auf_Koriander_003.jpg.

22 _ 14
(BIENE AUF KORIANDER /
BEE ON CORIANDER)
60 × 41,5 cm
NACH/AFTER: Amada44, Original file
2,431 x 1,620 pixels, 15. Juni / June 15, 2010.
IN: commons.wikimedia.org/wiki/File:
Biene_auf_Koriander_003.jpg.

21 _ 14
(DETAIL AUS DER VERSUCHUNG
DES HEILIGEN ANTONIUS /
DETAIL FROM THE TEMPTATION OF
SAINT ANTHONY)
27 × 19 cm
SØR Rusche Sammlung / Collection,
Oelde/Berlin
NACH/AFTER: Hieronymus Bosch,
Die Versuchung des hl. Antonius, Triptychon,
131 x 119/238 cm, Öl auf Holz, um 1501 /

The Temptation of Saint Anthony, triptych,
131 x 119/238 cm, oil on wood, circa 1501,
Museu Nacional de Arte Antiga, Lissabon /
Lisbon, Portugal.
IN: Jos Koldeweij, Paul Vandenbroeck,
Bernard Vermet, Hieronymus Bosch,
Stuttgart 2001, S. / p. 83.

20 _ 14
(QUAPPI IN BLAU / QUAPPI IN BLUE)
190 × 135 cm
Privatsammlung / Private Collection
NACH/AFTER: Max Beckmann, Bildnis
Quappi in blau, 60,8 x 35,2 cm, Öl
auf Leinwand / Portrait of Quappi in Blue,
60.8 x 35.2 cm, oil on canvas, 1926,
Bayrische Staatsgemäldesammlungen
München / Munich.
IN: Fundstück / From a photograph,
Frankfurter Allgemeine Zeitung.

18 _ 14
(MELANCHOLIA)
260 × 200 cm
NACH/AFTER: Giorgio de Chirico,
Melancholia, 79 x 63 cm, Öl auf Leinwand /
oil on canvas, 1912, Estorick Collection,
London, Großbritannien / Great Britain.
IN: tendreams.org/dechirico.htm.

16 _ 14
(CATHY IN GELB / CATHY IN YELLOW)
270 × 190 cm
Privatsammlung / Private Collection
NACH/AFTER: Wayne Lawrence, Cathy,
93,98 x 76,2 cm, Digital C-print, 2010.
IN: Fundstück / From a photograph,
Frankfurter Allgemeine Zeitung.

15 _ 14
(SIBYLLE VON KLEVE ALS BRAUT /
SIBYLLE OF CLEVE AS A BRIDE)
260 × 200 cm
NACH/AFTER: Lucas Cranach der Ältere,
Prinzessin Sibylle von Kleve als Braut,
55 x 37 cm, Öl auf Holz, nach 1526 / Lucas
Cranach the Elder, Portrait of Princess
Sibylle of Cleve, 55 x 37 cm, oil on wood,
after 1526, Schlossmuseum, Weimar.
IN: Eberhard Ruhmer, Cranach, London
1963, Tafel / plate 19.

14 _ 14
(URSPRUNG DER WELT / THE ORIGIN
OF THE WORLD)
181 × 147 cm
Privatsammlung / Private Collection
NACH/AFTER: Gustave Courbet, L'Origine
du monde
55 x 46 cm, Öl auf Leinwand / oil on
canvas, 1866, Paris, Musée d'Orsay, Paris,
Frankreich / France.
IN: commons.wikimedia.org/wiki/File:L%
27Origine_du_monde.jpeg#mediaviewer/
File:L%27Origine_ du_monde.jpg.

12 _ 14
(LA FEMME A LA VAGUE)
181 × 147 cm
Privatsammlung / Private Collection
NACH/AFTER: Gustave Courbet, La
femme a la vague, 65 x 54 cm, Öl auf
Leinwand / oil on canvas, 1868, Metro-
politan Museum of Art, New York, USA.
IN: commons.wikimedia.org/wiki/
File:Gustave_Courbet_009.jpg#mediavie-
wer/File:Gustave_Courbet_009.jpg.

11 _ 14
(UNTITLED FILMSTILL 15/1978)
181 × 147 cm
Privatsammlung / Private Collection
NACH/AFTER: Cindy Sherman, untitled
filmstill #15, 1978.
IN: The Complete Untitled Film Stills Cindy
Sherman, New York 2003, S. / p. 31.

10 _ 14
(UNTITLED FILMSTILL 13/1978)
120 × 135,5 cm
Privatsammlung / Private Collection
NACH/AFTER: Cindy Sherman, untitled
filmstill #13, 1978.
IN: The Complete Untitled Film Stills Cindy
Sherman, New York 2003, S. / p. 151.

9 _ 14
(DER TRAUM DES JOACHIM /
JOACHIM'S DREAM)
120 × 135,5 cm
NACH/AFTER: Giotto, Der Traum des
Joachim, 200 × 185 cm, Fresko, 1302–1305 /
Joachim's Dream, 200 x 185 cm, fresco,
1302–1305, Cappella degli Scrovegni,
Padua.
IN: Anne Mueller von der Haegen, Giotto,
Köln / Cologne 1998, S. / p. 56.

8 _ 14
(INCE HALL MADONNA)
46 × 36 cm
Sammlung / Collection Christian
Thilemann, Leipzig
NACH/AFTER: Van Eyck-Werkstatt
(Meister der Ince Hall Madonna), Madonna
mit Kind (Ince Hall Madonna), 26,3 x 19,4
cm, Öl auf Holz, nach 1433 / Workshop of
Van Eyck (Master of the Ince Hall Madonna),
Mary and Child (Ince Hall Madonna),
26.3 x 19.4 cm, oil on wood, after 1433,
National Gallery of Victoria, Melbourne,
Australien / Australia.
IN: Till-Holger Borchert, Van Eyck, Köln /
Cologne 2008, S. / p. 73.

7 _ 14
(THE SLITS)
60 × 50 cm
Sammlung / Collection Jocelyne & Fabrice
Petignat, Genf / Geneva
NACH/AFTER: The Slits, Cut, Schallplatten-
cover / record cover, Island Records, 1979.

5 _ 14
(MARIA MIT DEM KINDE / MARY
AND CHILD)
27 × 19 cm
Privatsammlung / Private Collection,
Paradiso
NACH/AFTER: Lucas Cranach d. Ä.,
Maria mit dem Kinde, Öl auf Holz, um
1518 / Lucas Cranach the Elder, Mary and
Child, oil on wood, circa 1518, Staatliche
Kunsthalle Karlsruhe.
IN: Postkarte / Postcard Julius Bard,
Verlag für Literatur und Kunst GmbH,
Berlin, Nr. / no. B 4.

4 _ 14
(MELANCHOLIA)
136 × 118 cm
NACH/AFTER: Giorgio de Chirico,
Melancolia, 79 x 63 cm, Öl auf Leinwand /
oil on canvas, 1912, Estorick Collection,
London, Großbritannien / Great Britain.
IN: Kestnergesellschaft (Hg. / ed.), Giorgio
de Chirico, Hannover / Hanover 1970,
S. / p. 85.

3 _ 14
(SEATED SCRIBE)
46 × 36 cm
Sammlung / Collection Thiery, Leipzig
NACH/AFTER: Gentile Bellini, Seated
Scribe, Gouache und Tinte auf Papier,
18,2 x 14 cm, um 1480 / gouache and ink
on paper, 18.2 x 14 cm, circa 1480,
Isabella Stewart Gardner Museum, Boston,
Massachusetts, USA.
IN: Hans Belting, Florenz und Bagdad,
München / Munich 2008, S./ p. 60.

2 _ 14
(GEWANDSTUDIE / STUDY OF
DRAPERY)
185 × 122 cm
Sammlung / Collection Christian Thielemann,
Leipzig
NACH/AFTER: Leonardo Da Vinci,
Gewandstudie für eine sitzende Figur,
26,5 x 25,3 cm, Tempera auf Leinwand, um
1475 / Study of Drapery for a Seated
Woman, 26.5 x 25.3 cm, tempera on
canvas, circa 1475, Musée du Louvre, Paris,
Frankreich / France.
IN: Frank Zöllner, Leonardo Da Vinci,
Jubiläumsausgabe, Köln / Cologne 2007,
S. / p. 360.

1 _ 14
(ANATOMIE DES DR. TULP /
THE ANATOMY LESSON OF DR. TULP)
230 × 180 cm
Privatsammlung / Private Collection
NACH/AFTER: Rembrandt van Rijn, Die
Anatomie des Dr. Tulp, 169,5 x 216,5 cm, Öl
auf Leinwand, 1632, Mauritshuis,
Den Haag, Niederlande. / The Anatomy
Lesson of Dr. Tulp, 169.5 x 216.5 cm, oil on
canvas, 1632, Mauritshuis, The Hague,
Netherlands.
IN: wikipedia.org/wiki/Die_Anatomie_ des_
Dr._Tulp.

Jochen Plogsties / Anaïs Goupy _ 13
I AM IN LOVE 1
55 × 46 cm
SØR Rusche Sammlung / Collection, Oelde/
Berlin
NACH/AFTER: Adriaen Coorte, Still life
with wild strawberries, 16,5 x 14 cm,
Öl auf Papier auf Holz / oil on paper on
wood, 1705, Mauritshuis, Den Haag,
Niederlande / The Hague, Netherlands.
IN: commons.wikimedia.org/wiki/
File:Coorte_5.jpg.

20 _ 13
(GREECE)
110 × 90 cm
Sammlung / Collection Kaiser, Leipzig
NACH/AFTER: Fundstück, Fotografie /
Found photography, 10,8 x 8,3 cm.

Jochen Plogsties / Anaïs Goupy _ 13
I AM IN LOVE 4
192 x 122 cm
NACH/AFTER: Raffael, Die Heilige
Margarethe / Saint Margaret, Öl auf Holz /
oil on wood, 1518, Louvre, Paris, Frankreich /
France.
IN: kunstkopie.de/a/raffael/hl-margarethe-1.
html.

13 _ 13
(ABBEY ROAD)
120 × 120 cm
Privatsammlung / Private Collection, Hanno-
ver / Hanover
NACH/AFTER: The Beatles, Abbey Road,
Schallplattencover / record cover, EMI 1969.

11 _ 13
(FENSTERBANK / WINDOW SILL)
27 × 19 cm
Privatsammlung / Private Collection, Eitorf
NACH/AFTER: Arne Linde, Einladungs-
karte Ausstellung / invitation to the exhibition „Portrait",
10,5 x 14,85 cm, 2013.

10 _ 13
(MONA LISA)
37 × 24 cm
Sammlung / Collection
Stefan Petraschewsky, Leipzig
NACH/AFTER: Leonardo Da Vinci, Mona
Lisa, 77 x 53 cm, Öl auf Pappel- holz /
oil on poplar wood, 1503–1517, Louvre,
Paris, Frankreich / France.
IN: Frank Zöllner, Leonardo da Vinci, Köln /
Cologne 2007, S. / p. 155.

9 _ 13
(ARABER, SEIN PFERD SATTELND /
ARAB, SADDLING HIS HORSE)
270 × 190 cm
Privatsammlung / Private Collection, Leipzig
NACH/AFTER: Eugène Delacroix, Araber,
sein Pferd sattelnd, 56 x 47 cm, Öl auf
Leinwand, 1855, Eremitage, St. Petersburg.
/ Arab, Saddling his Horse, 56 x 47 cm, oil
on canvas, 1855, Hermitage, St. Petersburg.
IN: Fundstück, Buchseite / From an
unknown book.

8 _ 13
(EGYPT)
30 × 30 cm, Öl auf Flugseide / oil on flight
silk nylon
Privatsammlung / Private Collection, Leipzig
NACH/AFTER: Detail aus der Grabkam-
mer des Tempelastronomen Pepi Nakht,
Fresko, um 1425 v. Chr., Nationalmuseum,
Kairo, Ägypten. / Detail from the Burial
Chamber of the Temple Astronomer Pepi
Nakht, fresco, circa 1425 BCE, National
Museum, Cairo, Egypt.
IN: Fundstück, Buchseite / From an
unknown book.

7 _ 13
(HOTSTEPPER)
37 × 24 cm
SØR Rusche Sammlung / Collection,
Oelde/Berlin
NACH/AFTER: Ronny Szillo, Einladungs-
karte Ausstellung / invitation to the
exhibition „O.D.B.", 10,5 x 14,85 cm, 2013.

6 _ 13
(SCHWEINE / PIGS)
14,8 × 14,8 cm
Privatsammlung / Private Collection,
Hamburg
NACH/AFTER: Fundstück, Memory /
From a card from the game „Memory", ca. /
about 6 x 6 cm, Ravensburger.

6 _ 13
(PORTRÄT EINES 39-JÄHRIGEN HERRN
MIT TOTENSCHÄDEL / PORTRAIT OF A
39 YEAR-OLD MAN WITH A SKULL)
37 × 24 cm
SØR Rusche Sammlung / Collection,
Oelde/Berlin
NACH/AFTER: Umkreis des Hermann
Tom Ring, Porträt eines 39-jährigen Herrn
mit Totenschädel, 52,3 x 38,3 cm, Tempera
auf Holz, 1554, Sammlung SØR Rusche
Oelde/Berlin, Deutschland. / Follower of

Hermann Tom Ring, Portrait of a 39 Year-
Old Man With a Skull, 52.3 x 38.3 cm,
tempera on wood, 1554, SØR Rusche
Collection Oelde/Berlin, Germany.
IN: Hans-Joachim Raupp (Hg. / ed.),
Stillleben und Tierstücke, Münster 2004,
S. / p. 315.

5 _ 13
(YELLOW)
37 × 24 cm
SØR Rusche Sammlung / Collection,
Oelde/Berlin

4 _ 13
(STRUMPFHOSEN / STOCKINGS)
270 × 190 cm
Sammlung Collection Kaiser, Leipzig
NACH/AFTER: Edgar Leciejewski,
Strumpfhosen / Stockings, Budapest,
2011.

2 _ 13
(PORTRAIT OF MARIA DE' MEDICI)
27 × 19 cm
Sammlung / Collection Köster,
München / Munich
NACH/AFTER: Agnolo Bronzino, Portrait
of Maria de' Medici, 52,5 x 38 cm,
Tempera auf Holz, 1551, Uffizien, Florenz,
Italien. / Portrait of Maria de' Medici,
52.5 x 38 cm, tempera on wood, 1551,
Uffizi, Florence, Italy.
IN: wikipaintings.org/en/agnolo-bronzi-
no/portrait-of-maria-de-medici-1553.

Jochen Plogsties / Anaïs Goupy _ 13
I AM IN LOVE 3
181 x 136 cm
NACH/AFTER: Fundstück / Found
photograph, 12 x 12 cm.

10 _ 12
(STRUMPFHOSEN / STOCKINGS)
46 × 36 cm
SØR Rusche Sammlung / Collection,
Oelde/Berlin
NACH/AFTER: Edgar Leciejewski, Fotografie, aus der Arbeit „Optimistic about
nothing", 2012, Tintenstrahlausdruck
der Originaldatei / photograph from the
work Optimistic About Nothing, 2012,
inkjet print of the original file.

9 _ 12
(BILDNIS EINES MANNES MIT ROTEM
TURBAN / PORTRAIT OF A MAN
WITH RED TURBAN)
46 × 36 cm
Privatsammlung / Private Collection,
Stuttgart
NACH/AFTER: Jan Van Eyck, Bildnis ei-
nes Mannes mit rotem Turban (Selbstbild-
nis?), 33,3 x 25,8 cm mit Rahmen, Öl auf
Holz / Portrait of a Man in a Red Turban
(Self-Portrait?), 33.3 x 25.8 cm with the
frame, oil on wood, 1433, The National
Gallery, London.
IN: Till Holger Borchert, Van Eyck, Köln /
Cologne 2008, S. / p. 37.

8 _ 12
(DETAIL AUS STRASSE IN DELFT /
DETAIL FROM STREET IN DELFT)
46 × 36 cm
SØR Rusche Sammlung / Collection,
Oelde/Berlin
NACH/AFTER: Jan Vermeer, Straße in
Delft, 54,3 x 44 cm, Öl auf Leinwand /
Street in Delft, 54.3 x 44 cm, oil on can-
vas, 1657/1658, Rijksmuseum, Amsterdam.

IN: Norbert Schneider, Vermeer
1632–1675, Köln / Cologne 1996,
S. unbekannt / p. unknown.

7 _ 12
(BILDNIS EINES MANNES MIT
ROTEM TURBAN / PORTRAIT OF A
MAN WITH RED TURBAN)
255 × 180 cm
Sammlung / Collection Hildebrand, Leipzig
NACH/AFTER: Jan Van Eyck, Bildnis eines
Mannes mit rotem Turban (Selbstbildnis?),
33,3 x 25,8 cm mit Rahmen, Öl auf Holz /
Portrait of a Man in a Red Turban
(Self-Portrait?), 33.3 x 25.8 cm with the
frame, oil on wood, 1433, The National
Gallery, London.
IN: Till Holger Borchert, Van Eyck, Köln /
Cologne 2008, S. / p. 37.

5 _ 12
(ANZEIGER HOCHHAUS / ANZEIGER
HIGHRISE)
173 × 132 cm
Privatsammlung, Hannover / Hanover
NACH/AFTER: Carl Dransfeld, Anzeiger-
Hochhaus, 57,5 x 56,5 cm, Fotografie,
1928, Sammlung Madsack, Hannover. /
Anzeiger Highrise, 57.5 x 56.5 cm, photo-
graph, 1928, Madsack Collection, Hanover.
IN: Ab + An, Göttingen 2007.

4 _ 12
(DRUM)
230 × 180 cm
Privatsammlung / Private Collection,
Stuttgart
NACH/AFTER: Drum, Africa`s Leading
Magazine, July 1955, Cover.
IN: Frankfurter Allgemeine Zeitung vom 6.
Dezember 2011, / of 6 December, 2011,
Nr. / no. 284, S. / p. 33.

2 _ 12
(DAME MIT DEM PERLENHALSBAND /
WOMAN WITH A PEARL NECKLACE)
46 × 36 cm
SØR Rusche Sammlung / Collection,
Oelde/Berlin
NACH/AFTER: Jan Vermeer, Junge Dame
mit Perlenhalsband, 55 x 45 cm, Öl auf
Leinwand, um 1662/1665 /
Woman With a Pearl Necklace, 55 x 45
cm, oil on canvas, circa 1662/1665,
Gemäldegalerie / Picture Gallery, Berlin.
IN: Norbert Schneider, Vermeer 1632–
1675, Köln / Cologne 1996, S. / p. 57.

1 _ 12
(MANN MIT BLAUEM CHAPERON /
MAN WITH BLUE CHAPERON)
260 × 200 cm
Museum der bildenden Künste, Leipzig
NACH/AFTER: Jan van Eyck, Bildnis eines
Mannes mit blauem Chaperon, 22,5 x
16,6 cm, Öl auf Holz, um 1430 / Portrait
of a Man With a Blue Chaperon,
22.5 x 16.6 cm, oil on wood, circa 1430,
Muzeul National de Arta al Românei,
Bukarest.
IN: Till Holger Borchert, Van Eyck, Köln /
Cologne 2008, S. / p. 34.

26 _ 11
(RASENSTÜCK / TURF)
270 × 190 cm
Privatsammlung / Private Collection,
Stuttgart
NACH/AFTER: Albrecht Dürer, Das große
Rasenstück, 40,8 x 31,5 cm, Aquarell

und Deckfarben, mit Deckweiß gehöht, auf Karton aufgezogen / Great Piece of Turf, 40.8 x 31.5 cm, watercolour and opaque colours, highlighted with white opaque colour, mounted on card, 1503, Grafische Sammlung Albertina, Wien / Vienna.
IN: zeno.org/Kunstwerke/B/Dürer,+ Albrecht%3A+Das+große+ Rasenstück? hl=rasenstuck.

25 _ 11
(RASENSTÜCK / TURF)
230 × 180 cm
Sammlung / Collection Müller, Frankfurt am Main
NACH/AFTER: Albrecht Dürer, Das große Rasenstück, 40,8 x 31,5 cm, Aquarell und Deckfarben, mit Deckweiß gehöht, auf Karton aufgezogen / Great Piece of Turf, 40.8 x 31.5 cm, watercolour and opaque colours, high- lighted with white opaque colour, mounted on card, 1503, Grafische Sammlung Albertina, Wien / Vienna.
IN: Norbert Wolf, Dürer, Köln / Cologne 2006, S. / p. 41.

24 _ 11
(LIEBESZAUBER / LOVE MAGIC)
97 × 128 cm
SØR Rusche Sammlung / Collection, Oelde/Berlin
NACH/AFTER: Niederrheinischer Meister, Der Liebeszauber, 24 x 18 cm, Öl auf Holz / Lower Rhine Master, The Love Magic, 24 x 18 cm, oil on wood, 1470/80, Museum der bildenden Künste Leipzig.
IN: Fundstück, Postkarte / From a postcard, F2371, Museum der bildenden Künste Leipzig, Deutscher Kunstverlag, München / Munich, Berlin.

23 _ 11
(MEHMET II)
54,5 × 45,5 cm,
Privatsammlung / Private Collection, Leipzig
NACH/AFTER: Nachfolger von Gentile Bellini, Bildnis des Sultan Mehmet II, 21 x 16 cm, Öl auf Holz, um 1510 / Follower of Gentile Bellini, Portrait of Sultan Mehmed II, 21 x 16 cm, oil on wood, circa 1510, Museum of Islamic Art, Doha, Katar.
IN: baluch-rugs.com/History/People/ Sultan_Mehmed_II .htm.

19 _ 11
(KOPF EINES JUNGEN MIT LANGEM BART / PORTRAIT OF A BOY WITH A LONG BEARD)
90 × 55 cm,
Privatsammlung / Private Collection
NACH/AFTER: Albrecht Dürer, Kopf eines Jungen mit langem Bart, 52,5 x 27,8 cm, Tempera auf Leinwand / Portrait of a Boy With a Long Beard, 52.5 x 27.8 cm, tempera on canvas, 1527, Musée du Louvre, Cabinet des Dessins, Inventaire du Musée Napoléon, Paris.
IN: Norbert Wolf, Dürer, Köln / Cologne 2006, S. / p. 82.

17 _ 11
(MANN MIT ROTEM TURBAN / MAN WITH RED TURBAN)
53 × 44 cm
Sammlung / Collection Hildebrand, Leipzig
NACH/AFTER: Jan van Eyck, Mann mit rotem Turban, 26 x 19 cm, Öl auf

Eichenholz / Man With Red Turban, 26 x 19 cm, oil on oakwood, 1433, The National Gallery, London.
IN: uploads5.wikipaintings.org/images/ jan-van-eyck/a-man-in-a-turban-1433.jpg.

16 _ 11
(MÄDCHEN MIT DEM PERLENOHR-RING / GIRL WITH A PEARL EARRING) 54 × 45 cm,
Kunstsammlung der / Art Collection of Sparkasse Leipzig
NACH/AFTER: Jan Vermeer, Das Mäd-chen mit dem Perlenohrring, 44,5 x 39 cm, Öl auf Leinwand, um 1665 / Girl With a Pearl Earring, 44.5 x 39 cm, oil on canvas, circa 1665, Mauritshuis, Den Haag / The Hague.
IN: gkue.de/Barock1_Site/ html/portrait. htm.

15 _ 11
(CHARITAS / CHARITY)
90 × 68 cm
Kunstsammlung der / Art Collection of Sparkasse Leipzig
NACH/AFTER: Lucas Cranach d. Ä., Charitas, 50 x 34 cm, Öl auf Holz, nach 1537 / Lucas Cranach the Elder, Charity, 50 x 34 cm, oil on wood, after 1537, Koninklijk Museum voor Schone Kunsten Antwerpen, Nachlass van Ertborn / van Ertborn Estate.
IN: lib-art.com/artgallery/8668-charity-lucas-the-elder-cranach.html.

14 _ 11
(MEHMET II)
23 × 18 cm,
Sammlung / Collection Jocelyne & Fabri-ce Petignat, Genf / Geneva
NACH/AFTER: Gentile Bellini (zuge-schrieben), Der Sultan Mehmet II, 69,9 x 52,1 cm, Öl auf Leinwand (wahrs. von Holztafel übertragen) / (ascribed), The Sultan Mehmed II, 69.9 x 52.1 cm, oil on canvas (probably transferred from a wood panel), 1480, The National Gallery, London, Layard Bequest, 1916.
IN: tankonyvtar.hu/historia-1979-03/ historia-1979-03-torok.

14 _ 11
(CHARITAS / CHARITY)
90 × 68 cm
Kunstsammlung der / Art Collection of Sparkasse Leipzig
NACH/AFTER: Lucas Cranach d. J. (?), Charitas, nach 1537, 120,5 x 82,4 cm, Öl auf Rotbuchenholz / Lucas Cranach the Younger (?), Charity, after 1537, 120.5 x 82.4 cm, oil on common beech-wood, Kunstsammlungen Weimar.
IN: Kunstsammlungen zu Weimar (Hg. / ed.), Lucas Cranach. 1472–1553. Ein großer Maler in bewegter Zeit, Weimar 1972, S. / p. 19.

13 _ 11
(CHARITAS / CHARITY)
90 × 68 cm,
Kunstsammlung der / Art Collection of Sparkasse Leipzig
NACH/AFTER: Lucas Cranach d. Ä., Charitas, 52 x 36 cm, Öl auf Buchenholz / Lucas Cranach the Elder, Charity, 52 x 36 cm, oil on beechwood, 1534, Sturze-negger-Stiftung Schaffhausen, Museum zu Allerheiligen Schaffhausen.
IN: clarus-cranach.de/Bilder% 20index 01/Stadel%20Museum/gros/big28.jpg.

12 _ 11
(LANDSCHAFT / LANDSCAPE)
97 × 128 cm
Privatsammlung / Private Collection, Hannover / Hanover
NACH/AFTER: Jochen Plogsties, Foto-grafie / photograph, 8,8 x 13 cm, 2006.

9 _ 11
(KATHARINENALTAR AUSSCHNITT LINKER FLÜGEL / ST CATHERINE ALTARPIECE, LEFT WING)
110 × 90 cm
Privatsammlung / Private Collection, Leipzig
NACH/AFTER: Lucas Cranach d. Ä., Katharinenaltar (linker Seitenflügel, Innen-seite), 121,4 x 64 cm, Öl auf Lindenholz, 1506, Staatliche Kunstsammlungen Dresden, Gemäldegalerie Alte Meister, 1996 Wiedererworben aus der Sammlung Maximilian Speck von Sternburg. / Lucas Cranach the Elder, Altarpiece with the Martyrdom of St Catherine (left wing, interior), 121.4 x 64 cm, oil on limewood, 1506, Staatliche Kunstsammlungen Dresden, Picture Gallery Old Masters, 1996 re-purchased from the Maximilian Speck von Sternburg Collection.
IN: Kunstsammlungen zu Weimar (Hg. / ed.), Lucas Cranach. 1472–1553. Ein großer Maler in bewegter Zeit, Weimar 1972, Umschlagabbildung vorne / front cover.

8 _ 11
(BILDNIS EINES MANNES MIT BLAUEM CHAPERON / PORTRAIT OF A MAN WITH A BLUE CHAPERON)
54 × 45 cm
Privatsammlung / Private Collection, Paradiso
NACH/AFTER: Jan van Eyck, Bildnis eines Mannes mit blauem Chaperon, 22,5 x 16,6 cm, Öl auf Holz, um 1430 / Portrait of a Man With a Blue Chaperon, 22.5 x 16.6 cm, oil on wood, circa 1430, Muzeul National de Arta al României, Bukarest.
IN: Till-Holger Borchert, Van Eyck, Köln / Cologne 2008, S. / p. 34.

7 _ 11
(LES ILLUSIONS PERDUES)
33 × 33 cm
SØR Rusche Sammlung / Collection, Oelde/Berlin
NACH/AFTER: Charles Gleyre, Le Paradis terrestre, Durchmesser / diametre: 24 cm, Öl auf Holz / oil on wood, um / circa 1870, Musée cantonal des Beaux-Arts, Lausanne.
IN: Stürzinger, Ursula et al. (Hg. / ed.), Charles Gleyre ou les illusions perdues, Zürich / Zurich 1974, Umschlagabbildung vorne / front cover.

5 _ 11
(DER POLNISCHE REITER / THE POLISH RIDER)
180 × 220 cm
Sammlung/ Collection Roth, Frankfurt am Main
NACH/AFTER: Rembrandt Harmensz. van Rijn, Der polnische Reiter, 116,8 x 134,9 cm, Öl auf Leinwand, um 1655 / The Polish Rider, 116.8 x 134.9 cm, oil on canvas, circa 1655, The Frick Collection, New York City, Henry Clay Frick Bequest.

IN: malerei-meisterwerke.de/bilder_gross/ rembrandt-harmensz.-van-rijn-der-polnische-reiter-%28tamerlan-verfolgt-bajesid-vor-istanbul%29- 07999.html.

4 _ 11
(MANN MIT ROTEM TURBAN / MAN WITH RED TURBAN)
26 × 33 cm
Sammlung / Collection Müller, Frankfurt am Main
NACH/AFTER: Jan Van Eyck, Bildnis eines Mannes mit rotem Turban (Selbstbildnis?), 33,3 x 25,8 cm mit Rahmen, Öl auf Holz, 1433 / Portrait of a Man in a Red Turban (Self-Portrait?), 33.3 x 25.8 cm with the frame, oil on wood, 1433, The National Gallery, London.
IN: Till Holger Borchert, Van Eyck, Köln / Cologne 2008, S. / p. 37.

2 _ 11
(DETAIL AUS DER ALLEGORIE DER MALEREI / DETAIL FROM THE ALLEGORY OF PAINTING)
23 × 18 cm
Privatsammlung / Private Collection Leipzig
NACH/AFTER: Jan Vermeer, Die Malkunst, 120 x 100 cm, Öl auf Leinwand, um 1665/1666, Kunsthistorisches Museum, Wien, Gemäldegalerie. / Allegory of Painting, 120 x 100 cm, oil on canvas, circa 1665/1666, Kunsthistorisches Museum Vienna, Picture Gallery.
IN: Norbert Schneider, Vermeer 1632–1675, Köln / Cologne 1996, S. / p. 2.

1 _ 11
(HALBAKT EINER BADENDEN / HALF-FIGURE OF A BATHER)
23 × 18 cm
Kunstsammlung der Art / Collection of Sparkasse Leipzig
NACH/AFTER: Jean-Auguste-Dominique Ingres, Halbakt einer Badenden / Half-figure of a Bather, 51 x 42,5 cm, Öl auf Leinwand / oil on canvas, 1807, Musée Bonnat, Collection Defresne - Collection Bonnat, Bayonne.
IN: Hans Ebert, Jean-Auguste-Dominique Ingres, Berlin 1982, Umschlagvorderseite / front cover.

43 _ 10
(HARLEKIN / HARLEQUIN)
23 × 18 cm
Privatsammlung / Private Collection
NACH/AFTER: Pablo Picasso, Sitzender Harlekin / Seated Harlequin, 130,2 x 97,1 cm, Öl auf Leinwand / oil on canvas, 1923, Kunstmuseum Basel, Depositum der Ein-wohnergemeinde der Stadt Basel / deposit of the municipality of Basel 1967.
IN: Fundstück, Postkarte / From a postcard of the Kunstmuseum Basel, Zürich / Zurich 2004, Foto / Photo: Martin Bühler.

38 _ 10
(WOLKE / CLOUD)
75 × 110 cm
Privatsammlung / Private Collection, Stuttgart
NACH/AFTER: Jochen Plogsties, Foto-grafie / photograph, 8,8 x 13 cm, 2006.

37 _ 10
(KIRSCHBLÜTE / CHERRY BLOSSOM)
55 × 52 cm
NACH/AFTER: Fundstück / Found object, Teedose / tea canister.

36_10
(KIRSCHBLÜTE / CHERRY BLOSSOM)
55 x 52 cm
Privatsammlung / Private Collection,
Zürich / Zurich
NACH/AFTER: Fundstück / Found object,
Teedose / tea canister.

35_10
(DETAIL AUS DER ALLEGORIE
DER ERLÖSUNG / DETAIL FROM THE
ALLEGORY OF SALVATION)
60×50 cm
SØR Rusche Sammlung / Collection,
Oelde/Berlin
NACH/AFTER: Lucas Cranach d. Ä. und
Lucas Cranach d. J., Allegorie der Erlösung,
Mitteltafel des Epitaph-Altars für Johann
Friedrich den Großmütigen, 1555, Stadt-
kirche St. Peter und St. Paul, Weimar. /
Lucas Cranach the Elder and Lucas
Cranach the Younger, Allegory of Salvation,
central panel of the Epitaph Altarpiece for
John Frederick the Magnanimous, 1555,
St. Peter and St. Paul parish church, Weimar.
IN: Kunstsammlungen zu Weimar (Hg. /
ed.): Lucas Cranach. 1472–1553. Ein gro-
ßer Maler in bewegter Zeit, Weimar 1972,
S. / p. 8.

16_10
(COMTESSE D' HAUSSONVILLE)
23×18 cm
Privatsammlung / Private collection,
Leipzig
NACH/AFTER: Jean-Auguste-Dominique
Ingres 131,8 x 92,1 cm, Öl auf Leinwand /
oil on canvas, 1845, The Frick Collection,
New York City.
IN: Hans Ebert, Jean-Auguste-Dominique
Ingres, Berlin 1982, Abb. / fig. 25.

14_10
(DETAIL AUS DER ALLEGORIE DER
ERLÖSUNG / DETAIL FROM
THE ALLEGORY OF SALVATION)
60×50 cm
Sammlung / Collection FH, Hannover /
Hanover
NACH/AFTER: Lucas Cranach d. Ä. und
Lucas Cranach d. J., Allegorie der Erlösung,
Mitteltafel des Epitaph- Altars für Johann
Friedrich den Großmütigen, 1555,
Stadtkirche St. Peter und St. Paul, Weimar. /
Lucas Cranach the Elder and Lucas
Cranach the Younger, Allegory of Salvati-
on, central panel of the Epitaph Altarpiece
for John Frederick the Magnanimous,
1555, St. Peter and St. Paul parish church,
Weimar.
IN: Kunstsammlungen zu Weimar (Hg. /
ed.), Lucas Cranach. 1472–1553. Ein
großer Maler in bewegter Zeit, Weimar
1972, S. / p. 87.

11_10
(BADENDE / BATHERS)
360×230 cm, 2-tlg. / 2-part
Sammlung der / Collection of the Leipziger
Volkszeitung
NACH/AFTER: Fundstück / Found photo-
graph, Die Zeit vom 28./29. März / from
28/29 March, 2009, Reise, S. / p. 9, Foto /
Photo: dpa.

1974
geboren / born in Cochem an der Mosel

1997–2002
Studium an der Akademie für
Bildende Künste, Mainz / Studies at the
Academy of Fine Arts, Mainz
(bei / with Friedemann Hahn)

2003–2008
Studium an der Hochschule für Grafik und
Buchkunst, Leipzig / Studies at the Academy
of Visual Arts, Leipzig (bei / with Arno Rink
und / and Neo Rauch)

2006
Diplom bei / Diploma with Arno Rink und /
and Neo Rauch

2008
Meisterschülerabschluss der Hochschule für
Grafik und Buchkunst, Leipzig / Graduation
as a master student at the Academy of
Visual Arts, Leipzig (bei / with Neo Rauch)

2009
Künstlerresidenz / Artist residency ISCP,
New York City, USA (gefördert durch die /
sponsored by Kulturstiftung des Freistaates
Sachsen)

2011
Projektstipendium / Project grant Am
Brunnen vor dem Tore (gefördert durch die /
sponsored by Kulturstiftung des Freistaates
Sachsen)

Kunstpreis der / Art award of the
Leipziger Volkszeitung

2013
Projektstipendium / Project grant Lokal-
kolorit (gefördert durch die / sponsored by
Kulturstiftung des Freistaates Sachsen)

Diese Publikation erscheint anlässlich der Ausstellung / This catalogue is published on the occasion of the exhibition

Jochen Plogsties. Küsse am Nachmittag / Kisses in the Afternoon

kestnergesellschaft, Hannover
21. November 2014 – 15. Februar 2015
November 21, 2014 – February 15, 2015

© 2014 kestnergesellschaft Hannover, Hirmer Verlag GmbH, München / Munich und die Autoren / and the authors

Herausgeber / Editors
Lotte Dinse, Veit Görner

Autoren / Authors
Lotte Dinse, Veit Görner, Andreas Reckwitz

Übersetzung Deutsch-Englisch / Translation German-English
David Sánchez

Lektorat Deutsch / Copyediting German
Susanne Ibisch

Lektorat Englisch / Copyediting English
Michele Tilgner

Redaktion / Editing
Lotte Dinse, Arne Linde

Gestaltung / Design
Gilbert Schneider, Tobias Wenig

Fotografen / Photographers
Stefan Fischer, Leipzig
Uwe Walter, Berlin

Dank an die Leihgeber / Thanks to the lenders
Dr. Friedhelm Haak
Steffen Hildebrand
Dr. Harald und Prof. Dr. Christine Langenfeld
Jocelyne & Fabrice Petignat
Stefan Petraschewsky
Dr. Dr. Thomas Rusche
Prof. Dr. Joachim Thiery

Erschienen im / Published by
Hirmer Verlag, München

Projektmanagement Verlag / Project management
Kerstin Ludolph

Produktion / Production
Katja Durchholz

Lithographie / Lithography
Joscha Bruckert

Druck und Bindung / Printing and binding
Passavia Druckservice GmbH & Co. KG, Passau

Bibliografische Information der Deutschen Nationalbibliothek:
Die Deutsche Nationalbibliothek verzeichnet diese Publikation in der Deutschen Nationalbibliografie; detaillierte bibliografische Daten sind im Internet über http://www.dnb.de abrufbar.

Bibliographical data of the Deutsche Nationalbibliothek:
The Deutsche Nationalbibliothek lists this publication in the Deutschen Nationalbibliografie; detailed bibliographic information is available on the Internet at http://www.dnb.de.

Deutscher Umschlag:
ISBN 978-3-7774-2338-8
English Jacket:
ISBN 978-3-7774-2357-9

Printed in Germany

www.hirmerverlag.de
www.hirmerpublishers.com

kestnergesellschaft
Goseriede 11
30159 Hannover
Deutschland / Germany
Fon +49 511 70120 0
Fax +49 511 70120 20
kestner@kestnergesellschaft.de
www.kestnergesellschaft.de

Das Land Niedersachsen fördert die kestnergesellschaft / The kestnergesellschaft is supported by the Federal State of Lower Saxony

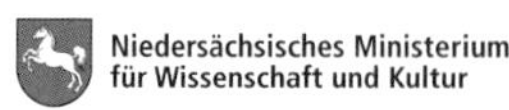

Die Ausstellung wird gefördert von der Kulturstiftung des Freistaates Sachsen und unterstützt vom Förderkreis der kestnergesellschaft / The exhibition is supported by the Kulturstiftung des Freistaates Sachsen and the Patrons` Circle of the kestnergesellschaft.

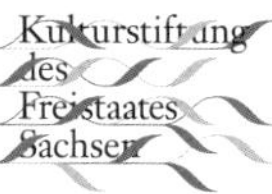

LEIPZIGER VOLKSZEITUNG

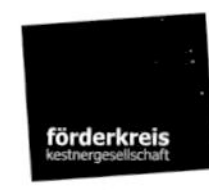

Steffen Hildebrand
Dr. Dr. Thomas Rusche, SØR Rusche Sammlung / Collection, Oelde/Berlin

Kulturpartner

NDR kultur

Dank an / Acknowledgements

HJÖRDIS BAACKE
JOSCHA BRUCKERT
LOTTE DINSE
MARKUS DRESSEN
THOMAS DÜFFERT
VEIT GÖRNER
ANAÏS GOUPY
FRIEDHELM HAAK
FRIEDEMANN HAHN
STEFFEN HILDEBRAND
KERRY INMAN
INGA KERBER
BIRGIT KULMER
EDGAR LECIEJEWSKI
ARNE LINDE
CAROLIN NITSCHE
SANDRO PARROTTA
URSULA PECHER
LOTHAR PLOGSTIES
NEO RAUCH
ANDREAS RECKWITZ
PATRICK REYNOLDS
ARNO RINK
CHRISTINE RINK
MARIE-THÉRÈSE RINK
THOMAS RUSCHE
HANS-WERNER SCHMIDT
GILBERT SCHNEIDER
ULRIKE THEUSNER
JOACHIM THIERY
TOBIAS WENIG
MARC ZEIMETZ
JANKA ZÖLLER

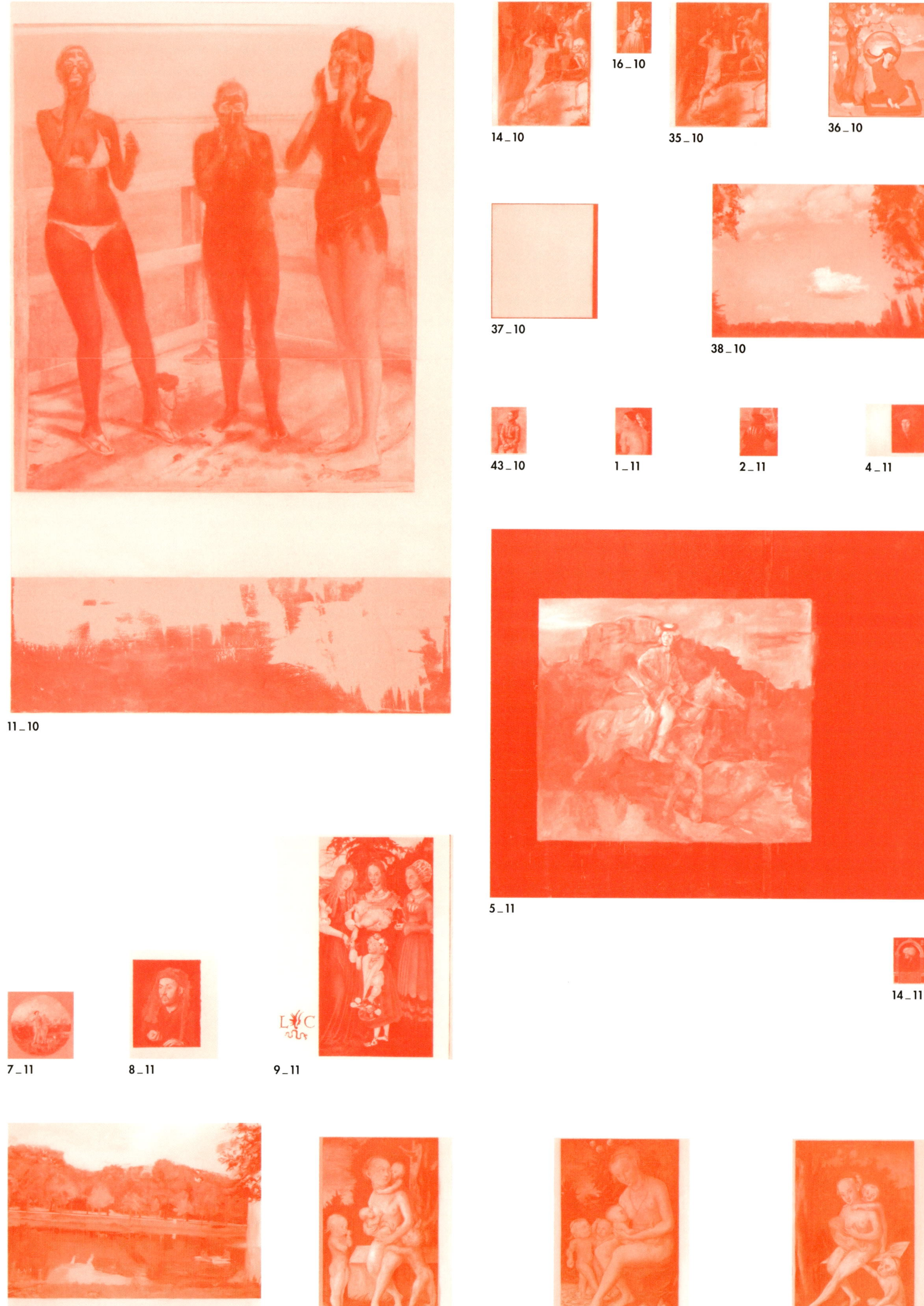

14 _ 10

16 _ 10

35 _ 10

36 _ 10

37 _ 10

38 _ 10

43 _ 10

1 _ 11

2 _ 11

4 _ 11

11 _ 10

5 _ 11

14 _ 11

7 _ 11

8 _ 11

9 _ 11

12 _ 11

13 _ 11

14 _ 11

15 _ 14

16_11

17_11

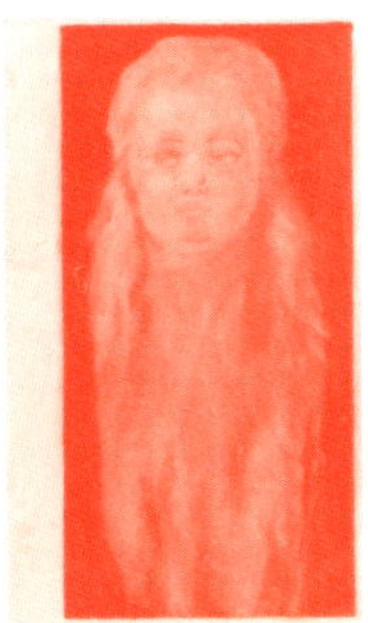

19_11

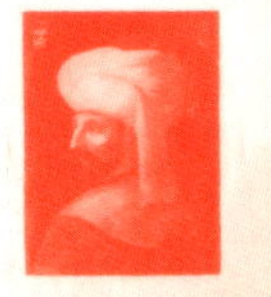

23_11

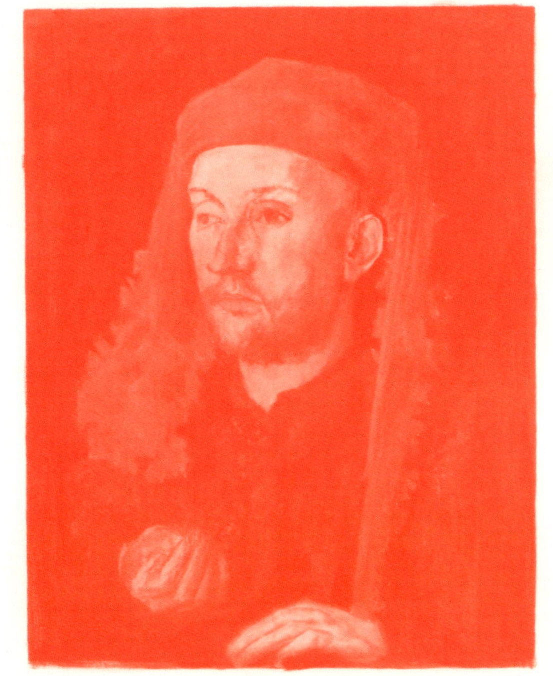

24_11

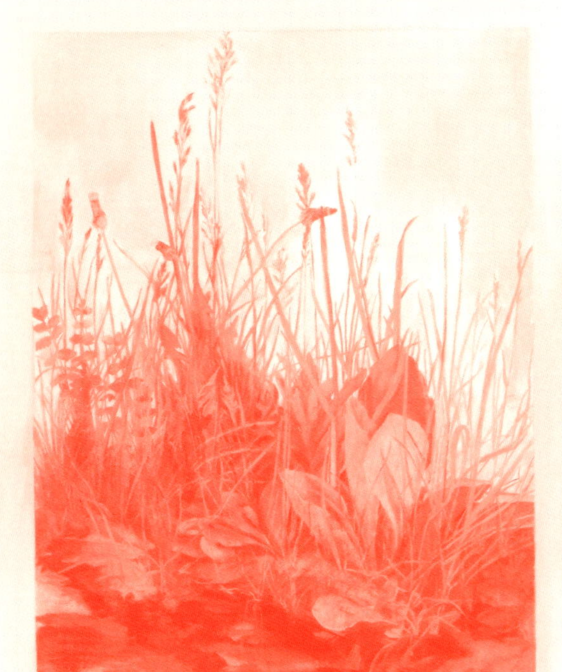

25_11

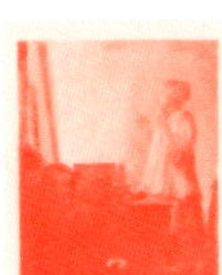

2_12

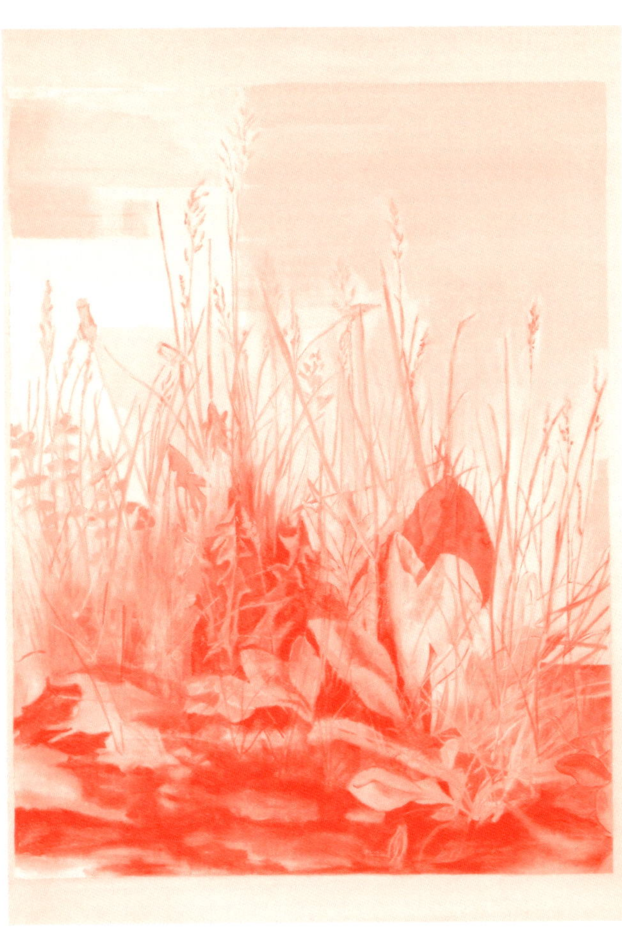

26_11

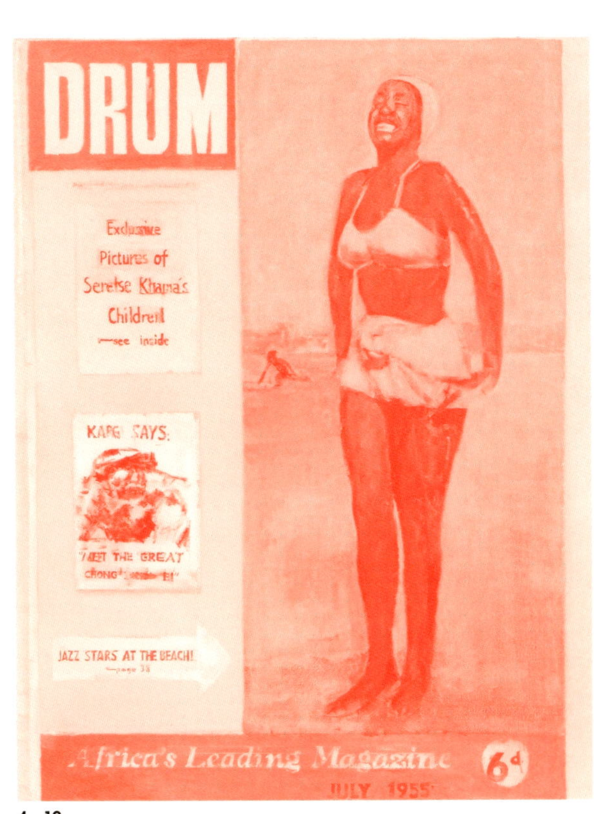

4_12

1_12

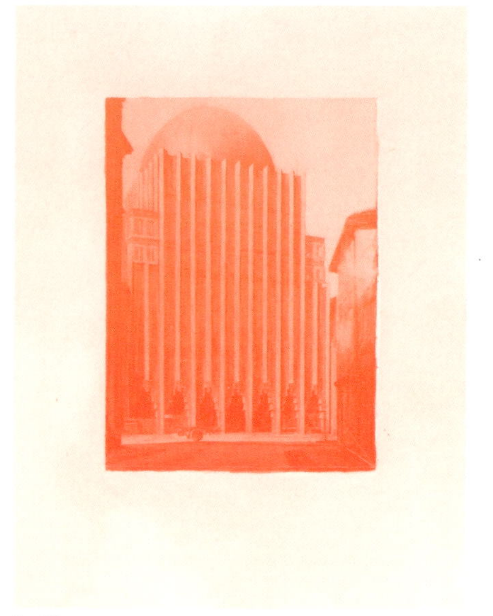

5_12

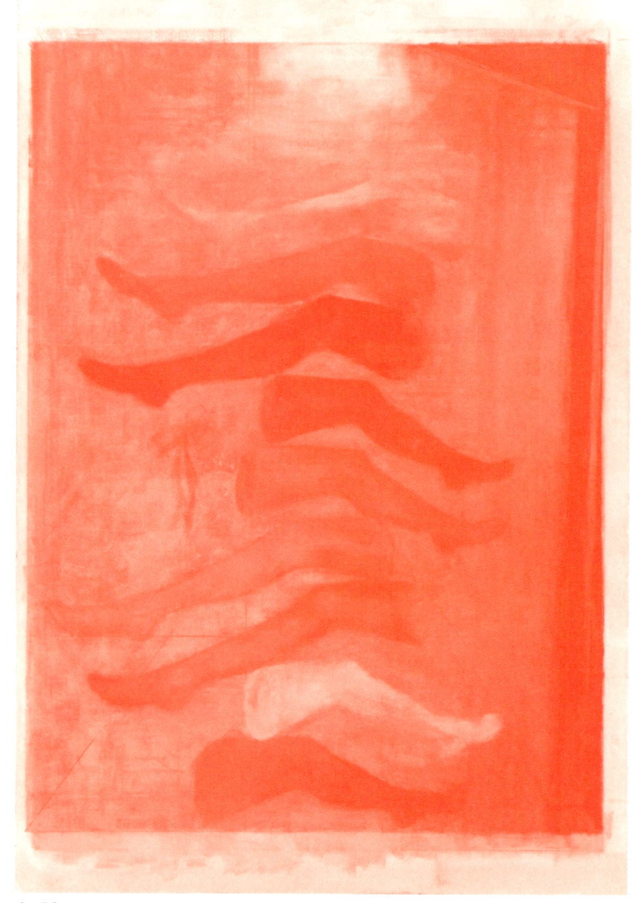

4_13

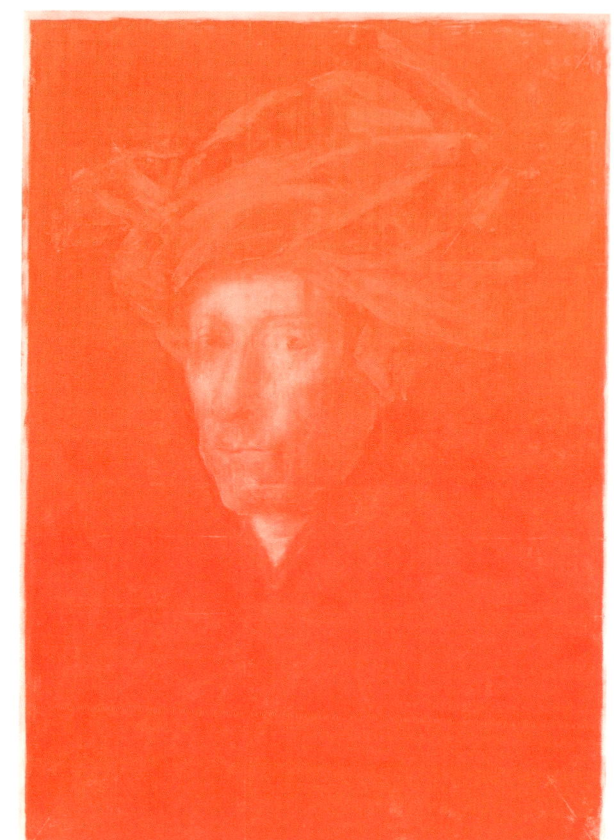
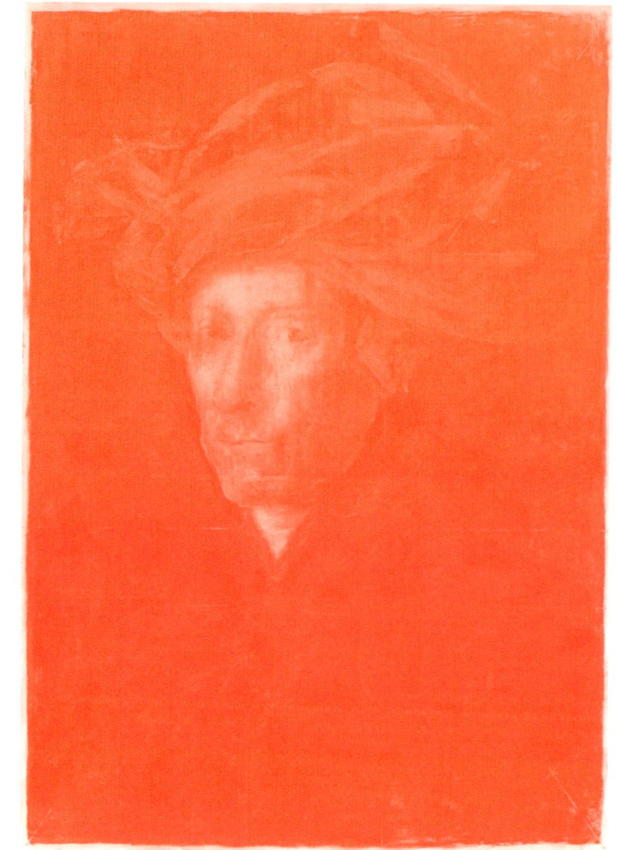

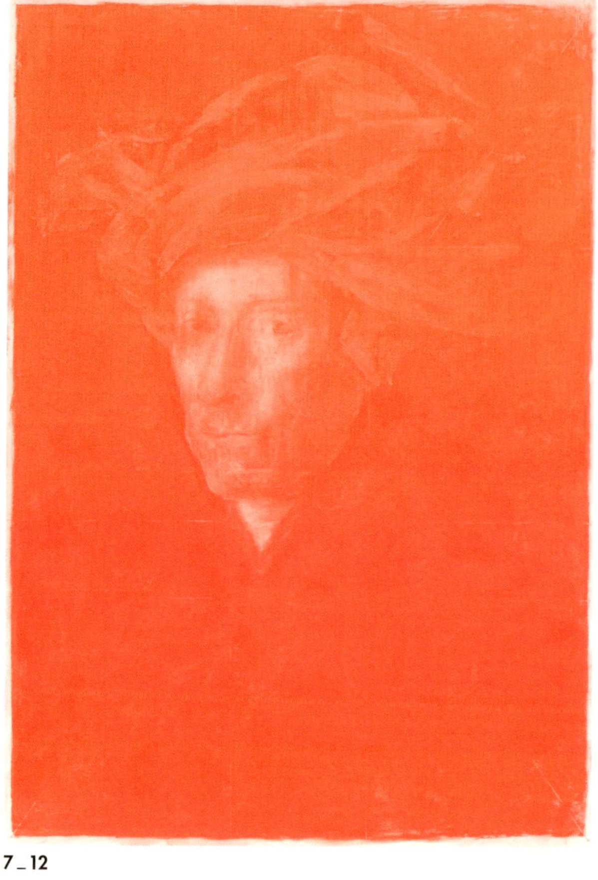

7_12

8_12

9_12

10_12

2_13

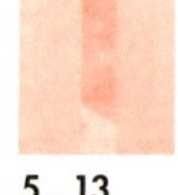

5_13

6_13

7_13

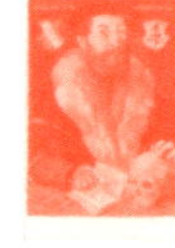

8_13

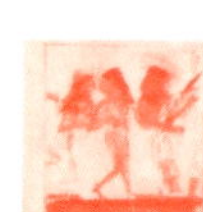

9_13

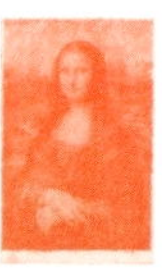

10_13

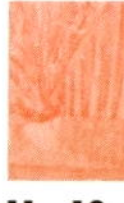

11_13

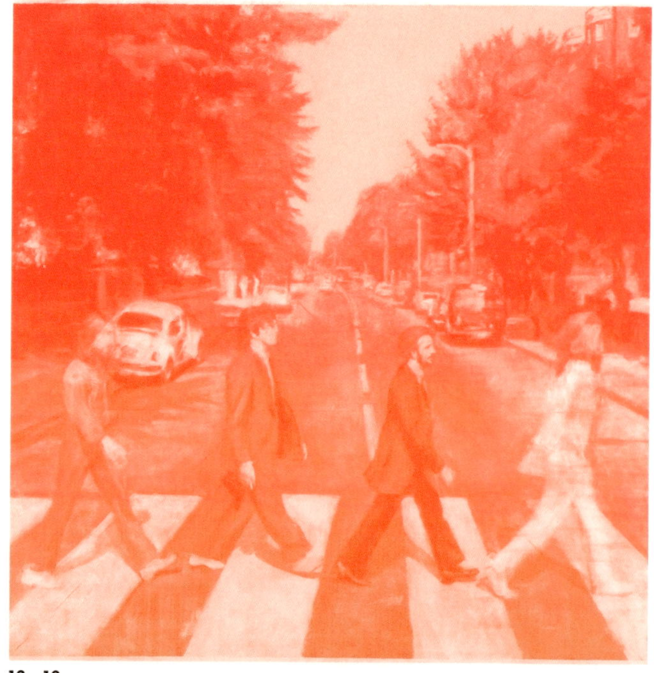
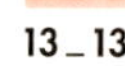

13_13

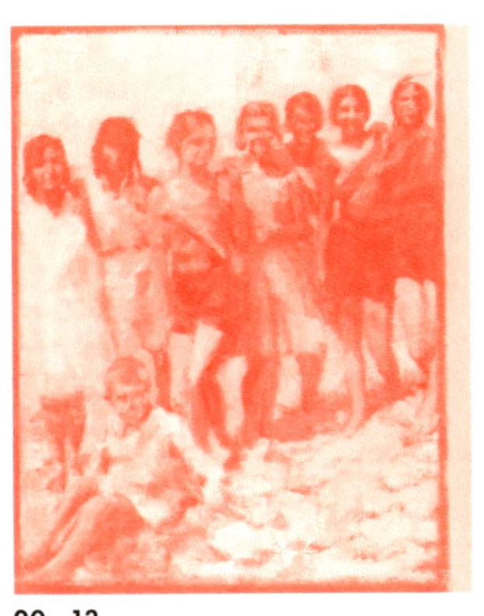

20_13

6_13

I AM IN LOVE 1

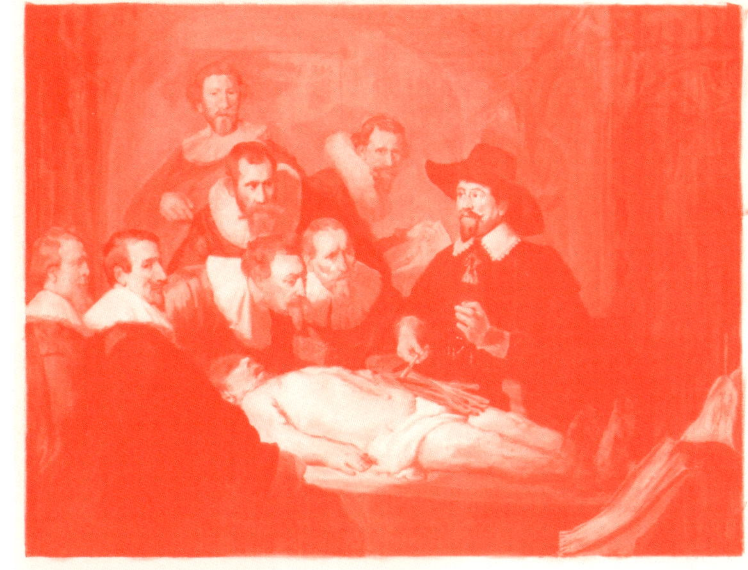

1_14

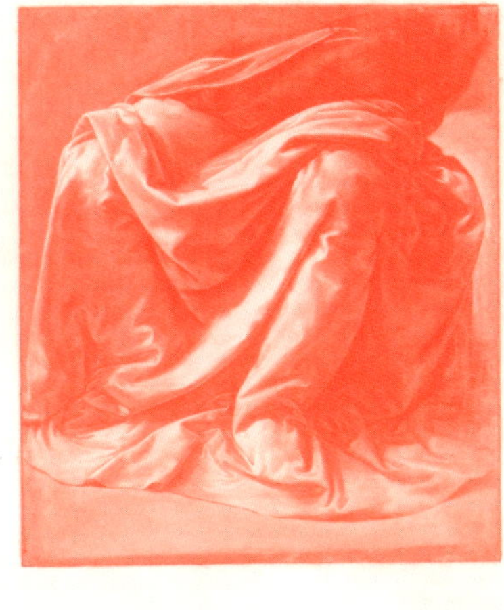

2_14

3_14

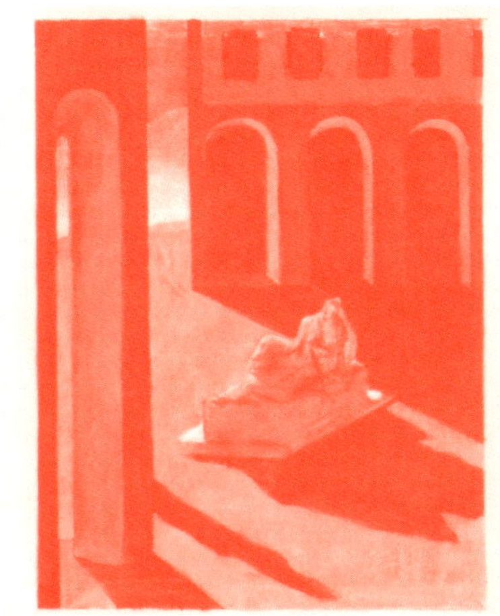

4_14

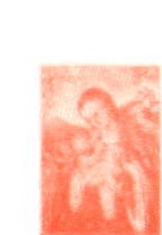

5_14

7_14

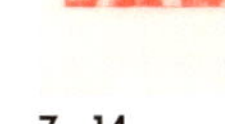

8_14

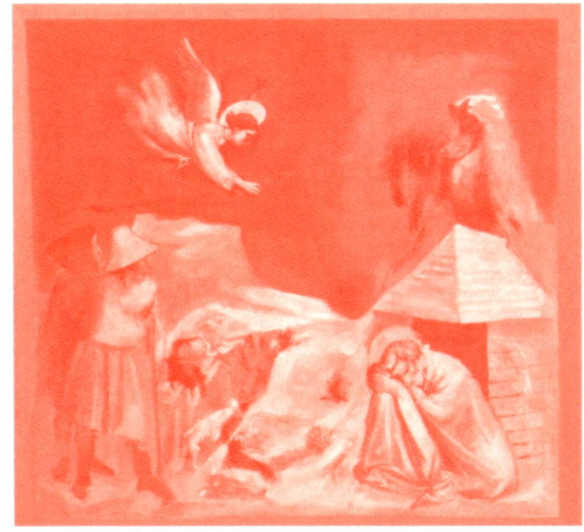

9_14

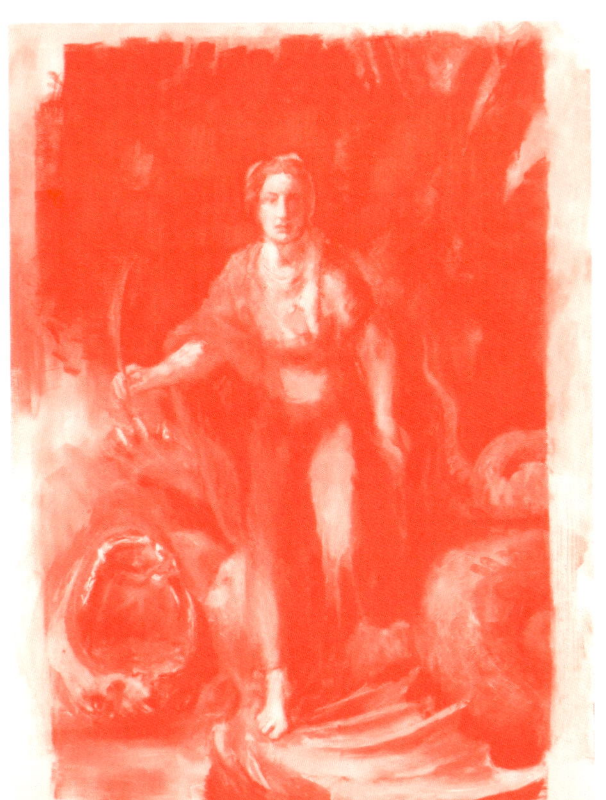

I AM IN LOVE 4

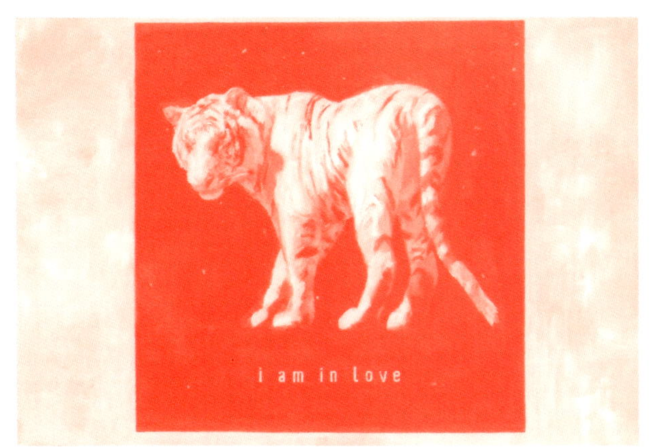

I AM IN LOVE 3

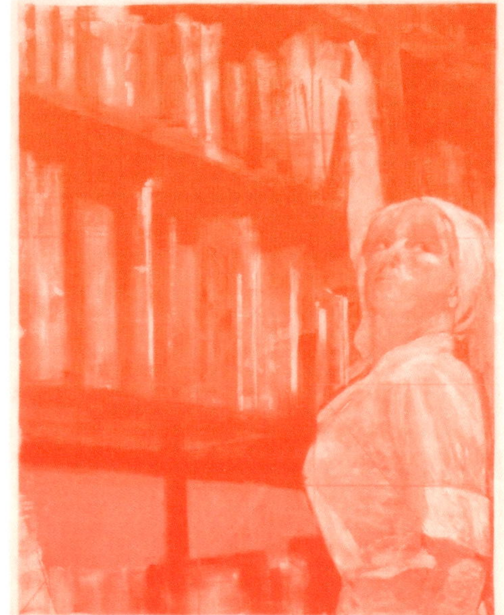

10 _ 14

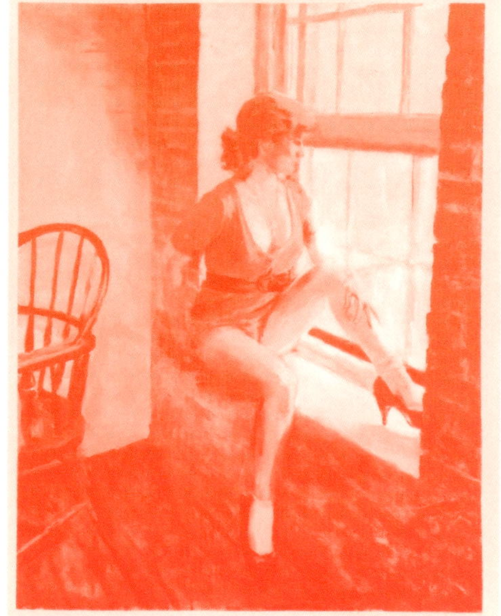

11 _ 14

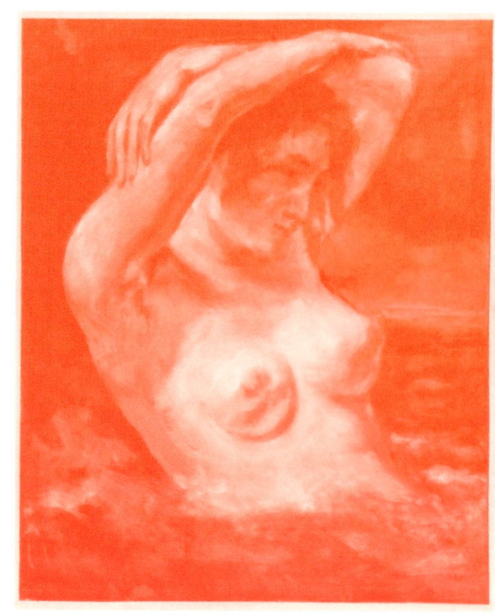

12 _ 14

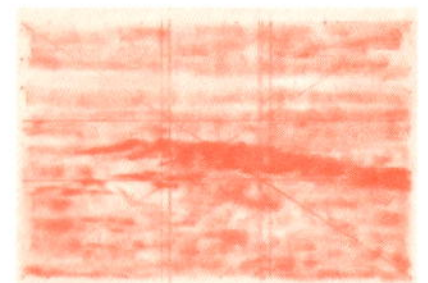

24 _ 14

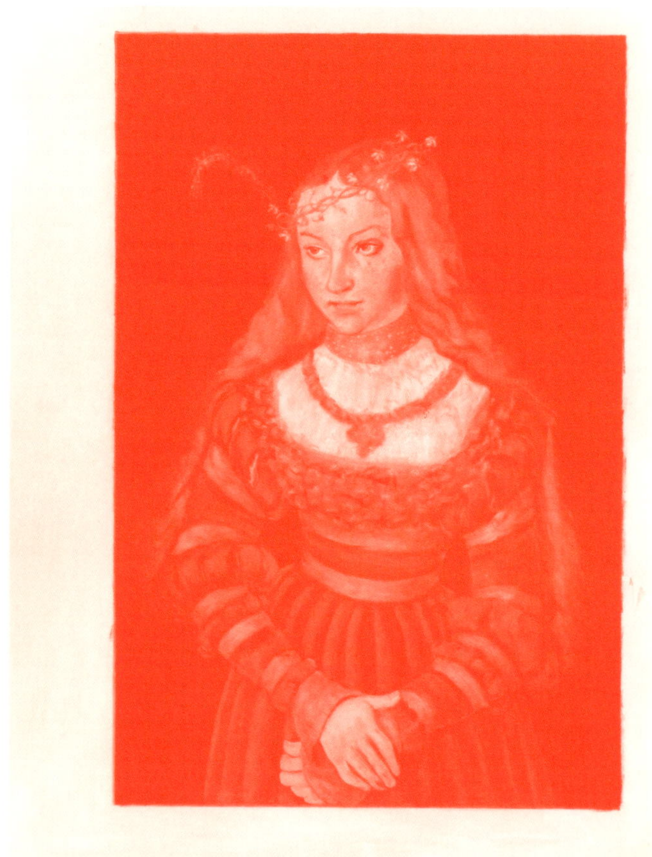

15 _ 14

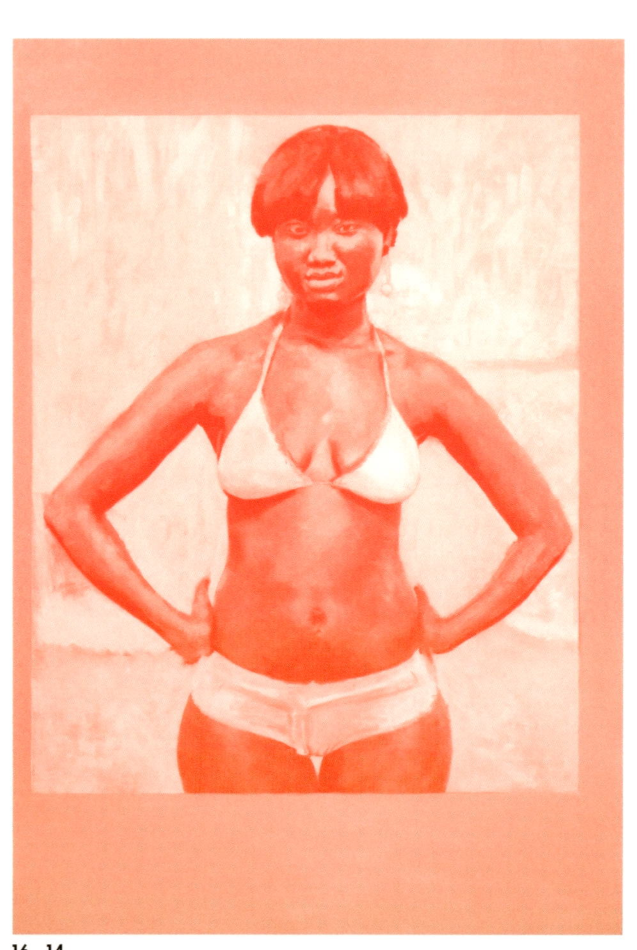

16 _ 14

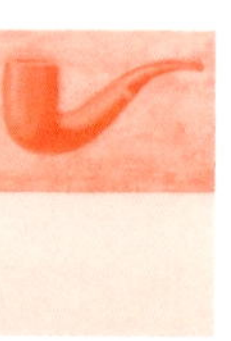

27 _ 14

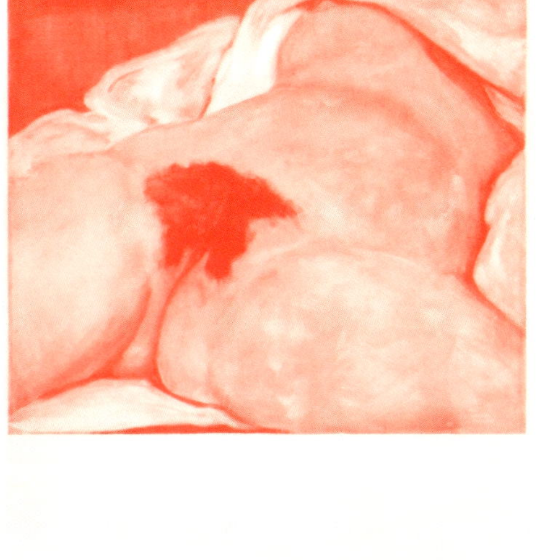

14 _ 14

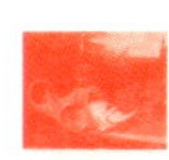

21 _ 14

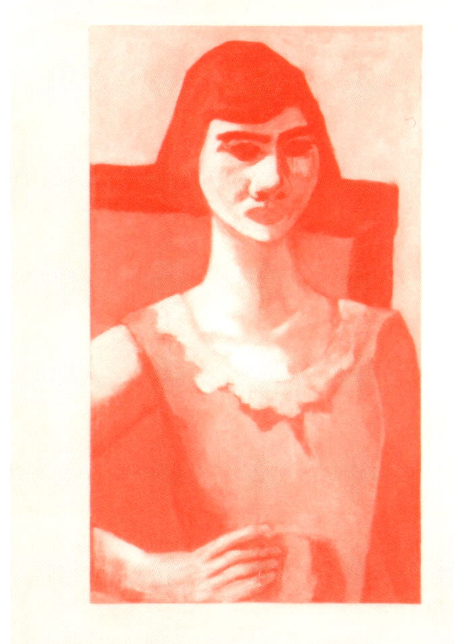

20 _ 14

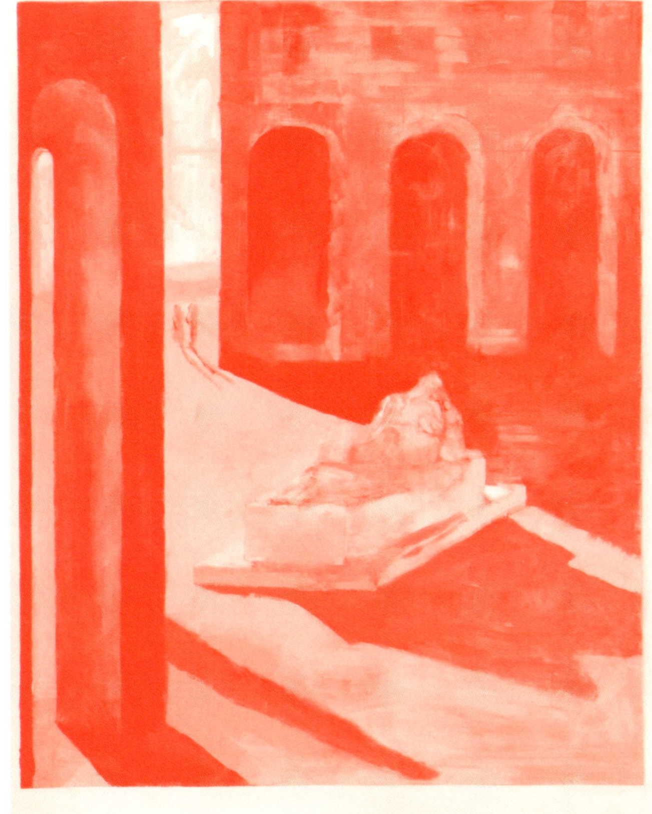

18 _ 14

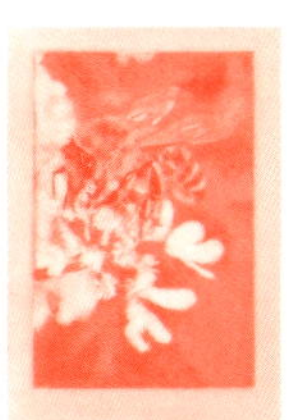
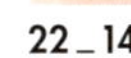

22 _ 14

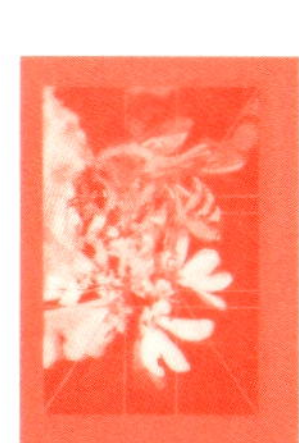

23 _ 14

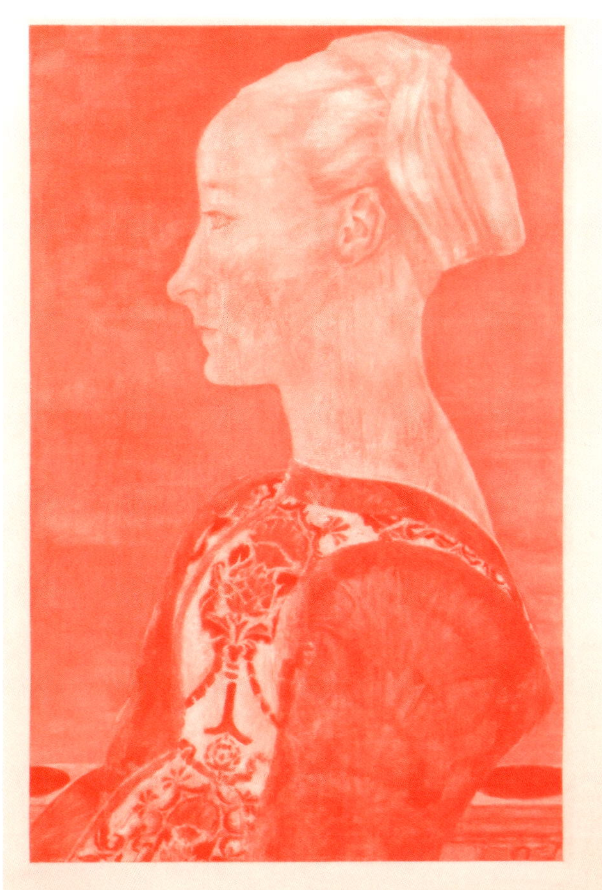

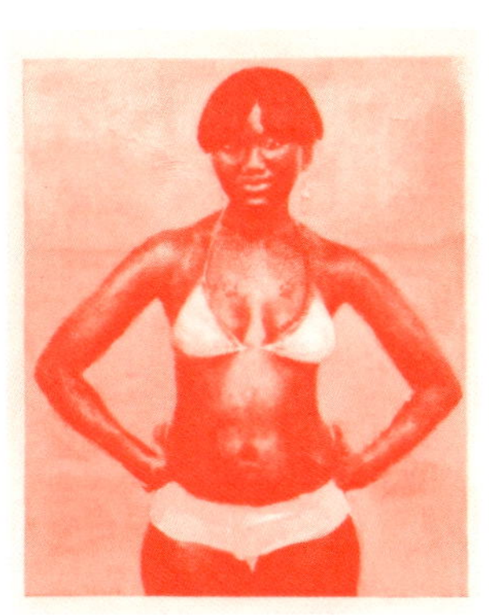

25 _ 14

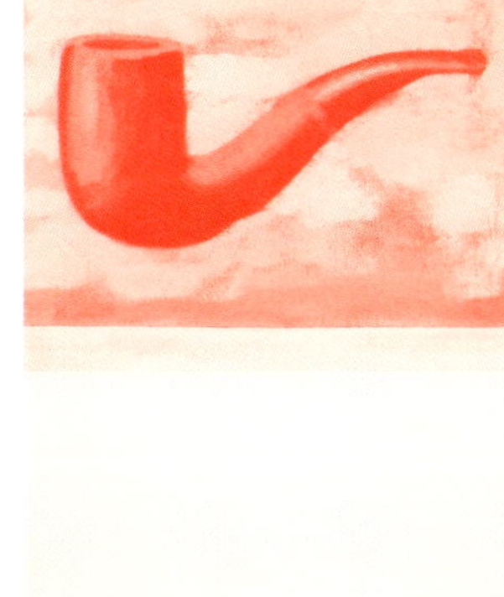

26 _ 14

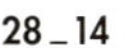

28 _ 14

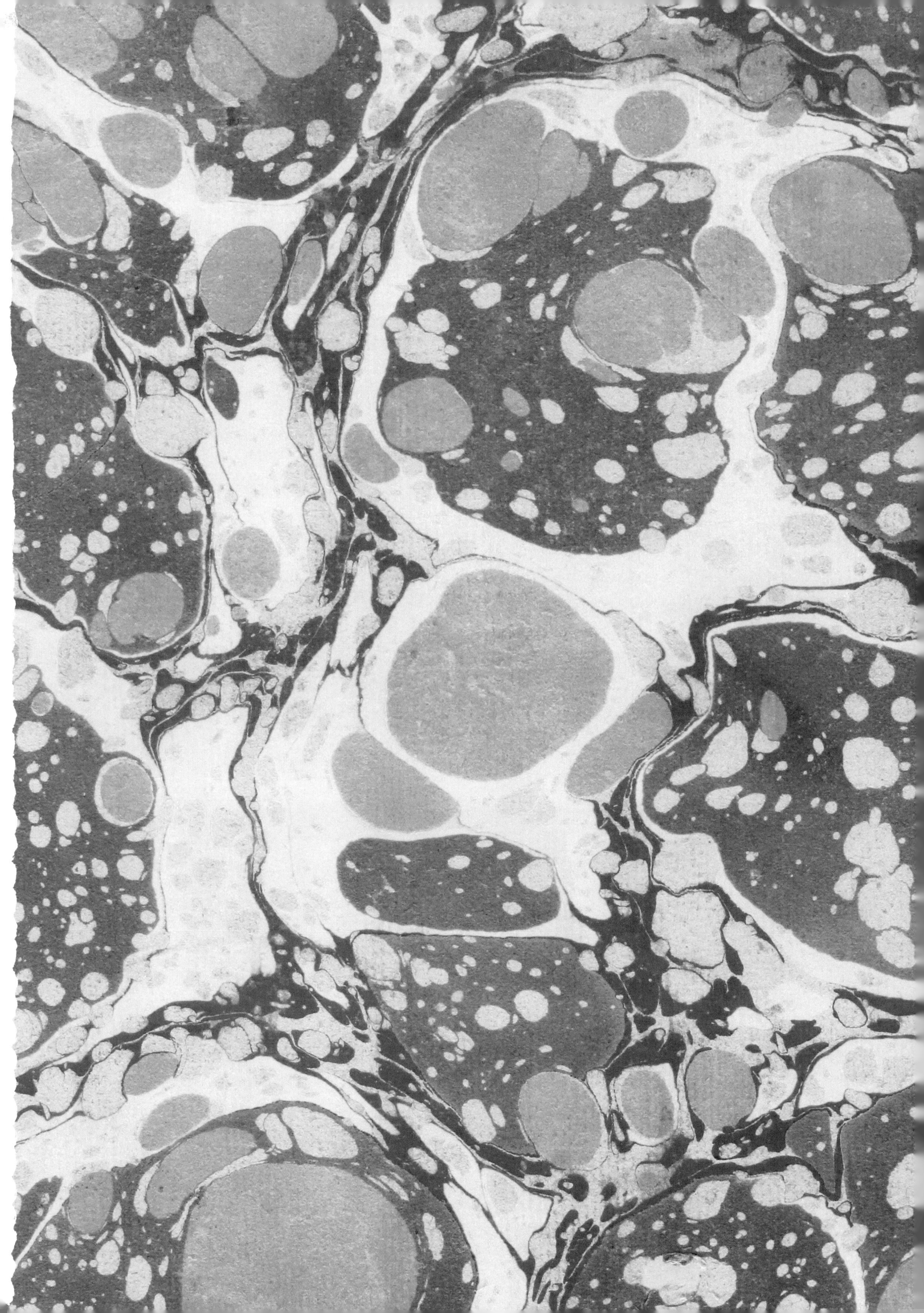

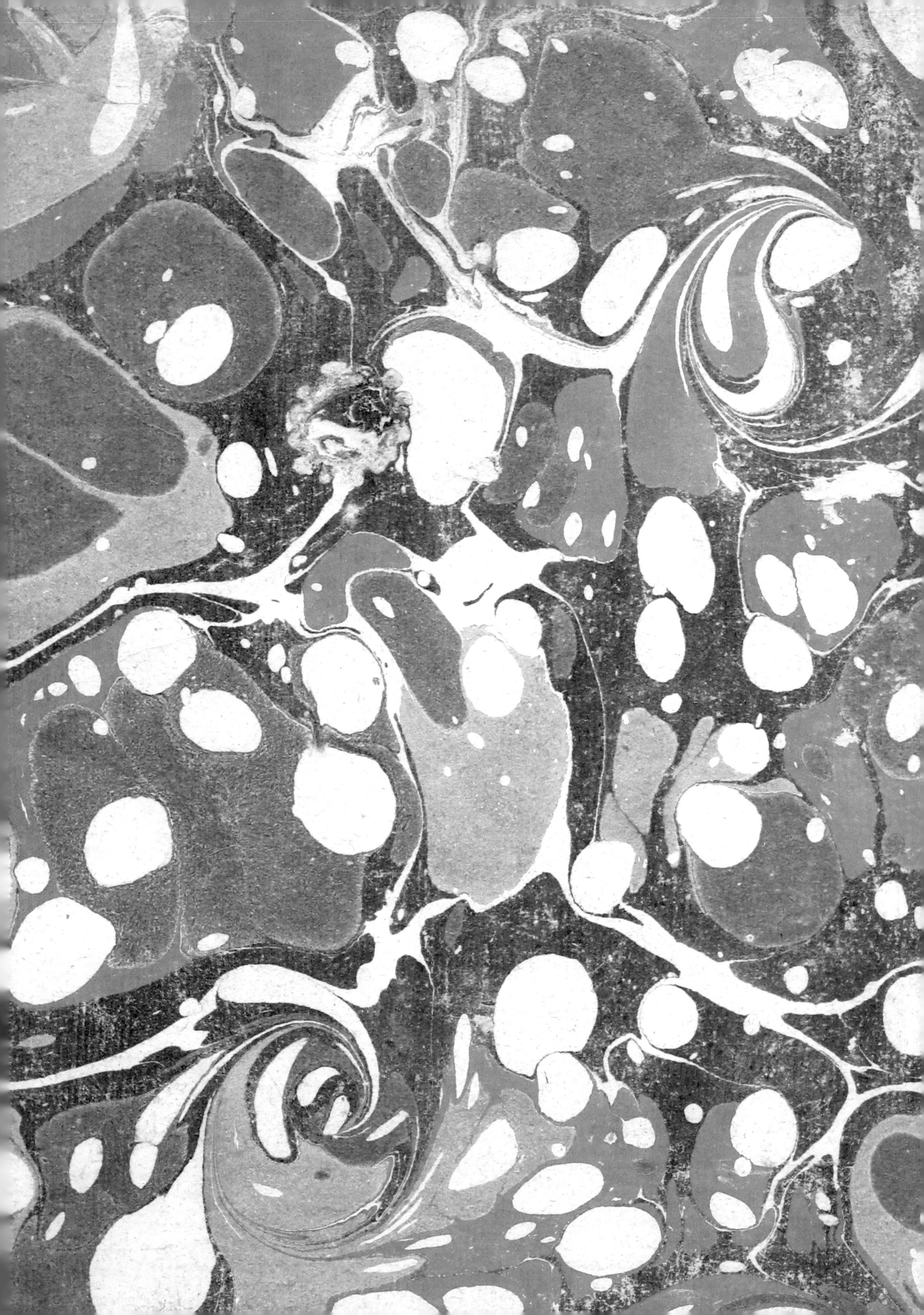